D0871764

T BONE BURNETT

AMERICAN MUSIC SERIES

David Menconi, Editor

T BONE BURNETT

A Life in Pursuit

LLOYD SACHS

University of Texas Press
AUSTIN

Printed in the United States of America
First edition, 2016

Requests for permission to reproduce material
from this work should be sent to:
Permissions
University of Texas Press
P.O. Box 7819
Austin, TX 78713-7819
http://utpress.utexas.edu/index.php/rp-form

The paper used in this book meets the minimum requirements of
ANSI/NISO Z39.48-1992 (R1997) (Permanence of Paper). ♾

LIBRARY OF CONGRESS CATALOGING-IN-PUBLICATION DATA

Names: Sachs, Lloyd, author.
Title: T Bone Burnett : a life in pursuit / Lloyd Sachs.
Other titles: American music series (Austin, Tex.)
Description: Austin : University of Texas Press, 2016.
Series: American music series
Identifiers: LCCN 2016005519
ISBN 978-1-4773-0377-1 (cloth : alkaline paper)
ISBN 978-1-4773-1155-4 (library e-book)
ISBN 978-1-4773-1156-1 (nonlibrary e-book)
Subjects: LCSH: Burnett, T-Bone. | Sound recording executives and producers—United States—Biography. | Musicians—United States—Biography.
Classification: LCC ML429.B927 S23 2016 | DDC 780.92—dc23
LC record available at http://lccn.loc.gov/2016005519

doi:10.7560/303771

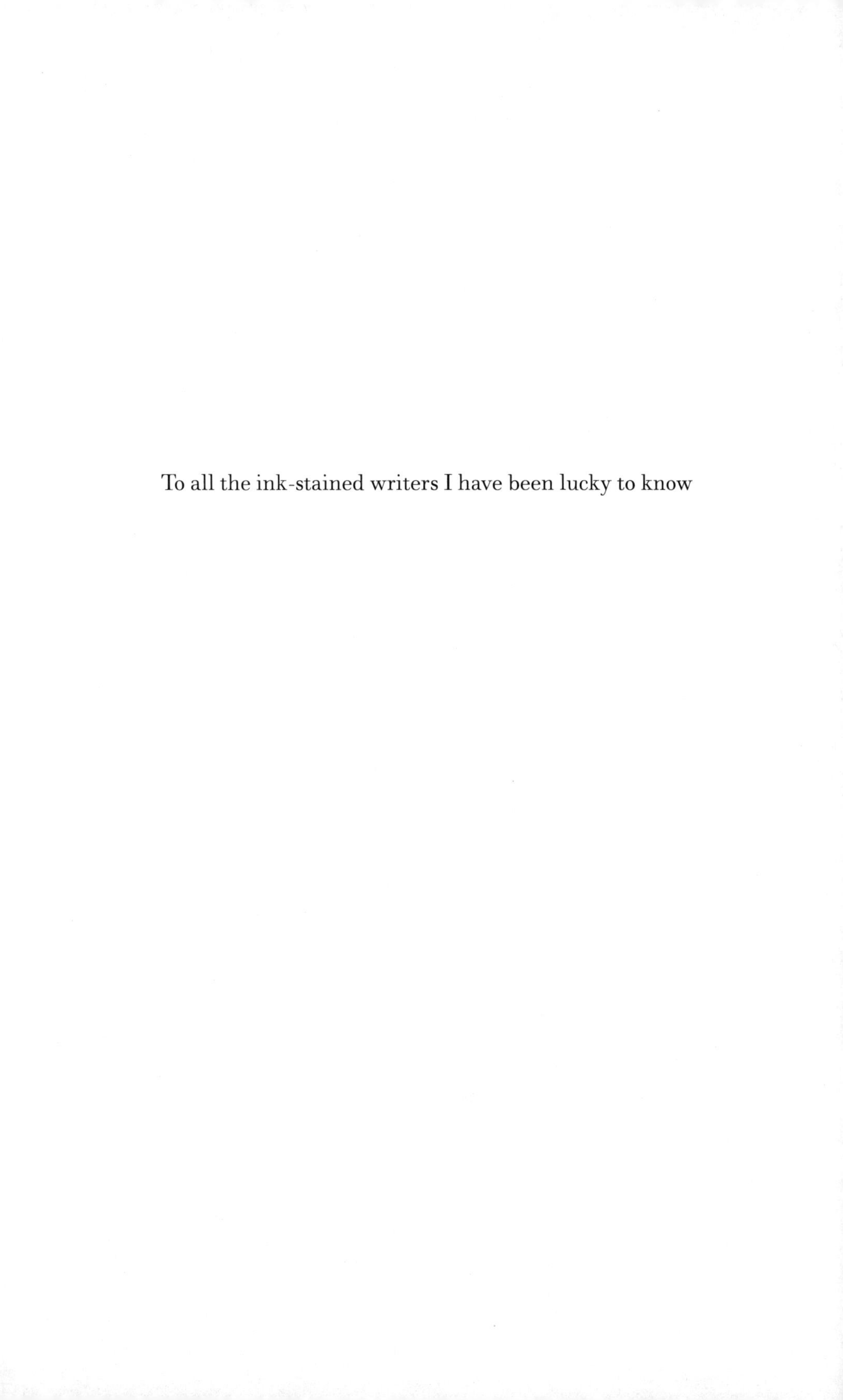

To all the ink-stained writers I have been lucky to know

CONTENTS

T BONE BURNETT

INTRODUCTION

Opening Chorus

ON TOP OF THE WORLD (OR CLOSE)

Fish were jumpin' when T Bone Burnett conducted his first conference call with Alison Krauss and Robert Plant to discuss making an album together. The famed producer was up in Vancouver, British Columbia, at the Capilano Salmon Hatchery, perhaps thinking of Lou "The Salmon King" Kemp, the tour manager of Bob Dylan's Rolling Thunder Revue. Surrounded by God's wonders—steep granite cliffs, lush rainforest vegetation, roaring waterfalls—the spiritual seeker who some people think led Dylan down the path of Christianity was in an elevated state when he connected with Krauss, who was in Nashville, and Plant, who was in Bali—"or somewhere," as Burnett would later say.

The geographical distance between the artists was a perfect metaphor for the vast stylistic distance between Krauss, a bell-toned sweetheart of modern bluegrass, and Plant, the leonine former wailer of Led Zeppelin. The thought of Krauss putting fiddle to the metal on "Black Dog" was only slightly odder than the thought of Plant going back porch. But Krauss, who grew up not in bluegrass country but in the university town of Champaign, Illinois, was a heavy metal fan. And Plant, a blues-loving native of England's Midlands, was such a fan of hers that he had asked her to perform with him as part of the Rock and Roll Hall of Fame's 2004 American Music Masters Tribute to Lead Belly.

"Singing that Lead Belly stuff wasn't in the right range for us," Krauss said in a 2008 press teleconference, according to the *Cleveland Plain Dealer*, but the encounter piqued the singers' interest in further collaborations, and naturally led them to Burnett. He had recorded Krauss for *O Brother, Where Art Thou?*, the 2000 soundtrack album that ignited the roots music revival. And Burnett had been in talks with Plant about producing a sequel to *The Honeydrippers: Volume One*, the 1984 EP of fifties-era rock and R&B that the Brit recorded with his former Zep mate Jimmy Page. Krauss told Burnett that she wanted to do something darker than usual. Plant said he wasn't interested in recording a conventional duo album. Leave it to Burnett to satisfy both their visions while surprising and challenging them with one of his own.

For Burnett, who with his vast knowledge of American music redefines the old throwaway line (and Dylan cover title) "I forgot more than you'll ever know," everything starts with the song. He went into full scuba mode, diving down deep into the vast stream of recorded history for tunes he envisioned Plant and Krauss covering. He came up not with a mere handful of singles and the like but with stacks of them. Listening to playlists ranging from the 1950s R&B group Li'l Millet and His Creoles' tune "Rich Woman" to the prototypical alt-country artist Townes Van Zandt's "Nothin'," Plant felt as if he were attending a master's class in spinology. "I thought I was pretty knowledgeable about American music, but I'd missed out on an entire area," he told Jon Pareles of the *New York Times*. "I now know that American music is a total panorama. I was cutting it off and thinking it was redneck hell down there."

Collaborations between well-known artists frequently go awry either because their styles don't jibe (as with *Eric Clapton & Wynton Marsalis Play the Blues*), because there is too much of one star and not enough of the other (as with *All the Roadrunning*, on which Emmylou Harris disappears for long stretches opposite Mark Knopfler, who produced the recording), or because there is no chemistry between them (as with virtually all the cuts on Frank Sinatra's phoned-in *Duets*). Burnett, however, heard *Raising Sand* less as a collaboration than as a convergence—a meeting of open-minded artists for whom one plus one equaled not two but one. If Plant and Krauss had any second thoughts about softening or departing from their signature styles to level the interpretive playing field, the relaxed atmosphere Burnett created in the studio enabled them to get past their doubts. Both were rewarded by finding sides of their talents of which they themselves had perhaps been unaware.

Plant was an obvious choice to sing Little Milton's "Let Your Loss Be Your Lesson," a mid-1970s B-side delight from the blues and R&B artist's years with the Stax label. But Burnett asked Krauss to sing it instead. She initially begged off, feeling "too white" to do it (as she told National Public Radio's *Weekend Edition Sunday*). Prodded by the producer, however, she rose to the challenge, bringing a soulful depth to what became a plucky, Loretta Lynn–type vehicle. Plant, rock's quintessential lead singer, had rarely sung harmony, but opposite Krauss, a skilled arranger who showed him how to sing his parts, he sounds as pure as a choirboy. Their hushed communion on "Killing the Blues," on which Greg Leisz's sighing pedal steel arches over the singers like a rainbow over gold, is spine-tingling. Burnett first heard that song decades earlier when its composer, Roly (Rowland) Salley, Chris Isaak's longtime bassist, played it in the Bay Area home of the Chicago-born bluesman Nick Gravenites.

As we will see, great music producers approach their work as uniquely as great film directors approach theirs, employing different methods to get the best performances out of their actors, different levels of formality to frame the performances, and different conceptions of the imprint they should or shouldn't leave on the finished product. Burnett now carries such weight in the entertainment capitals of

Hollywood and Nashville that the title "record producer" can contain him no more than "film director" could contain Orson Welles. His *O Brother* soundtrack altered the landscape of American music so markedly that it may well have affected our culture as significantly as *Citizen Kane* did. From his own critically acclaimed work as a singer and songwriter to his close associations with Bob Dylan and Sam Shepard—one of the greatest songwriters of our time and one of the greatest playwrights—to his outspoken efforts to overhaul digital recorded sound, Burnett's accomplishments have made the musician-producer one of the most significant figures in popular culture during the past forty years.

His success is particularly amazing because, in many ways, he is an outsider playing an insider's game. A fierce intellectual, he finds cultural enrichment in a paradise of anti-intellectualism. A man of deep religious faith, he thrives in a den of moneylenders. Burnett is part Don Quixote, charging at digital windmills in his quest to restore analog truth, and part Southern politician, crossing palms with hyperbolic play money: he says that Justin Timberlake is "the closest we have to Bing Crosby," claims the mandolinist Chris Thile is "the Louis Armstrong of his time," and calls Alison Krauss "the one . . . [just as] Ray Charles was the one."

For all that, Burnett has never been able to get past his own self-consciousness and self-doubt as a recording artist. While scoring success after big-time success for others—whether breaking bands, such as Counting Crows, or reviving legends, such as Elton John—he is stuck as a singer-songwriter on the mezzanine level of critics' favorite. As acclaimed as some of his albums are, they have all withered on the commercial vine. That the once rail-thin, six-foot-five Texan has never been comfortable performing before crowds hasn't helped.

That isn't to say he hasn't invested each of his own albums with high hopes. Such was the case with his 2006 effort, *The True False Identity*—his first album under his own name in fourteen years, and, alas, his last major one at this writing. Standing in an alley outside Chicago's Vic Theater that May, a few hours before launching his first concert tour in nearly twenty years, he was wired with expectation. With a newspaper photographer preparing to take aim, he fidgeted against a brick wall, tugging at a pesky nose hair, a study in spasmodic motion. Gone for a fractured moment was the fastidious image the once scrawny, mop-topped Burnett had created for himself with his Miles Davis sunglasses, perfectly parted and tossed hair, and regal, high-button outfits. Gone was the music industry sophisticate, chased by a minor eruption of what Sam Shepard once called his "peculiar quality of craziness." I imagined the competing aspects of his outsize personality speeding through him like the notes of his favorite Charlie Parker solo, the one on "Night in Tunisia."

Burnett had called earlier in the day to invite me to the sound check. I had interviewed him several times for the *Chicago Sun-Times*, where I was a music columnist, and *No Depression* magazine, where I was a senior editor. He had always made himself available—sometimes on short notice—not only for pieces I was working on about him or his former wife and close collaborator, Sam Phillips, but also for ones about artists he had produced. I had visited him after one or two shows in the Windy City and met him for lunch in Los Angeles. As enthusiastic a listener as he is a talker, he laughs at all your jokes, making you feel like you're the sharpest tack in the box. A bookish Lenny Bruce, he's a spritzer who fills the air with quotations from literary figures, philosophers, and jazz greats—not to show off but rather because he just can't help himself and also, one senses, because he feels a personal need to elevate words and ideas at a time in our culture when they are taking it on the chin from visual images.

For all that, when I approached him in the summer of 2008 to propose writing a book about him—not a commercial offering, which would have entailed digging through his personal life, but a critical appreciation of his extensive body of work as an artist and producer—he hemmed a bit and referred me to his manager in Los Angeles. Well, I hadn't picked the best time or place to talk book: backstage at the Ravinia Festival in the Chicago suburbs following a *Raising Sand* concert. Burnett, who had played a supporting role on guitar, was wiped out from the heat. In subsequent weeks and months, determined to sell him on the book directly rather than go through the guy in charge of his business affairs, I made numerous attempts to follow up on our Ravinia conversation. But he was never at the numbers he told me to call, and he didn't respond to my e-mails. I wasn't yet familiar with his Houdini-like proficiency for disappearing.

Finally, he sent me an e-mail saying that he just wasn't ready to have a book written about him, that he still had a lot left to accomplish and didn't have time to gaze back at his past. "He dreads shuffling off this planet, and the thought of anyone writing his story makes him queasy," Phillips told me many months later, during a long lunch in the Polo Lounge in the Beverly Hills Hotel. On another occasion, his seventeen-year-old daughter with Phillips, Simone, speculated that I might have just asked him on the wrong day. "Once he says something, he always feels like he has to stick to it, to uphold his reputation," she said.

Aside from a few seasonal greetings, Burnett and I had no further contact for the next few years. I have to admit that when the University of Texas Press, with whom I had been discussing possibilities for its American Music Series, expressed interest in a Burnett bio in early 2014, I groaned. As much as I still wanted to do the book, I had no desire to go on the chase again. And I certainly didn't want to make an enemy of Burnett, whom, I felt, I could call a friend, at least on some level.

But the more I thought about it, the more I couldn't shake the fact that he was the artist—the cultural force—I most wanted to write about. Only a small percentage of music fans, even those who considered themselves deep into "Americana," had ever heard or heard of such acclaimed albums of his as *Truth Decay*, *T Bone Burnett*, and *The Criminal under My Own Hat*. I had the opportunity here to awaken the public to the complete T Bone. And however universally he was known as a producer—rarely did his name appear in print without "legendary" or "visionary" before it—few people understood what a crucial role he had played in furthering the larger cause of American music, which he views not through the museumy lens of Ken (*Jazz*) Burns but as a collection of living and breathing documents of who we are.

When I contacted Burnett to tell him I had agreed to do this book, with or (sigh) without his participation, and proposed that we meet over lunch to talk things over, he wrote back, "We can have lunch any time you're not writing a book about me. (Insert smiling type face deal here.)" Saying he had no time at that moment to "look backward," he added, "The one thing I will say is, if you do this, please don't say I have had a career. I haven't had a career. That is not what I did."

I later found out that Burnett has been rejecting the notion of a "career"—he prefers "pursuit"—since he and his artist friends in high school struck the word from their vocabularies. I also realized I needn't feel spooked by his use of the past tense. For all the times he has talked about walking away from producing or recording or performing—"The door has closed behind me to a life in music," he told *Rolling Stone* in 2012—he has rarely been without a full dance card.

Still, the man was approaching seventy. Who knew how long he could continue waging war against the technology community, which he called out in a 2014 op-ed column in the *Los Angeles Times* for devaluing music? Who knew how much longer this radical in plain sight could rage against government corruption and surveillance and the slavery of outsourcing? "T Bone is always advocating for musicians and artists," Phillips told me. "He'll never stop. A lot of people come to mind who don't like him because he is kind of a wild man. He's always fighting to make things better, to achieve breakthroughs, whether that means fighting himself or the people he loves or butting heads with the company men, the business people, the people who aren't treating his crew right."

Burnett, whose Christian mysticism shares a lot with Zen, believes in the discipline of "beginner's mind," the basic tenet of which is to treat every moment as your first, not as a preparation for or a bridge to the next moment, and to keep starting over from square one. For all his successes, for all his clout, he is still finding his way, still stopping and starting over in pursuit of a higher truth in art and life. "That's the only way to really learn," he once said. The closed door is actually open. The end of the road is actually the beginning. Consider this book one longtime follower's modest attempt to chart the progress he has made so far.

CHAPTER 1

Sound Citizen

In September 1983, a \$5.5 million avant-garde arts center and performance space called Caravan of Dreams opened in Fort Worth, Texas. Designed by an architect with a degree from London's Institute of Ecotechnotics—where they "integrate the 'ecology of technics' and the 'technics of ecology'"—and financed by Ed Bass, one of the city's oil-rich Bass brothers, the facility boasted a nightclub, a restaurant, an art gallery, and studios dedicated to recording, dance, and karate. On opening weekend, the free jazz pioneer Ornette Coleman, a Fort Worth native, was honored. Among other offerings, he had a string composition of his performed in a rooftop garden boasting a thirty-two-foot-high, neon-lit geodesic dome and a cactus preserve. Beat movement hero William S. Burroughs also attended the festivities.

For all the cultural clashing occasioned by this zany convocation of business leaders, artist types, and ecotechnicians, locals cheered the transformation of what had been a desolate stretch of Cowtown into a much-needed cultural attraction. But it wasn't long before reports of a bunch of weird stuff—like the chanting of Tibetan mantras in the restaurant and bizarro theater productions about the end of the world—had people thinking that "Caravan of Pipe Dreams" (as it was dubbed by *Texas Monthly*) was a sham, perhaps even a scam. And then things got even stranger: "Edward Bass Funds 'Intellectual Cult,' Ex-Members Say," read a headline in the March 30, 1985, edition of the *Dallas Morning News.*

According to *Texas Monthly*, the citizen who blew the whistle on the cult, from outside the organization, was none other than "Fort Worth musician and record producer" T Bone Burnett. (The description tells you how little known he still was in his home state after recording six albums, three under his own name, and appearing in Bob Dylan's Rolling Thunder Revue.) Reportedly identifying himself as a member of the Spiritual Counterfeiters League, Burnett helped get Bass's brother Sid to step in and save Ed from the "mental torture" being practiced on him by his business partner, systems ecologist John P. Allen. More than thirty years on, the story reads like a parody Burnett might write. But as different as he and Ed Bass were, they shared serious concerns about the future of civilization.

Bass was also an investor in the $100 million Biosphere 2 project, dedicated to constructing "portable Earths" to carry people away from our sure-to-be-devastated planet to some safe destination—like Mars. Burnett, who grew up near Carswell Air Force Base, had never gotten over the continual presence of B-52s circling overhead, either returning home from Southeast Asia to refuel or heading back to drop more bombs. "They told us that [the B-52s] were protecting the strategic air force base there because we were the third Russian target in order of priority," Burnett told *Smoke Music Archive.* "That puts no pressure on a six-year-old kid at all."

Joseph Henry Burnett III, an only child, was born in St. Louis on January 14, 1948. His grandfather Joseph Henry Burnett Sr. was for twenty-eight years the Georgia-based secretary of the Southern

Baptist Convention. Having had his dreams of playing professional baseball or football erased by World War II, Burnett's father—who was vigorously pursued by the Brooklyn Dodgers, among other teams—settled for a life in business. By the time T Bone Burnett was four, the family had moved to New Orleans and then Fort Worth, where his father got a job with the Tandy Corporation.

By all accounts, his parents were happy-go-lucky types who led a lively social life and resisted the town's hard-core conservative element. An Episcopalian, Burnett's mother, Hazel, raised him in that faith. ("As maligned as the Episcopal Church is, they give you the whole Gospel every time you go in," he told *Today's Christian Music* in 1982.) For reasons he says he can't remember, Burnett acquired his nickname when he was four or five. Like an old tie clip, the hyphen between "T" and "Bone" has a way of disappearing and reappearing. Reputedly razzed by blues artists for comparing himself to T-Bone Walker, another local music legend, Burnett went by J. Henry professionally for a while before reclaiming his nickname without the dash. For the sake of consistency, I will refer to him as T Bone Burnett from here on.

He was a determined kid. When older boys in the neighborhood wouldn't let him help them build a fort out of discarded Christmas trees, telling him he was too little, he went up and down the block gathering his own trees and dragged them back with a coat hanger hook. The boys changed their tune and let him play. "I was such an idealist that every time I got disappointed it would infuriate me," he told *Rolling Stone*. "I wanted everything my way." His feelings still overwhelm him as an adult. "My dad has mellowed as he has gotten older," Simone Burnett told me, "but he has such a deep well of emotion that when he analyzes his own thoughts relating to how he can better himself, it can be too much for him."

He took up golf at an early age. By the time he was seven, he was a regular on the nearby Texas Christian University golf course. "We all wanted to be Ben Hogan," he told the *San Francisco Chronicle*, referring to the Fort Worth fairway legend, whose wife was a friend of his mother. At the driving range, he said, Hogan "would come stand behind us and watch us hit balls. It would just be incredibly daunting.

He wouldn't say anything, and then he would go back inside." Burnett never became Ben Hogan, or Byron Nelson (another PGA great from Fort Worth, also home of the satiric golf writer Dan Jenkins), but he did make it onto the golf team at Paschal High School. And he got good enough to be a 5 handicap at the 2014 Pebble Beach Pro Am, where he played in a foursome with the actor Ray Romano.

His first exposure to music came via his parents' ample collection of 78s by such greats as Louis Armstrong, Ella Fitzgerald, Duke Ellington, Dinah Washington, Count Basie, and Mahalia Jackson, and songwriter collections by the likes of Rodgers and Hart and Cole Porter. He was most taken with songs that transported him somewhere mysterious or exotic: Porter's "Begin the Beguine"; "Hernando's Hideaway," from *The Pajama Game* (the Ella version); "The Naughty Lady of Shady Lane," a hit for the Ames Brothers. "That's when I started realizing you can create place with music," he told the *Daily Beast*. "Music is a place. Music is atmosphere and environment. That's something that's been very important to me. Everything I do I try to do with a sense of place."

The radio was his gateway to a world of places. Top 40 stations, he recalled, "would play Peggy Lee and Little Tommy Tucker and Hank Williams, and then the Beatles, four songs in a row." He listened to a steady diet of the West Texas prodigy Buddy Holly, whose rockabilly beat left a permanent imprint on him, and Johnny Cash, who had "the stature of Whitman or Emerson." He absorbed the music of the blues greats Howlin' Wolf ("a shaman"), early Skip James ("conjuring music"), and Jimmy Reed, whose "Big Boss Man" was "big-time sex music." "When we were teenagers in Fort Worth," he told *Vulture*, the *New York Magazine* site, "we would dance to Jimmy Reed all night long."

Among the musical greats who had called Fort Worth home were the blues-gospel legend Blind Willie Johnson, Lead Belly (who was a street singer there), Western swing king Bob Wills and his Texas Playboys, the soul saxophonist King Curtis, the R&B guitarist Cornell Dupree, and the jazz modernists Ornette Coleman, Julius Hemphill, and Dewey Redman. "For me, the kinds of distinctions people make between styles didn't exist," Burnett told me in a 2003 interview.

"The Beatles, John Lennon doing 'I'll Cry Instead,' were cut from the same cloth as the Carter Family, and it came from the same place as [Bobby "Blue" Bland's] 'Turn On Your Love Light.'"

When Burnett was twelve, he began his lifelong investigation of music with his friend Stephen Bruton, who would become Kris Kristofferson's longtime sideman and gain a following as a singer-songwriter himself. The boys spent Saturdays hanging out at the T. H. Conn Music store, poring over catalogs and playing around with instruments, including the beat-up Epiphone Texan guitar Bruton talked the owner into selling him for a reduced rate. (He was still playing it on his final project, *Crazy Heart*, the 2009 film starring Jeff Bridges for which he wrote songs and provided inspiration.) The two friends also hung out at Record Town, the specialty shop on South University Drive near the TCU campus owned by Bruton's father, Sumter Bruton Jr., a seasoned jazz drummer whose deep interest in all forms of music was reflected in the unusual—nay, spectacular—range of records he carried: records, Burnett told Terry Gross, host of NPR's *Fresh Air*, "that we wouldn't have had the wherewithal to find ourselves"; records that proved the legends he had been told about—Skip James, Robert Johnson, the Stanley Brothers, so many others—actually existed.

Burnett credits Bruton, a preteen bluegrass banjo prodigy who was obsessed with field recordings from the 1920s and 1930s, with teaching him half of what he knows about music. Bruton introduced him to Dock Boggs's original recording of "Oh Death," which as "O Death" became one of the key components of the Coen Brothers' film *O Brother, Where Art Thou?*, the soundtrack of which Burnett produced. Burnett was also in thrall to the live 1956 version of "Wrought Iron Rag" by the trombonist Wilbur De Paris and his New New Orleans Jazz. With a lineup boasting the former Jelly Roll Morton clarinetist Omer Simeon and trumpeter Sidney De Paris, Wilbur's brother, this Dixieland revival band ignites the form. One pitched solo follows another, each player upping the ante with brash wit and woolly intensity. "It's like a supersonic jet taking off," Burnett told NPR. "When it breaks the sound barrier, the audience goes into ecstasy." A dedicated breaker of sound barriers himself, he added, "That was something I always wanted to be part of, an event that created this much pandemonium."

If hearing such artists on record was transporting, hearing the music live raised Burnett's excitement level even higher. "We would hear that there was this great band playing down the street, and the next thing you know, we'd be hiding under a pool table because we were under age, watching King Curtis and Cornell Dupree," Stephen Bruton told the *Tone Quest Report* (his older brother, Sumter Bruton III, would sneak them in). The low-rent clubs on the Jacksboro Highway, known equally as a sin strip and a guitar player's paradise, exposed both spectators and many backing musicians to a wide range of styles.

Burnett said he was ten when he picked up an old Gibson guitar and became hooked on playing music: "I hit the low E string, and it did its thing," he told *Performing Songwriter*. "I thought, 'OK, what is that?' I was gone, right there." His mother said he started playing at age twelve. "One year I went to Mexico and bought him an eight-dollar guitar," she told the TCU alumnus newspaper. "He never put it down." The first song he learned to play was Maybelle Carter's finger-picking classic "Wildwood Flower."

That folk stuff didn't last. In the wake of the British invasion of the early 1960s, a mighty wave of young Fort Worth rock bands with long hair, tight outfits, newly bought guitars, and names like the Jades and the Barons staged nightly battles, with as many as ten groups on a single bill. Singles were hawked. Teen clubs flourished. Races mixed. The Beatles' February 9, 1964, appearance on *The Ed Sullivan Show* was life changing.

"Two days later, I sensed a presence in my room," Burnett's high school friend David Graves told me. "It was Terry Burnett—that's what we called him at the time—hammering away on a guitar. He had always played folk before then. But he had the same response to the Beatles that I did. He was totally smitten. Two weeks later, we had a garage band we put together with three other high school kids. It wasn't much; we played high school parties and stuff. But that was the start."

Graves had Burnett's father, then working at a furniture manufacturer, refurbish a bass Graves had purchased for ten dollars at a pawnshop. The boys formed the Shadows, whose gigs included a department store fashion show. They went on to perform at frat parties in a band called the Loose Ends, which often featured Stephen Bruton knocking out Chuck Berry riffs. Burnett would "get a job someplace and he'd say, 'You're playing electric guitar,'" Bruton told *Fretboard Journal*. "And I'd go there, and he'd put a guitar on me, and then he'd just reach over and turn up the volume and say, 'Go!'"

In the summer of 1965, after graduating from high school, Burnett and Graves practically lived at Sound City, the four-track basement studio located beneath the local KXOL radio station. That's where the shady, Colonel Tom Parker–like promoter Major Bill Smith had produced two "cotton-pickin' smashes," Bruce Channel's "Hey! Baby" (1962) and Paul and Paula's "Hey Paula" (1963). Burnett quickly became taken with the recording process. "I loved the idea that you could go in and nothing was there, but you come out and something was there, something beautiful," he told the *Telegraph*. And, he said in a *New York Times* interview, "We just jumped in and started plugging things in. Every once in a while they'd make a really good sound, and every once in a while a really horrible one. I found both equally mysterious and fascinating."

As John Morthland pointed out in his *Austin Chronicle* review of *Fort Worth Teen Scene! Vols. 1–3*, a collection of sides from 1964 to 1967, most local bands of the time had little interest in melody and harmony. They were more disposed toward the "fuzz, distortion, and raunch" of such British exports as the Rolling Stones, the Yardbirds, and the Kinks. Burnett, who saw the Beatles perform in Houston on August 19, 1965, was quickly converted to their experimental style of pop. "Free Soul," the Loose Ends' main contribution to the anthology, stands out with its brooding melodicism and rudimentary effects. Written under the name Jon T. Bone, the single—Burnett's first—boasts his best petulant John Lennon vocal ("I won't be owned by you / There's too much I've got to do / I want to be a free soul") while aspiring to a Byrds-like Rickenbacker sound with a newly acquired twelve-string acoustic guitar.

Recorded in the spring of 1966, "Free Soul" was, Graves told me, "T Bone's first legitimate attempt to put out something saleable." In his fledgling efforts as a producer, he had done little more than record bands live. Though Burnett enticed a Vietnam chopper pilot living in the apartment complex his mother managed into buying some new box amps and guitars in exchange for a co-producer credit, Sound City's antiquated equipment made it difficult to achieve any kind of artful, layered sound. With the help of the engineer Phil York, who would gain prominence through his work with Willie Nelson and the Rolling Stones, Burnett increased the number of tracks at his disposal through the "bouncing down" or "mixing down" technique. That involved recording the four tracks from one machine over to one track on a second four-track machine, then recording more music on the first machine and mixing those tracks down to one track.

The previous fall, Burnett had recorded "He's a Nobody," the even more Beatles-esque B-side included on *Fort Worth Teen Scene!* This harder-edged, garage-style rocker features Burnett's attempt at a British pronunciation of "girl." He revealed just how smitten he was with the Beatles when, after laying his hands on a prerelease radio promo copy of *Sgt. Pepper's Lonely Hearts Club Band* in May 1967, he and Graves performed all the songs on it at a teen club. The actual album came out on June 1, 1967. "Since no one else had heard the songs yet, some had the impression they were our work," Graves wrote on Facebook. "We didn't say one way or the other. . . . For a few days, we had *SPLHCB* to ourselves."

The music provided an escape from what Burnett described to *Rolling Stone* as "a dark upbringing." By the time he was in high school, his parents had divorced. His mother, an enthusiastic supporter of his musical efforts, moved into an apartment building; Burnett lived in the house with his ailing father, who would die in 1967. "T Bone was something of a lone wolf," Graves told me.

While attending TCU with Bruton, Burnett, deferred from military service because of an asthma condition, worked as an A&R man for the producer Charles Stewart, who was leasing Sound City. As noted in the September 2002 issue of *TCU Magazine*, Burnett's "stint as a Horned Frog was short-lived. His passion for music and his [flair] as a record producer helped him march straight from campus to the music industry." "He knew what he wanted, and he didn't let anything stop him," Bruton told *Los Angeles Magazine*. "T Bone looked at this like a big chess game, and he knew how to play."

Stewart, who had produced an R&B hit by the Van Dykes, helped get the Loose Ends' "Free Soul / He's a Nobody" released on the Mala label. Burnett became partners with Stewart and, with a bank loan of $12,000 plus inheritance money, purchased the studio with Jim Rutledge, future star of the hard rock band Bloodrock. "We were the first folks in there to develop it for the recording of real band music," Graves told me.

In 1968, Burnett took an oddball Texas singer dressed in leather chaps and a white ten-gallon hat into the studio. Two vacuum cleaner salesmen (or so the legend goes) had spotted the singer performing on the roof of a 1959 Chevrolet Bel Air sedan, the sides of which had "NASA Presents the Legendary Stardust Cowboy" painted in black and the roof of which boasted a map of the moon. Accompanying himself on a broken Dobro and bugle, the Cowboy—Lubbock native Norman Carl Odam—unleashed a torrent of blood-curdling screams and hillbilly yelps, as if on a bad acid trip. Burnett thrashed away, perhaps in self-defense, on drums. "T-Bone Burnett was just hog wild," the Cowboy claimed in his promotional bio. "He was orbiting the moon."

However elevated he was, Burnett heard something in the record. In what may have been the first demonstration of his sixth sense about what the public wants to hear even when it doesn't know it, the young producer ran upstairs to KXOL with his two-track monaural tape of "Paralyzed." Given some airplay, the Cowboy's inchoate screaming fit drew a positive response. Co-authoring one of the strangest chapters in rock history, Burnett proceeded to press five hundred copies of the song on Major Bill Smith's Psycho-Suave label and distributed it to other radio stations. Amazingly enough, it became a regional hit.

And that wasn't all: Mercury Records signed Ledge, as his fans called him, to a singles deal; in October 1968, "Paralyzed" got a mention in *Billboard*'s Special Merit Spotlight. The man who claimed to have written "more space songs than anybody" (even, presumably, his fellow intergalactic traveler, the visionary jazz bandleader Sun Ra) made an unlikely landing on *Rowan & Martin's Laugh-In*, NBC's popular sketch comedy show. To his dismay, he was mocked and laughed at by the cast. But that memory is no doubt eased by the fact that, while Rowan and Martin are history, the Stardust Cowboy is still Legendary.

"Paralyzed," which according to the musicologist Irwin Chusid's book *Songs in the Key of Z: The Curious World of Outsider Music*, has actual lyrics ("I ran to the 'frigerator / Hungry as an alligator / I opened the door, and what did I see? / I saw my baby starin' right back at me"), was but one of many records Odam cut at Sound City and Delta, another local studio. Don Duca, a drummer from Tulsa who was in Burnett's circle, told me that Burnett laid down one stipulation for those recordings: "You couldn't play an instrument on which you had any experience."

Soon after helping immortalize the Legendary Stardust Cowboy, Burnett produced what some rock fans consider a lost classic of the sixties, *The Unwritten Works of Geoffrey, Etc.* Recorded in September 1968, the album featured an ad hoc group of top-notch young local players—all either high schoolers or dropouts—who had played on the Cowboy sessions. Released under the name Whistler, Chaucer, Detroit, and Greenhill, *Unwritten Works* was an apt title for what David Bullock, Scott Fraser, Eddie Lively, and Phil White had going into the sessions. Most of the songs were written on the fly, frequently in a drug haze, over five days and nights. Borrowing liberally from leading California bands of the day—Buffalo Springfield, Jefferson Airplane, Moby Grape—Whistler and his pals brought a larkish high-mindedness to country-rock, baroque folk, and full-blown psychedelia.

In revealing the ambition and restless creativity of a young producer working on the cheap and with outmoded equipment, *Unwritten Works*—all twenty-eight minutes of it—is a fascinating document. For one of the songs, Burnett took tracks from the master tape of a tune he had previously recorded with a string quartet, played them backward, and combined them with plucked piano strings. On another number, Stephen Bruton produced a quirky banjo sound by playing a six-string acoustic guitar in open tuning with the capo high up the neck.

"We spent hundreds of hours decorating our tracks with plucked pianos, backward guitar solos, accordions, sand blocks, you name it," Bullock wrote in a letter to the producers of TV's beloved mother-daughter series *Gilmore Girls* after the show's aspiring girl drummer character, Lane (Keiko Agena), spoke of needing to find a copy of *Unwritten Works* to complete her collection of must-have albums. (Lane may well have been reading *The Mojo Collection: The Ultimate Music Companion*, in which *Unwritten Works* is included among the six hundred greatest albums ever made. Burnett no doubt appreciated the subhead on the entry, "Showcase of the sophisticated scene in Ft. Worth, Texas"—especially having arranged for go-go girls from *Sump'n Else*, a Saturday afternoon teen dance show out of Dallas, to come to Sound City to sing on a few songs with Whistler and company.)

Burnett wrote four of the tracks on *Unwritten Works*. Rendered in cozy folk-rock style, with soulful harmonica and fiddle solos, "The Viper (What John Rance Had to Tell)" is an early manifestation of his interest in crime themes. Its parenthetical phrase was taken from a chapter title in *A Study in Scarlet*, the first Sherlock Holmes book by Arthur Conan Doyle. In the story, Rance is a constable who discovers a dead body. Exactly what is going on in the song is unclear, but take care, dear listener: "When you ask about the sniper / You may find a black spot in the palm of your hand."

"As Pure as the Freshly Driven Snow," a mere snippet at one minutes and thirty-nine seconds, is a jaunty, string-infused love tune with echo effects. "On Lusty Gentlemen" is noteworthy for its discordant touches, spooky organ and flute, pounded piano chords, distant voices, and a long sustained tone at the end. And then there's "Street in Paris," a melodramatic art-rock number with rickety upright piano and violin about a life-changing encounter with a girl that leaves the shy singer in a painful daze. Sung with megaphone effects (the Roaring Twenties idol Rudy Vallée lives!), the tune climaxes with a demented crying jag that might have been inspired by "Paralyzed." A "horrible, trippy, music-hall influenced tune," pronounced the mononymous Jason in 2007 on the vintage music site *Rising Storm*.

According to Bullock, as reported in "Lost in Space: The Epic Saga of Fort Worth's Space Opera," an extensive, multipart article about his next band, published on the *Rock & Reprise* site, Major Bill helped Burnett get the Whistler group a deal with UNI, an MCA imprint. But after a good initial offer was made, recalled the band's singer, John Carrick, Burnett told them, "If this is what they are willing to offer right off the bat, I should push for more." Indeed, he did just that, resulting in UNI taking the offer off the table and giving it to the Houston psychedelic band Fever Tree. "What we finally got," said Carrick, "was kind of a cut-out bin deal." *The Unwritten Works of Geoffrey, Etc.*—which, trivia fans take note, boasted a cover designed by the rising singer-songwriter Guy Clark—floated away in a sea of barely noticed albums.

Following an acrimonious split by the band that never really was a band, three of its members went on to form the well-regarded, Byrds-influenced Space Opera. After Burnett impressed on them the importance of complete artistic control, they spurned a modest offer from Clive Davis at Columbia Records that didn't give them that autonomy, and signed instead with Columbia Records of Canada, which did. Branded a Canadian band—probably not a label you wanted stuck on you if you weren't the Guess Who—Space Opera was one album and out. Well, Burnett was still finding his groove as a deal maker.

During his time at Sound City, Burnett produced dozens of regional hits, among them the Van Dykes' horn-boosted, glockenspiel-dappled "Sunday Kind of Love" and a live album by the blues artist Robert Ealey & His Five Careless Lovers, featuring Sumter Bruton III on guitar. He also had name artists such as Conway Twitty, Doug Kershaw, Doug Sahm, and Marc Benno stop by for midnight tapings after their club dates.

In some ways, Burnett never left Sound City. During his time there as a producer, he strived to capture the spacious sound of the Skyliner Ballroom, a juke joint and sometime strip club where young T Bone stayed out late hearing Bobby Bland, Junior Parker, and the local bandleader Ray Sharpe, best known for "Linda Lu." Years later, listening to the recordings he made at Sound City alongside *Live! The Ike & Tina Turner Show*, recorded in 1965 at the Skyliner, he was struck by how much that sound had followed him. The Ike and Tina recording, he told *Tape Op*, "sounded like everything I've done my whole life and I realized that everything I've been trying to do from the beginning was to recreate this excitement of sound." If the recordings he most prized as a child had the mysterious ability to transport him to different times and places, these recordings were equally special for their ability to transport him back to a specific time and place with the same sense of wonder.

While coming of age in Fort Worth, Burnett never put much stock in the hippie movement. He didn't trust it, he said. For him, the visual artists he befriended in high school were the real counterculture. "They looked at things in a way that no one I grew up with had even thought of," he told *Smoke Music Archive*. "They were funny, smart and there was also more of that sense of escape and getting out that was real. Those people felt free." In an interview with *Mix*, he said, "I always thought of making records as the equivalent of what my friends who painted did."

Jim Meeker, a local oil man and art collector, facilitated Burnett's and his high school friends' interest in art by bringing to town such celebrated modernists as Andy Warhol, Robert Rauschenberg, Ed Ruscha, and Kenny Price. The Jackson Pollock school had an especially powerful impact on Burnett. Inspired by the bold statements the abstract expressionist made through the uncontrolled spreading of dripped paint across a canvas, he became devoted to uncontrolled waves of sound in the studio, to allowing musical overtones and blooming after-tones to emerge naturally. He also learned to let the music unfold on its own terms when it didn't want to conform to preconceived strategies.

However much was going on in Fort Worth in a cultural sense, the city was too isolated to provide more than the occasional gig. "We were living under such a low ceiling," Burnett told the *Riverfront Times* of St. Louis. "There were no roads out. It seemed like we were trapped." Given its open persecution of free-spirited sixties types—young guys with long hair and beards were refused service at gas stations and restaurants—Texas as a whole was too conservative for someone with Burnett's brand of individualism. It certainly wasn't a place where you could perform your own songs without having people scream out for songs they already knew.

Los Angeles beckoned.

CHAPTER 2

The Outsider

During his first visit to Los Angeles in 1967, Burnett discovered that the cool and carefree California in which the late-fifties and early-sixties TV stars Ricky "Hello Mary Lou" Nelson and Edd "Kookie" Byrnes existed was nowhere to be found—and that the rednecks on acid he hoped he had left behind were there as well. Still, "the Athens of the modern world," as he calls Los Angeles (when not comparing it to Andy Griffith's Mayberry), offered all kinds of opportunities to play. In 1969, he fell in with a group of musicians living in the Valley in a small group of houses called the Plantation, including Ry Cooder and Taj Mahal, late of the Rising Sons; the southern soul transplants Delaney and Bonnie Bramlett; and the Oklahomans Leon Russell, J. J. Cale, Bobby Keys, and Jesse Ed Davis. Some were coming off a stint with the Shindogs, the house band of TV's short-lived rock variety show *Shindig!*, while others had played with the unsung session greats known as the Wrecking Crew. While living in Laurel Canyon, Burnett and Bruton went to the Troubadour in West Hollywood most nights and forged connections with Dr. John (who, lest anyone forget, got his start in Los Angeles writing for Sonny and Cher), the Flying Burrito Brother Chris Ethridge, and other exceptional players.

For years, Burnett spent much of his time in transit between Fort Worth and Los Angeles. Darrell Leonard, a trumpeter with whom he became friends after Leonard's touring Oklahoma band cut a bunch of tracks at Sound City, remembers Burnett tracking him down at a Sunday jam session in 1971 immediately after returning from a road trip to Los Angeles. "T Bone said his car was acting funny and he needed a ride to California, did I want to go?" Leonard told me. "I thought it over and said sure."

Their extended stay in Los Angeles proved rewarding. Leonard became a working member of Delaney & Bonnie and Friends, the celebrated rock 'n' soul road band whose most noteworthy Friend was Eric Clapton, and got Burnett a gig as substitute guitarist in the ensemble for a few shows on the West Coast. "T Bone was like a skinny little kid, a great big twelve-year-old kid," singer Bonnie Bramlett told me. "I wanted to slingshot his little butt. But he had big dreams."

Burnett struggled to attain those dreams in a scene dominated by the sensitive singer-songwriter confessions of Joni Mitchell, Jackson Browne, and James Taylor, the zipless country-rock of Linda Ronstadt, and the peaceful, easy, decreasingly countrified rock of the Eagles. As a Texan whose band, the B-52s, was mostly made up of Lone Star players, he lacked the cosmic LA vibe of such blues-bitten artists as Tom Waits and Captain Beefheart.

He led a vagabond existence, staying with friends, including a wedding musician who once brought home cake on which they subsisted for an entire week. For a time, he rented a former hunting lodge in Tujunga—on a good day, a thirty-minute drive from Hollywood—with Leonard and other musicians. The Lodge, as it was known, had a big living room space in which to rehearse and record. According to Leonard, Burnett played a lot of fingerpicking acoustic blues—"Mississippi Fred McDowell, that type of thing. He was a thoughtful player, with solid fundamentals in the blues stuff. He also was a good

R&B player in a Steve Cropper–ish way. He always came up with cool parts, and a good sound, and he knew a gazillion songs."

At another point, Burnett found himself living next door to Burt Bacharach, the artist he likes to say was his role model when he was plotting his escape from Fort Worth: someone who wrote songs for the movies, had race horses and, oh yes, was married to Angie Dickinson. (For the record, Burnett also wanted to become Phil Spector, producer of giant-sounding hits by Ike and Tina Turner, the Ronettes, and the Righteous Brothers; Don Kirshner, who orchestrated the TV success of the Monkees and produced the syndicated show *Don Kirshner's Rock Concert*; and the Four Seasons songwriter and producer Bob Crewe.)

In 1972, Burnett married Stephanie Harrison, a hippie girl (as one friend described her) he had met the previous year on Dennis Hopper's ranch in Taos, New Mexico, where the actor retreated—stumbled, actually—following the commercial flop of his ambitious film *The Last Movie*. (Hopper hosted all kinds of painters, rock artists, and poets.) During that notable year, Burnett co-produced his first major album, *Delbert & Glen*, the debut of Fort Worthians Delbert McClinton and Glen Clark, and the first and only album by the artist known as J. Henry Burnett, *The B-52 Band & the Fabulous Skylarks*.

Burnett, who was seven years younger than McClinton, didn't know him well personally but certainly knew him as an artist. In 1960, McClinton's "Wake Up Baby" became the first song by a white artist to land on local blues station KNOK. He played harmonica on Bruce Channel's "Hey! Baby"; led one of the early blue-eyed soul groups, the Ron-Dels; and backed a host of blues legends at the Skyliner. Burnett wasn't well acquainted with Clark either, who was the same age as him but attended a different high school and ran in different circles in Fort Worth.

Burnett was brought into *Delbert & Glen* by his friend Daniel Moore, a seasoned musician and songwriter who would become best known for "Shambala," a 1973 smash for Three Dog Night, and "My Maria," a Top 10 hit that same year for co-writer B. W. Stevenson. Burnett and Moore had worked together on demos by a Texas band called the Fare that was later signed under the name El Roacho by CBS. Using their connections, they got the regal chief of Atlantic

Records, Ahmet Ertegun, to listen to a three-song demo by McClinton and Clark. Not long after, Ertegun and his close friend, art collector Earl McGrath, pulled up to the Lodge in a stretch limo to ink a deal. Released in 1972, *Delbert & Glen* was the first release on Clean Records, an Atlantic-distributed label headed by McGrath.

Though Burnett is widely credited as sole producer of the LP, Moore called the shots in the studio; in fact, his name precedes Burnett's in the credits. Burnett's main contribution, Moore told me, was as "a facilitator." Burnett cast the project, bringing in members of his band, not least the accomplished keyboardist Tom Canning. "Without T Bone's wheeling and dealing and putting on the dog, the album might not have happened," Clark told me. "He provided the wherewithal to get it done."

Though the cover of *Delbert & Glen* boasts abstract cow art by proto-pop painter Larry Rivers, McClinton and Clark refused to buy into the cosmic-cowboy image that record labels were using to promote Texas acts, and didn't want any part of country-rock either. McClinton spoke to me of the "madness" of the sessions, alluding to the free flow of drugs and alcohol—and, perhaps, the spooky vibe that still lingered in Los Angeles following the 1971 conviction of Charles Manson. But the album is an unassuming mix of honky-tonk, rock, and blues—Texas barroom music, performed by musicians who knew it floor to ceiling.

Clean Records, which disappeared as suddenly as it appeared, did little to promote *Delbert & Glen.* Voilà: a collector's item. A few months later, however, with the project under his belt, Burnett felt ready to record an album by the B-52s. As a producer, he again played second fiddle to Moore. But with its eager testing of styles and mixing of genres, *The B-52 Band & the Fabulous Skylarks* is clearly Burnett's album.

This is that rare debut that feels like a transitional album, one that is frequently a step ahead of itself. Coming from someone known for much of his career for a stripped-down approach as a producer, *The B-52 Band* may catch you by surprise in the way it pulls out stops and hoists up walls of sound. Part soul revival (the rollicking "We Have All Got a Past"), part Texas blues workout (the four-to-the-floor

"Mama, Please Don't You Lie"), part Beatles homage (the dark, chiming "Sliding By," which cops the melody from "Don't Let Me Down"), and part religious hymn (the aching piano ballad "Bring Me Back Again," featuring a second lead vocalist, Gary Montgomery), *The B-52 Band* keeps you off guard with its leapfrogging of styles.

Burnett, whose reedy voice has always set him apart, hadn't yet settled on a vocal identity. He ranges from sinister swamp man on "Now I Don't Mind No Light Sermon" ("Why you make it hard on me and my friends for something you yourself did?") to sensitive John on "You Been Away So Long," with its stark Lennonism, "Please, mama, stand alone." And the Skylarks, Rita Jean Bodine and Linda Carey Dillard, aren't so fabulous as background singers. They can wear you out with their answering choruses. But as easy as it is to dismiss *The B-52s* as an inconsistent early effort, or write it off as a minor offshoot of the rock 'n' soul revival instigated by Leon Russell and Joe Cocker (with whom Moore was familiar from his work with their Mad Dogs and Englishmen troupe), this is anything but a "straightforward collection of bluesy rock tunes" (*Encyclopedia Britannica*) or an otherwise conventional effort.

In its own way, *The B-52s* revealed Burnett's ties to the singer-songwriter Randy Newman, an outsider who had made himself an LA rock favorite. The charismatic Burnett and super-laconic Newman (whose masterpiece *Sail Away* had just been released) were very different in style and temperament. But like his Louisiana-born counterpart, Burnett infused LA rock culture with southernisms. Like Newman, a latter-day Stephen Foster, Burnett embraced bedrock American song forms. And though Burnett hadn't yet cranked up his social commentary, he would prove to be as committed a Swiftian as Newman—and as "loving" of "El Lay." "The constant unbelievable backstabbing here has taught me never to say a bad word about anyone," Burnett told me in 2003. "It's not possible to hate people because if you start, you'll never stop."

It took Burnett a while to record another album under his own name. When Bob Dylan hijacks you, it is easy to set your personal goals aside.

CHAPTER 3

Player in the Band

One of Burnett's blessings, and sometimes one of his curses, is an inability to think small—to approach a song or a project without seeing its larger meanings and possibilities. Long before he told the graduates at the University of Southern California that "the goal of art is to create conscience," he was measuring things in those terms. Individual successes were great, but how can we change the mind-set of popular culture? How can we instill in people the need for change? What alternatives to what Burnett calls "music for people who don't like music" can we create?

According to Don Duca, a onetime club owner who for many years was a regular at Burnett's weekly poker game at the tall Texan's oceanside condo in Santa Monica, Burnett came up with the idea for Bob Dylan's Rolling Thunder Revue. Burnett, he said, proposed it several months before it came to pass, when they were staying at the Tujunga Canyon lodge in 1975. "T Bone was always talking at the breakfast table about what he thought Dylan should do, what Dylan needed to do at that point, what direction he needed to take as a performer," Duca told me. "He had all sorts of ideas. One morning, he brought up the idea of the tour. The next day, he flew to New York. A couple of weeks later, someone brought in the latest issue of *People* magazine. In it was a large picture of T Bone, at a table at a fancy New York restaurant with Dylan and his manager Al Grossman. T Bone never had any qualms about going straight to the top with a project proposal."

Bob Neuwirth, Dylan's onetime sidekick, road manager, poetic muse, and musical consigliore ("If ever there was a renaissance man leaping in and out of things, he would have to be it," Dylan wrote in *Chronicles: Volume One*), remembers things differently. "Dylan and I decided after two beers that it would be hilarious if he and I and Ramblin' Jack [Elliott] got into a station wagon and played pop-up shows," he told me in 2015, flashing back to the summer of 1975. They would drive from city to city, performing where they could, with whom they could.

During an engagement at the Other End in New York's Greenwich Village the first week in July, Neuwirth hosted an unlikely assortment of performers. Through the week, the likes of Ian Hunter, David Bowie guitarist Mick Ronson, Gordon Lightfoot, Ringo Starr, the Blues Brothers John Belushi and Dan Aykroyd, celebrities such as Muhammad Ali and Caroline Kennedy—and Dylan—turned the gig into a cultural happening. "I was asking people who wandered by the bar to play with me," said Neuwirth, an Ohio native who made his name on the Cambridge, Massachusetts, folk scene. "T Bone was in Texas, hiding out or making records. I called him and said you gotta come up here. He said send me a ticket. So I did."

According to Neuwirth, he first encountered Burnett a few years earlier in Woodstock, where Stephen Bruton moved in 1970—hoping, among other things, to play with his idol, Van Morrison, who was living there. (Their only encounter, alas, was at the local bank, where the

Belfast Cowboy was withdrawing money in order to move to California.) When Burnett came up for a visit, Neuwirth, who was among the musicians hanging out in upstate New York, was invited to meet him. Girls and tequila were on the program. "I liked the surrealistic songs he was writing," Neuwirth told me.

Burnett, who had never been in the Village, was overwhelmed by all the music happening there. "It was Valhalla," he told *Uncut.* "It was freedom." In addition to joining Neuwirth's amazing, expanding band at the Other End, Burnett accompanied him for a song at Gerdes Folk City, where Dylan was among those celebrating owner Mike Porco's birthday, and participated in late-night jam sessions at the Broadway loft of the abstract painter Larry Poons. Holding forth on guitar and grand piano, Dylan aired out songs from *Desire*, which he was in the process of recording.

"I had to twist T Bone's arm into going on Rolling Thunder," Neuwirth told me. But Burnett seemed to be in mid-tour form at a pre-Thunder party. As recounted by Larry "Ratso" Sloman in *On the Road with Bob Dylan*, "T Bone had a bag of golf clubs on his back, a driver in his hands, and Neuwirth was screaming, 'Playing through, playing through.'"

Neuwirth is credited with putting together the touring band, which became known as Guam; bassist Rob Stoner was the musical director. The players included the violinist Scarlet Rivera, who became famous for her searing solo on "Hurricane," Dylan's fiery epic about wrongfully imprisoned boxer Rubin "Hurricane" Carter, and the boyish nineteen-year-old string prodigy David Mansfield. With Frank Zappa providing transportation for the musicians and their significant others via his bus, Phydeaux, the Rolling Thunder Revue kicked off on October 30, 1975, in Plymouth, Massachusetts. Neuwirth acted as emcee and sang harmony with Dylan. The core cast included Joan Baez, the Byrds' Roger McGuinn, and Mick Ronson. They were joined along the way by such artists as Joni Mitchell, Gordon Lightfoot, Ronee Blakley (a star of the Robert Altman film *Nashville*), and Roberta Flack.

Though a virtual unknown to audiences, Burnett couldn't help drawing their attention: Who the heck was that skinny kid with the Big Bird look towering over his fellow musicians (not to mention tour companions like Allen Ginsberg)? "I stood at the back of the stage and didn't move," Burnett told the *Telegraph*. "It's inhibiting when you're a foot taller than anyone else and you have to bend down to the mike. I wasn't made for that."

David Mansfield recalled a less-reserved Burnett. "He would use his height sometimes to lunge across the stage," Mansfield told me. "He would make stage moves that because of his appearance were very striking. Mick Ronson, in comparison, would strike all these guitar-god poses." In what became a regular feature of the concerts, Burnett, lampooning his Texas image, lassoed Roger McGuinn from the wings following the singer's rendition of his Byrds hit "Chestnut Mare." Quipped Joan Baez in her best Newport Folk Festival hillbilly accent, "Roger dang near got himself lassoed to death!" And, accurately characterizing Burnett, she proclaimed, "He's one of them rushed-up fellas!"

Some members of the troupe, put off by Burnett's antics, wanted Dylan to cut him loose. With all the guitarists in the show (as many as five), Burnett's absence as a musician might not have mattered. His guitar skills, as good as they were, were not the reason he was on the tour to begin with, said Neuwirth, who as band organizer had been drawn to his outsize personality and overall talent. But, Mansfield told me, Burnett was "the only guy in the Rolling Thunder Revue who could play a Texas shuffle properly." He added, "Dylan liked the idea of this ragtag gypsy caravan, this oddball collection of people. I mean Bob appeared in whiteface the whole time. This tall, string bean cowboy fit right in."

Dylan incorporated footage from the tour into *Renaldo & Clara*, his misbegotten, four-hour theatrical film extravaganza. Burnett, who doesn't like to be photographed or filmed, asked to be left out of the epic, but he was cast in it anyway, briefly showing up as the Inner Voice and "Buddy Holly." In his book *Hard Rain: A Dylan Commentary*, Tim Riley describes Burnett as "the most unselfconsciously comic presence in the film . . . and a major discovery."

The playwright Sam Shepard, who was invited by Dylan to join the tour sight unseen, ostensibly to fashion a script for *Renaldo & Clara*, writes in his *Rolling Thunder Logbook* that Burnett had "a peculiar quality of craziness about him. He's the only one on the tour I'm not sure has relative control over his violent, dark side. He's not scary; he's just crazy." Shepard cites the destructive behavior that his future collaborator would unleash in restaurants "if he wasn't served when the hunger hit him."

In a 1983 *Rolling Stone* interview, Burnett admitted to being "mean and sarcastic" during the tour and "laughing in the face of death." In a 1996 interview with *Los Angeles Magazine*, though, he said, "I was never really all that crazy. But I would behave metaphorically at times." He followed that up by saying, "I wanted to know how far I could go, that's for sure."

Burnett made his presence felt in a more agreeable way by singing harmony on various tunes and hustling songs, including two by his Texas friend Roscoe West (né Bob Barnes). Ronson sang "Life on Mars" (not to be confused with David Bowie's "Life on Mars?") and Burnett sang "Hula Hoop," a slap at corporate types he co-wrote with West. With its seething lyrics ("I've never been to art school / But I kinda like Picasso / If I had one of his paintings / I'd only piss it off in Reno"), sung over a slinky, conga-fed groove, the tune provided a peek into the songwriting persona Burnett was developing. Another of the spotlight numbers he sang during the marathon sets, which could run as long as five hours, was Warren Zevon's "Werewolves of London." Burnett had met the brash Los Angeles rocker in 1973 at a Sunday gathering hosted by Don Everly following the contentious breakup of the Everly Brothers, the legendary act for whom Zevon was musical director. Burnett and Zevon became friends and chess partners. Burnett said he first heard "Werewolves" the day after Zevon wrote it (LeRoy Marinell and Waddy Wachtel received co-writing credits). He began performing his reggae-tinged version of the song two years before Zevon recorded it. "It seemed like a good tune to do for a crowd who had never heard me, or it, before," Burnett says in Sid Griffin's *Shelter from the Storm: Bob Dylan's Rolling Thunder Years.*

Singing over a lacerating steel guitar, Burnett left his own manic imprint on the knife-in-cheek classic. Among the celebrity dance pairings he imagined "doing" the Werewolves were Babe Ruth and Brigitte Bardot and the British film stars Glenda Jackson and Oliver Reed of Ken Russell's 1969 film *Women in Love.* He name-checked the Texas soul great Joe Tex, Carl Douglas (of "Kung Fu Fighting" fame), and the Band's Rick Danko.

By most accounts, the second leg of Rolling Thunder, which began in early 1976 and featured such new faces as the Texas singer-songwriter and humorist Kinky Friedman, lacked the galvanizing power and cohesion of the first half. But one of its highlights was Burnett's "Silver Mantis," a folk song co-written with his high school artist friend John "Flex" Fleming about a Japanese warlord's daughter who is saved from a kidnapping by a lowly servant only to see her father toss the servant in prison in a jealous rage.

"There's T Bone!" Dylan said, introducing Burnett to the hometown crowd at the Tarrant County Convention Center Arena in Fort Worth. "Sing a song called 'Sashiko'!" Never mind that Dylan got the title wrong and mispronounced the name of the princess. He was so fond of the song that he positioned it nicely between "Lay Lady Lay" and "Idiot Wind," played bass on it, and had Joan Baez sing harmony. Burnett, who played some piano, also got to sing "The Dogs," another Fleming co-write, this one inspired by COYOTE (Call Off Your Old Tired Ethics), the 1970s rights group dedicated to the repeal of prostitution laws.

The impact that Dylan had on Burnett, who reportedly teared up during the great one's renditions of "You're a Big Girl Now," was enormous. "Dylan opened the borders and wrote about life from a whole other point of view," Burnett told the *Los Angeles Times.* "I had started trying to do that. Writing songs that weren't just about girlfriends and boyfriends and cars." Less simply, Burnett was influenced by the freedom Dylan enjoyed in departing from realism in his lyrics and indulging in righteous anger. Burnett also was impressed by the looseness and changeability of Dylan's music, as well as the pacing of his shows. "Dylan doesn't give you an arrangement; you busk along . . ." he told Sid Griffin. "He wasn't one for getting everything all bolted down." Indeed, as Mansfield recalled, what was a waltz one night might become a blues shuffle the next.

Beyond all that, the Rolling Thunder experience instilled deep community values in Burnett. Though Dylan was the obvious focal point, and the reason fans filled the seats, these shows weren't just about him. They were about a group of diverse artists who were striving for unity, for common cause, for an uplifting grassroots vision at a time when the United States (with Gerald Ford in the White House) was sorely missing one. Burnett has never stopped pursuing that kind of group experience. Again and again, whether performing with a troupe called Void at Chicago's Steppenwolf Theatre in 1999; joining Jackson Browne and Nanci Griffith in a 2001 benefit for Minnesota's Gyuto Monastery hosted by Jessica Lange and Sam Shepard; putting together stage extravaganzas like the 2010 Speaking Clock Revue with the likes of Elvis Costello, Neko Case, and the Punch Brothers; recording the all-star ensemble album *Lost on the River: The New Basement Tapes*; or teaming up with John Mellencamp and Stephen King on the musical *Ghost Brothers of Darkland County*, Burnett has found greater meaning in "we" than "I." He has strived, as he would sing on his next recording, to "keep it in the family."

CHAPTER 4

Alpha Male

Disillusioned, burnt out, drugged out, or all of the above, many survivors of the sixties turned to religion as part of what *Time* magazine dubbed "The Jesus Movement" on its cover of June 21, 1971. "There is an uncommon morning freshness to this movement, a buoyant atmosphere of hope and love along with the usual rebel zeal," read the accompanying story. "Their love seems . . . deeper than the fast-fading sentiments of the flower children."

Well, maybe and maybe not. But coming off the positive energy and uplift of Rolling Thunder, Burnett was drawn to a nascent spiritual movement in Southern California—one that embraced rock music as a powerful medium for Christians to fellowship with God, at a time when conservative churchgoers distrusted the metaphor. Spearheaded by musicians like the "Jesus rock" singer Larry Norman (whose 1969 Capitol recording *Upon This Rock* is considered by some to be the first Christian rock album) and the former Righteous Brothers pianist (and manager) John Wimber, these churches offered a more open and casual form of Bible study.

In the mid-to-late 1970s, around the time that Burnett, Steven Soles, and David Mansfield began embracing religious expression as the Alpha Band—and the born-again Christian Jimmy Carter became president—Burnett and his wife began attending Bible classes at the Vineyard Christian Fellowship in West Los Angeles. Soles, Mansfield, and other friends followed. Reportedly prodded by his girlfriend at the time, Dylan began studying there in 1979 with his personal pastor, Kenn Gulliksen. Some of the musicians (not Dylan, who sat in the back, incognito) performed in the church band, for which Soles wrote songs. "People in the arts were flocking to the place," Mansfield told me. "Sometimes, people were dragging their friends there just to hear the music."

Burnett, who in the face of attempts to stereotype him as born-again has always personalized his approach to religion, drew from these studies what he wanted and needed in consolidating his beliefs and renewing his faith (which didn't include the speaking in tongues, divine healing, and "signs and wonders" promoted by some branches of the Vineyard). "T Bone talked about this stuff all the time," said Mansfield, who as one of the last members of the circle to commit to Christianity—he had not yet done so when he joined the Alpha Band—came under some intense pressure. "T Bone and Steven were laying it on pretty thick," he told me. "They challenged me pretty hard."

In other ways, there was nothing typical about the Alpha Band. Rather than create noise for themselves in the music capital, the new band left Los Angeles in the summer of 1976 and set up shop in the historic New Mexican town of Tesuque, outside of Santa Fe. Dylan's longtime road manager and aide Victor Maymudes (whose recollections are the basis for his son Jacob's 2014 book, *Another Side of Bob Dylan*) had remodeled a property in the town and turned it into a nightclub. The Alphas rehearsed by day and performed bar-band style by night. In a short amount of time, they created their own scene. When they felt ready, they invited the major record labels down to hear them. Arista Records founder Clive Davis sent his young associate (and future film producer of note) Roger Birnbaum, who flipped for the band and urged his boss to see them for himself. Davis came and did a double flip. "He practically got down on bended knee to sign us," Mansfield told me. "It was very bizarre."

After dishing out a reported $6 million for them, Davis proclaimed the Alpha Band the most important act since the Beatles ("We should have quit then—our case was hopeless," said Mansfield) and installed them as co-headliners at Arista's August convention in Camelback, Arizona. They shared the bill with the Funky Kings, a short-lived LA country-rock band featuring Jack Tempchin (writer of such Eagles hits as "Peaceful Easy Feeling") and Jules Shear (a future songwriting hero known for such hits as the Bangles' "If She Knew What She Wants"). In his 2013 memoir *The Soundtrack of My Life*, Davis says the Alpha Band "brought the house down." Carried by the momentum and media exposure of Rolling Thunder, how could this group fail?

The fact that they took their name from *Alphaville*, the chilly 1965 sci-fi film by nervy French director Jean-Luc Godard, should have been a sign that Burnett, Soles, and Mansfield (plus a rhythm section including B-52 Band members David Jackson and Matt Betton) weren't going to be rolling out any easy-feeling FM hits. To be sure, there were whiffs of the Band and Little Feat, Bo Diddley, and Buddy Holly in their sound—and plenty of Texas blues and border music. Early on, Mansfield told me, Burnett gave him a cassette tape of songs by Elmore James, Jimmy Reed, and other blues greats "to absorb and study." But couched in Marxist parables, sci-fi scenarios, existential dramas, and snarling performance art, *The Alpha Band* (released in late 1976) did not connect with mainstream listeners.

Burnett was settling into what Mansfield called "the Jeremiah phase of his new-found Christian faith" (Jeremiah being the great prophet who spoke against false prophets in warning his people that Jerusalem would be destroyed unless they mended their ways). And though as a social critic he largely took aim at corrupt institutions rather than individuals, there was a little Professor Harold Hill as well in his warnings of doom with a capital D for people who didn't reorder their priorities, rein in their excesses, and find a higher power in which to believe.

Set to a throbbing beat, "Interviews" is a spooky rip on skewed modern values from fifty million years in the future. One of its star attractions is a circus barker who resembles the soft porn king Russ Meyer. Broken in during Rolling Thunder, "The Dogs" is a surrealistic, Spanish-tinged tale of "forbidden women" in "Hollow wood." The honky-tonk noir "Last Chance to Dance" could be a sketch for a Robert Rodriguez film. "Your knife is on the table," sings Burnett, "My gun is in my boot / If you promise not to cut me / I'll promise not to shoot." Among the lighter tunes are the twangy ballad "Dark Eyes," an excuse for Mansfield's airy violin and mandolin solos, and "Keep It in the Family," which boasts an irresistible shuffle and bounce along with collegial group vocals.

The Alpha Band fell far short of Beatle-like—or Bay City Roller–like—heights. Pressured by a mortified Clive Davis to be more listener-friendly, the group did its best to follow his directive—to a point, and with mixed results—on their 1977 follow-up, *Spark in the Dark*. Burnett's treatment of Bob Dylan's infrequently heard "You Angel You" is one of his most delectable covers. On the rock bard's underrated 1974 album *Planet Waves*, "You Angel You" got the full Band treatment, with Robbie Robertson at his most cutting on guitar, Garth Hudson pouring out lyrical insight on organ, and Rick Danko and Levon Helm locking down the rhythm with soulful strength. Burnett transforms the song into an elegant, sweetly galloping rockabilly number, with guest Ringo Starr providing a buoyant backbeat on drums and singing harmony.

"Silver Mantis," though boasting an exotic arrangement featuring Osamu Kitajima's kora and Mansfield's haunting cello, here occasions one of Burnett's most agreeably unaffected performances. The story of the warlord's daughter and the servant who gets thrown in a dungeon for saving her is told in slow, unhurried fashion (at six minutes and thirty-three seconds, it's one of Burnett's longest songs), boasting rare, meaningful silences between sections. Kris Kristofferson and Rita Coolidge would soon record "Silver Mantis" for their 1979 album *Natural Act*.

Had the rest of *Spark in the Dark* been as strong, Clive Davis might have had his high hopes for the Alpha Band validated. But the album, "humbly offered in the light of the triune God," is weighed down by preachiness. "Born in Captivity" is a smug attack on corporate brainwashing set to a clip-clop beat, in which helpless consumers are portrayed as "Cossack children of the bourgeoisie." And on the group-written "East of East," Burnett, cast as an "absent-minded priest," ruminates on sin with church bells pealing over slide guitar. (The latter song was inspired, he writes in the notes to his 2006 anthology, *Twenty Twenty: The Essential T Bone Burnett*, by the disquieting sight late one morning at the Chateau Marmont Hotel of a beautiful thirteen-year-old German girl joining her mother and a stoned-out Roman Polanski in his room. The girl was future film star Nastassja Kinski.)

Filled out by a flowery piano piece by Soles and a new-agey acoustic number by Mansfield, *Spark in the Dark* awakened little more interest than did *The Alpha Band*. Burnett, worn out from Arista's efforts to make the group more accessible—"I was ready for the wigwam," he told *Rolling Stone*—informed Davis that the Alphas were going to jump the commercial tracks even more on the third and final album of their deal. If the label wanted to let them out of their contract, it could. Perhaps holding out hope for a miracle, Davis let them complete their religious trilogy.

Throwing himself into his songwriting, Burnett turned out the most explicitly Christian Alpha Band album—and the boldest, widest reaching, and biggest sounding. Featuring an expansive cast of Burnett regulars, plus a church choir directed by the famed gospel artist Andraé Crouch, *The Statue Makers of Hollywood* (1978) made the country-rock tag that some reviewers insisted on sticking on the band seem even sillier than before. For all its messages from on high, the album came down to earth with its interjections of humor, irony, and playfulness.

The opener, "Tick Tock," is a bumptious, eight-minute telling of Genesis, carried by a low-riding funk groove that might have been stolen from the multiracial LA band War. The song features a rare trick vocal by Burnett, whose teasing, drawn-out "Ohhh yeaaaaahhs" provide the hook. On "Mighty Man" and "Perverse Generation," Burnett takes the modern age to task for achieving "progress" at the cost of hardened hearts. The faithless Everyman in the first song, which channels the work of the Italian film composer Ennio Morricone with its whistling high notes and stentorian male chorus, "can fly to the moon but . . . can't get to heaven in his rocket" (and the lowly mortal "can't even keep his car from stalling").

Best of all is "Rich Man," which is unlike anything Burnett had done before. "Oh, you rich man weep and howl" is the basic theme, but repeated over the earthy, swooping sound of the church choir the phrase takes on all-inclusive power. Mansfield's mandolin is first heard dancing through Darrell Leonard's burly, dissonant horn arrangement. Then, playing off congas with unlikely sitar-like effects, Mansfield fashions what can only be described as a Caribbean raga sound. The song is nothing short of epic and yet, in the end, has the airiness of a hit single. Following "Back in My Baby's Arms," a happy dose of Texas-meets-Memphis soul, Burnett brings things full circle with Hank Williams's "Thank God," one of the ultimate mergers of secular and sacred. "In this world of grief and sorrow / Filled with selfishness and greed," he sings, "There remains the Glory Fountain / To supply our every need."

The Statue Makers of Hollywood was another commercial flop. In his autobiography and in various interviews, Clive Davis has singled out his signing of the Alpha Band as one of his biggest misfires. In his estimation, the band failed to win an audience because, though their albums were "perfectly respectable" (ouch), they didn't yield the "signature song" needed to "fully establish a group's identity with the public." If anyone in the music business can claim to have solved the vexing riddle of how to make a hit record, it's Davis, who has scored with everyone from Barry Manilow to Patti Smith to Whitney Houston. But the Alpha Band's failure to ignite seems to have had less to do with its lack of "a signature song" than its preachy intellectualism.

Burnett has said the band never had real direction and became temperamental. Hoping they could pull off a Steely Dan—take on only choice gigs and make records when they felt like it—the Alphas hit the road only when they needed to cover debts. "We were a bit full of ourselves," Mansfield told me.

In 1979, Dylan shocked the world (again) with his own religious album, *Slow Train Coming*, which announced his conversion to evangelical Christianity. "Well, it may be the devil or it may be the Lord / But you're gonna have to serve somebody," he sings, pointing a threatening finger at "All nonbelievers and men stealers talkin' in the name of religion." Speculation was rife that Burnett, playing pied piper for the Vineyard, had "turned" one of the world's most famous Jews. But while Soles spoke openly about religiously lobbying Dylan—"I kept telling him that I was so glad that I didn't have to place my faith in man any longer," he told *New Musical Express* in 1979—Burnett repeatedly denied that he played any such role.

In a 1987 interview with the *Los Angeles Times* critics Robert Hilburn and Chris Willman bearing the headline, "Rock of Ages: There's a New Spirituality in Pop Music," Burnett said he thought the former Robert Zimmerman had gotten caught up in a worldwide spiritual moment that also had touched Ireland's U2 and Australia's INXS as well as musicians in his own backyard, such as Roger McGuinn, Richie Furay of Poco, and Barry McGuire of "Eve of Destruction" fame. "Maybe rock 'n' roll has finally begun to grow up," Burnett said. "It has gone through its infancy and its adolescence, which was the '60s, and probably its yuppie, material stage. Now, the artists are free to look a bit deeper into life and search for some eternal truths . . . the kind of search that has been part of literature and art for ages. Rock 'n' roll is a very powerful medium, and it helps us all to get something through this medium that is about life rather than death."

Burnett would continue to express and explore his religious faith through music, but the Alpha Band was history, leaving behind little in the way of bonus tracks, bootlegs, or boo hoos. Still as much of an outsider in Los Angeles as he had been in Fort Worth, Burnett was again left looking for artistic purchase. He returned to Texas, played a lot of golf, and worked on a sci-fi novel, thinking that kind of writing would become his life's work. Kris Kristofferson helped set him straight.

CHAPTER 5

Spiritual Gumshoe

In the spring of 1979, while Burnett was regrouping and de-discombobulating post-Alpha Band, Kristofferson the matinee idol was up in Montana's Glacier National Park filming *Heaven's Gate*, Michael Cimino's ill-fated Western epic. He invited Bruton, Burnett, and David Mansfield to join him. They each were given a cameo role: Burnett was the leader of the Heaven's Gate Band (he got to count in a tune), Bruton the band member D. B. Schultz and, in a charming roller rink scene, Mansfield the skating violinist John DeCory. (Mansfield ended up scoring *Heaven's Gate*, winning the job over several big-name movie composers, after the soundtrack superstar John Williams bowed out to become conductor of the Boston Pops Orchestra.) Rolling Thunder Revue trouper Ronnie Hawkins, who played "Bob Dylan" in *Renaldo and Clara*, also appeared in Cimino's film.

During the weeks that stretched to six months in Big Sky Country, Burnett and Mansfield had plenty of time and opportunities to preach religion. "We were like two little Bible thumpers," Mansfield told me. "T Bone was on fire. He was seeing everything in black and white." Burnett was set back on his heels a bit when he asked John Hurt whether he had read any C. S. Lewis, an important writer for the Christian movement, and the British actor replied, "Oh, yes, my father was friends with Jack Lewis." A fellow free spirit, Hurt ended up commandeering a six-seat private plane with Burnett. "We felt like we were escaping across the Rockies!" the actor told *Vulture*.

More productively, Burnett and his cronies worked on a bunch of new songs back at their Kalispell hotel, the Outlaw Inn (now unfortunately called the GuestHouse Inn & Suites & Outlaw Convention Center). Kristofferson lent them members of his band, including the Louisiana guitar wiz Gerry McGee, a latter-day member of the Ventures. The revered composer of "Me and Bobby McGee" (no relation) and "For the Good Times," who didn't often cover other people's tunes, had become one of Burnett's major patrons by including not only "Silver Mantis" but also "Hula Hoop" and "Back in My Baby's Arms" on his album *Natural Act*. A few years earlier, Kristofferson had tried to get "Hula Hoop" into the rock music remake of *A Star Is Born*, but his co-star and executive producer Barbra Streisand wanted ownership of the publishing. Refusing to give away those rights, Burnett reportedly walked away from a big payday.

The gathered players at the Outlaw Inn worked out the songs by day and performed them by night in the hotel bar. Ultimately, they recorded acoustic versions of them in Mansfield's room on his two high-powered Nakamichi cassette decks. "We nailed the songs, the feel of them, the directions we wanted to go, without drums," Mansfield told me. "They were nice-sounding little recordings. T Bone was really eager to get them out."

Back in Los Angeles, Burnett signed a deal with Takoma, an indie label founded and made semi-famous by the fingerpicking guitar god John Fahey (though he no longer owned it). It was run by Denny Bruce, a respected industry figure and former drummer who had managed Burnett's B-52 Band and produced the folk artist Leo Kottke. Bruce reportedly told Burnett to make an album like Buddy Holly would make in Las Cruces, were he alive in the last year of the 1970s. That album, largely consisting of the songs recorded in Montana, was *Truth Decay*, the 1980 release widely regarded as Burnett's bona fide solo debut.

Buddy Holly certainly would have been right at home in the garage where the *Truth Decay* sessions took place—the Valley garage studio of Burnett friend Reggie Fisher. Nothing if not resourceful, Fisher created the album's trashy-ambient sound by leaving the door leading from the garage to the attached house half-open and miking the room next to it—which may seem like a far cry from the sophisticated techniques Burnett would later employ as a producer, but reflected a shared desire to capture old sounds in new ways. The rockabilly spirit couldn't be more alive on tunes like "Quicksand," on which the basic Outlaw Inn band stirs the catchy melody over a shaking groove and Burnett's ringing guitar chords reflect off the sizzle of the cymbals.

With the great, perennially undervalued Billy Swan singing harmonies behind him, Burnett performs with understated confidence. The low-boil, bluesified swing of "Talk Talk Talk Talk Talk" and the high-octane, hard-edged Western swing of "Driving Wheel" reveal Burnett's feel for jazz. The thwomping power-pop workout "Boomerang," a leftover from the Alpha Band, is both the hookiest tune on the album and the one with the most skewed narrative—one in which "thieves and debutants talked in italics." On the mournful, lovely piano ballad "Madison Avenue," Burnett asks, "Who is the father of lies?"—an ageless question that might be directed at *Mad Men*'s advertising legend Don Draper and the empty, manufactured values he promotes.

"Power of Love," a stately, high-stepping ballad later covered by Arlo Guthrie, radiates beams of steadfast belief, as does the tender country-spiritual ballad "I'm Coming Home," which is lifted by Mansfield's gorgeous guitar solo. In contrast to the harsh visions Burnett expressed in his Jeremiah mode, these smart, probing songs unfold in a soft-spoken, nonthreatening manner. The emptiness of "Talk Talk Talk Talk Talk" ("They don't say nothing") is counterbalanced by the full emotions of "Tears Tears Tears," on which Burnett declares, "Know that truth is truth and I love you." The false values of "House of Mirrors" ("This suit is you, this car is you, this studio is you") are neutralized by the power of love, which "can make a skeptic believe."

Like the soul singer Al Green, who released his great *Belle Album* three years earlier, Burnett was adept at ambiguity. Home could be where you live or where He lives. Love could lift you romantically and save you from your loneliness or lift you higher and forgive you of your sins. But on *Truth Decay*, Burnett came clean with his direct expression of religion, presenting himself not as a Christian rocker, and not as a rock artist with a "Christian" point of view, but a rock artist of Christian faith with wholly personal beliefs. Asked in 1982 by *Today's Christian Music* about his religious message, he said, "I'm not really conscious of it but I know what my message is not. It's not: 'I-used-to-be-miserable-but-now-I-found-Jesus—but-you're-still-miserable-so-why-don't-you-find-Jesus-and-be-happy-like-me.'" He added, "I don't find myself needing to go out and find people to tell about Jesus. My ministry is to make doubters out of unbelievers."

At the same time, he felt cut off from believers: "I'm out there doing it. I'd appreciate some support. I am a Christian and I think what I'm doing is healthy." Bono, among other young, religious-minded rock artists looking for role models, agreed, embracing *Truth Decay* as a breakthrough album. The Takoma debut, wrote Ken Tucker in *Rolling Stone*, "suggests that T Bone Burnett is the best singer-songwriter in the country right now. No one this year will make music more forthright, more tender, more scrupulously free of cheap irony and trumped-up passion." The *Village Voice*'s Robert Christgau called it the best rockabilly album of the year.

For all that, *Truth Decay* failed to find an audience, partly because people had trouble finding it. When the album was reissued on CD by the British Demon label in 1986, a time when people were excited about acquiring digital versions of their favorite LPs, *Truth Decay* was long absent from the vinyl racks. These days, it is not commercially available in any format. Burnett did remix three of the songs for *Twenty Twenty*, but as good as those reconstituted tracks sound, you miss the garage-band immediacy of the originals.

In early 1981, Burnett and his wife mutually decided, following this latest disappointment, that it was time for him to get more aggressive in pursuing success—"to dance or get off the floor" as he put it in a November 1983 *Rolling Stone* profile. For long stretches over the next couple of years, leaving his wife, Stephanie, and their daughters Angelina (born in 1978) and Molly (born in 1981) behind in Fort Worth, he lived in Los Angeles, crashing in his manager's rented house and driving a maroon 1965 Cadillac with "TEXAS" emblazoned on the license plate.

Burnett, who hadn't played much live outside of Rolling Thunder, began regularly appearing at Hop Singh's, a jazz and rock joint in the West Los Angeles community of Marina Del Rey, and Madame Wong's, a Chinese restaurant with spots in Chinatown and Santa Monica. His unusual shows, which drew on his love of show tunes and standards as well as roots music, and showed off his offbeat wit, drew attention. Warner Bros., which expressed interest in signing him, rejected his proposal to do an album consisting of personal interpretations of show and film tunes. But his first major label, which like other record companies was dabbling with the "mini-album" or extended-play format in the days preceding the arrival of the compact disc, had no trouble making his insouciant treatment of "Diamonds Are a Girl's Best Friend" the centerpiece of a six-song EP, *Trap Door* (1982).

There have been few notable rock covers of Broadway tunes: Janis Joplin's "Summertime" from *Porgy and Bess*; the Mamas and the Papas' "My Heart Stood Still" from *A Connecticut Yankee*; the Beatles' "Till There Was You" from *The Music Man*; and I suppose we must include the Fifth Dimension's "Aquarius / Let the Sunshine In" from *Hair*. In his notes to *Twenty Twenty*, Burnett says he always found it strange to hear a man sing "House of the Rising Sun" (a 1964 smash for the Animals), being that it was written about a girl working in a New Orleans brothel. "Diamonds Are a Girl's Best Friend," written by Styne and Robin for the iconic character of Lorelei in *Gentlemen Prefer Blondes*, was his own experiment in gender reversal.

In the annals of popular music, the words "Let's rock" have never been uttered with cooler reserve than they are when Burnett kicks his "Diamonds" into gear. He recites the words in song-speak as if imparting some kind of secret knowledge; you picture him in front of a fireplace in some fancy boîte, his spectators swigging wine; maybe there are imported olives and nuts in brilliant cut crystal bowls. "Diamonds" does indeed rock, just fine, its chiming folk-rock guitars and thrumming percussion and his bandmates' bright harmony vocals making for good company. But anyone who has heard the song delivered from Lorelei's point of view in *Gentlemen Prefer Blondes*—especially as performed by the super-seductive Marilyn Monroe in the film version—may need a few moments to adjust the vertical hold.

The prefeminist joke in the lyrics is that if a woman has to suffer the consequences of living in a man's world, she is going to make the opposite sex pay through the nose for her . . . attention. So, is Burnett sharing Lorelei's delight, as a friend of hers, admiring her wiles? Or, is he playing the part of devil, in full control of the game and in full possession of his power? Sounding like they are in on the game, the answering vocalists have us leaning toward the latter interpretation. And then there is a third possibility: What if Burnett is singing as a willing victim? Who wouldn't go into hock to spend some quality time with Marilyn? Rock on, indeed.

It is difficult to imagine Burnett pulling off this stunt earlier in his career: "Men grow cold as girls grow old / And we all lose our charms in the end." But at thirty-two, he had started absorbing the theatrical influences—Kurt Weill, Bertolt Brecht, Lotte Lenya—he had dipped into on the cabaret-derived material on *The Unwritten Works of Geoffrey, Etc.* A postmodern art song in rock clothing, his "Diamonds" casts a gentle irony that, coming from such a jigsaw-jagged commentator, is doubly winning.

Elsewhere, the EP spotlights a very different kind of blonde. On "I Wish You Could Have Seen Her Dance," a barroom attraction in a low-cut black satin dress, black velvet gloves, and rhinestone bracelets shows off her moves before a group of sexed-up teens: "She did a pirouette and then a kung fu step" and also "the flavo and the tango and the flamenco." The song has more cute asides than it can bear, but its surging, new wave energy—and underlying compassion for a girl marked by disappointment—make up for that. With guitars jangling (and burning in the case of the solo near the end), "Ridiculous Man" exposes the follies of wealth and power. And then, wiping the slate clean, Burnett makes a powerful declaration of belief on "Poetry."

Reminiscent of a Brill Building ballad with its tailored melody, the song depicts being broken and scared, "hiding in the blackness of the darkness of night," and then finding a burning presence to love not only "more than dreams and poetry / More than laughter more than tears, more than mystery"—but also "more than rhythm, more than song."

Coming from someone so profoundly invested in music, that is quite a statement. That said, the deeper you get into Burnett's body of work, the more you get a sense that music in and of itself is for him a source of transcendent beauty and truth—not only in service of a higher authority, as in the Vineyard services, but on its own. "We talked a lot about how music in itself is enough, making it beautiful is enough, how you don't need to weigh it down with a [religious] agenda," Sam Phillips told me. A beautiful chord sequence or captivating rumble, whether it has roots in Howlin' Wolf or Irving Berlin or an African tribal band, can lift us out of ourselves and into a dimension of spiritual feeling—of being connected to forces greater than ourselves. "I was beginning to go through a rough personal time, as were a lot of people around me," Burnett says in the liner notes to the 2007 Rhino reissue of *Trap Door*. "I think I was trying to reassure those friends, and myself."

Though the running time of the EP, produced by Burnett and Reggie Fisher, is only twenty-two minutes, it doesn't feel slight the way most efforts in this format do. There is a lot to digest. Reviews were strong. "The most profoundly elegant and powerful rock release of 1982," wrote Joseph Sasfy in the *Washington Post*, holding out hope the artist would cease to be "somewhat unknown to the record-buying public." He went on, "If Dylan is the only relevant comparison, you would have to return to 'John Wesley Harding' for a comparable experience."

His reputation rising, Burnett got a plum spot as opening act for several American "farewell" concerts by the Who in October 1982. His Rolling Thunder crony Mick Ronson reportedly turned down a lucrative offer from Bob Seger to accompany Burnett instead. Going on before Pete Townshend, Roger Daltrey, and the blokes was no picnic for Burnett, a marginal figure at best for Who fanatics. According to coverage of the Seattle Kingdome concert on *The Who Concert*

Guide site, he "suffered a particularly bad response of almost incessant booing and jeering . . . for the duration of their thirty-minute set." And on Halloween eve at the Los Angeles Memorial Coliseum, Burnett suffered the odd indignity of having to open not only for the Clash and the Who, but also a complete playing on the PA system of *The Best of the Doors.*

The booers didn't know what they missed. To hear Burnett, Ronson, and company perform at the Old Waldorf in San Francisco the same week, via an archival recording on the *BB Chronicles* blog, is to hear a unit that gave away nothing in slashing power and punkish concision. They opened the first set with a crunching reading of Eddie Cochran's "C'mon Everybody," closed the second set with a Ronson guitar freak-out on Burnett's "Love at First Sight," and poured corrosive power into most everything in between. "Can I Get a Witness" was treated to a blistering, call-and-response, reggae-rock sermon ("Religion is so much easier now that God is gone / We don't have to think about the things like right and wrong"). After giving "Diamonds Are a Girl's Best Friend" a showbiz-style intro—"Jule Styne song, Jule Styne and Leo Robin wrote this for Carol Channing"—Burnett turned it into a hard-edged romp. (Among the less satisfying numbers was his wobbly rendition of Roger Miller's "King of the Road.")

The other club dates Burnett was playing around the same time, without Ronson, "were always a total blast," Mansfield said. On one memorable night at McCabe's Guitar Shop, the Santa Monica landmark, the songs included Kris Kristofferson's "The Pilgrim Chapter 33" (inspired by the "walkin' contradiction" Bob Neuwirth); "Be Careful of Stones That You Throw," originally recorded by Hank Williams as "Luke the Drifter" and later by Bob Dylan during the *Basement Tapes* sessions; and the spoken word and piano number "Art Movies," which became a B-side obscurity ("They're usually made by very small Germans," Burnett informed the crowd).

He was, in fact, a serious filmgoer, at a time when the American cinema was going through a golden period—directors like Martin Scorsese, John Cassavetes, Blake Edwards, and Jonathan Demme were turning out masterpieces—and new and revived European classics by the likes of Ingmar Bergman, Jean-Luc Godard, Eric Rohmer,

Bernardo Bertolucci, and Germany's Rainer Werner Fassbinder were being widely distributed. With his investment in darkness, and the truth about humanity that can be found there, Burnett was a big fan of film noir, including works based on or inspired by Raymond Chandler, one of Los Angeles' greatest contributions to popular culture, and mysteries by such authors as his LA friend James Ellroy, widely known for *The Black Dahlia.* The presence of these works was strongly felt on his first full-fledged Warner album, *Proof through the Night* (1983).

If any album seemed to prime him for stardom, this was it. It boasted guest shots by a murderer's row of guitarists in Pete Townshend, Ry Cooder, Mick Ronson, Richard Thompson, and David Mansfield, not to mention the Tom Petty and the Heartbreakers drummer Stan Lynch. And the songs, in the year of *The Year of Living Dangerously*, were edgy and atmospheric, marked by smeared red lipstick, the lingering scent of cigarette smoke, and the sound of heels clicking against darkened sidewalks. We encounter a disappeared girl who had "a whisper you could hear across an ocean"; a girl who "once made people faint" but "crumbled like a dream"; and, on the Townshend-fired "Fatally Beautiful," a Marilyn Monroe–like character who was sexually abused as a foster child, got taken advantage of by a film producer, and became a centerfold before being murdered by an admirer.

At its best, *Proof through the Night* has the moral complexity of Roman Polanski's *Chinatown* and the offhand brilliance of Robert Altman's Chandler adaptation, *The Long Goodbye.* "When the Night Falls," written with Roy Orbison in mind, is a heart-wrenching portrait of existential despair in which a man, overcome with remorse over a lost love, leaves his hotel every twilight to "follow my shadow till morning" and climbs back to his dark room "through the litter of Sunday newspapers." The visionary "Hefner and Disney," spoken with a resigned anger bordering on wistfulness, portrays the *Playboy* founder and Mickey Mouse inventor as interchangeable threats to the moral fabric—evil men "who wanted to rob the children of their dreams." Despite running only three minutes and forty seconds, this twisted fable has the feel of an epic with its spaghetti Western crescendos, modern classical touches, and muted female vocal choruses. (In 2014, Burnett named Uncle Walt as his "most despised living person" in *Vanity Fair*'s Proust Questionnaire.)

Too often, though, Burnett gets caught up in easy moralizing and intellectual gamesmanship (e.g., he says the women in the songs are metaphorical stand-ins for America in its diminishing states of glory). The main offender is "The Sixties," which purports to lament the tossing out of important 1960s ideals like social responsibility along with love-ins and tie-dyed shirts, but comes off as a contemptuous indictment of the "new breed of man"—the man in faded Levis and Gucci loafers whose idea of applying counterculture values is not questioning authority or putting larger purposes ahead of his immediate needs, but smoking "the best marijuana," paying for "free love," and talking the talk: "You know I'm a sports freak / I'm a jazz freak / I'm a video freak."

"I was writing about self-deception and deceiving myself while I was doing it," Burnett told me in 2003. But responding to criticism at the time, he said that any moral judgments in the songs were meant to be self-inclusive. "I've written a lot of really tough songs; I've been really tough on my characters a lot of times," he told the *Los Angeles Times*. "But at the same time I know any discussion of morality begins with one's self, and the person I was really dealing with in all those things *was* myself." He is no Jimmy Carter, but then again, Burnett has never made any bones about struggling with impure desires. "All the greed and lust and confusion and ambition is all part of me," he told *Rolling Stone*.

What made Burnett most unhappy about *Proof through the Night*—which, it should be pointed out, earned him the top spot in a *Rolling Stone* critics' poll for songwriter of the year, and is regarded by many people as one of his best albums—was the way the songs were handled in the studio. Plans to have the Who regular Glyn Johns produce it in London fell through. The job went to Jeff Eyrich, a young LA studio bassist who went on to produce the Blasters, Rank and File, and Thin White Rope but at the time had produced only "A Million Miles Away," the hit single by the power pop band the Plimsouls. Burnett had not yet acquired the clout to produce himself—or, as he prefers, co-produce with a trusted ally ("We all need editors"). With Eyrich at the controls, *Proof* became a study in excess.

"It was decided that we needed more muscular rock 'n' roll stuff," Burnett wrote in his liner notes for the 2007 Rhino reissue of *Proof* (packaged in a two-disc set with *Trap Door* and *Beyond the Trap Door*, an EP of odds and ends that had been released in England). Posting on the mastering engineer Steve Hoffman's *Music Forums* message board, Burnett lamented "some echo unit that the producer and engineer loved. They used it all over the record. It just went on and on." In the end, he wrote in the Rhino notes, he was forced to write two songs on the spot "that I never really felt confident in."

It's a measure of just how distressed Burnett was about *Proof*—which, he posted on Hoffman's site, "was released prematurely and half-baked and overdone"—that it didn't appear on CD until twenty-seven years after its initial release on vinyl. That is one of the longest stretches an album of its stature has remained undigitized. And the Rhino version came out only after he had had a chance to redo and in some cases lengthen no less than seven of the songs for *Twenty Twenty*.

"I stripped off all the production," he posted, "rewrote a couple of songs, re-sang a couple, and remixed the whole thing except for one song, 'Shut It Tight,' which was recorded before we began production on the album and therefore was not subject to the nonsense that went on during the actual production of the album, if you will forgive me for saying so. I always thought there was a pretty good record underneath all that and have now proven so to myself at least."

The alterations are pretty striking, conceptually as well as aurally. Burnett's voice on the original version of "Hefner and Disney" has no definition; he is a talking head with no stake in the music going on around him. The remake gives his vocal a devilish dimension with its depth of focus: the medium meets the message. Out-of-sync acoustic guitars add a modern classical element to "Fatally Beautiful." With its drums removed, the antinuclear rant "The Murder Weapon" makes a considerably subtler statement.

"There were things that I know a lot more about now, things that had gnawed at me for years, things that I'd let go out that I wish I had paid more attention to, that I could have done a whole lot better," he wrote in the *Proof* liner notes. He added, "Back then I used to make records and then go out on the road, and when you go out on the road you learn so much about how the song is speaking. There were a couple of songs that I re-sang because I thought that I could sing them so much better—I wish I had sung everything better. And I did some remixing where things got lost or covered up in production, where I couldn't hear the song or even what I meant at the time."

For those purveyors of art who are opposed to after-the-fact tampering or repackaging—whether it's Ted Turner colorizing classic films, an academic "restoring" Robert Penn Warren's *All the King's Men* to the point of changing Willie Stark's name (meet the new boss, Willie Talos?), or Bob Dylan releasing an alternate *Self-Portrait*—Burnett's changes are objectionable on their face. Many fans of *Proof* prefer the sound of the original, echoes and all, to the resounding, deep tones and chamber-like sound of the remake. But as Burnett's followers well know, there is no place for permanence in his ongoing pursuit of truth—aural, spiritual, poetic. Historical recordings need to be preserved, but for him, music—including or especially his own—is there for the renewing and reimagining. And in rare cases like *Proof*, where someone thinks it is a good idea to keep T Bone from being T Bone, music is there for the rebuilding—no matter how long that may take.

CHAPTER 6

Master Builder

The brass at Warner Bros. may have had doubts about entrusting Burnett with the production of *Proof through the Night.* But during the making of that album, the Warner subsidiary, Slash Records, which was enjoying national success documenting the LA punk and roots-revival scene, asked him to produce a promising band from East Los Angeles. That band was Los Lobos, a long-standing unit that had developed from an acoustic group specializing in traditional Mexican music into an electric band with a blistering, punk-friendly attack.

Lobbied by one of his leading acts, the Blasters, to sign Los Lobos, the head of Slash Records, Bob Biggs, a painter and art collector, put them on his roster. But he didn't know what to do with them. His close friend Hudson Marquez, a conceptual artist (part of the art group

Ant Farm, creators of Texas' popular *Cadillac Ranch* installation) and video producer (known for TVTV), who knew Burnett from his Alpha Band days and had himself co-produced an album by the Blasters keyboardist Gene Taylor, urged Biggs to hire him. "I played Biggs the Alpha Band albums and other tapes I had of Bone," Marquez told me. "He said he liked the simple, bare-bones production of T Bone's recordings and his ease with R&B. And, of course, he knew Tex-Mex music."

Burnett, who had never seen Los Lobos live, was knocked out when he saw them perform at a club. Los Lobos knew next to nothing about him, but when the band members Cesar Rosas and Conrad Lozano met with him at Hollywood's Ocean Studio, per Chris Morris's *Los Lobos: Dream in Blue*, they were impressed with what he had been working on lately. Their shared love of *norteño* music and Buddy Holly clinched the deal. "They understood all the connections, how it all made sense," Burnett tells Morris.

Continuing the record-release strategy they had used with Burnett, Warner had Los Lobos record an EP as their Slash debut, with Burnett producing. The Blasters saxophonist Steve Berlin, who had been playing a lot with Los Lobos and had a strong desire to produce them, was hired as Burnett's backup in the studio. Biggs, Berlin said in an e-mail to me, had been impressed by his production of Los Lobos' "We're Gonna Rock" on the Rhino collection *LA Rockabilly*, compiled by the original Blasters manager Art Fein. "He thought T Bone and I would work well together."

As things turned out, Burnett and the hard-edged Philly native Berlin butted heads from the start, to the point where, Berlin claims in the Morris book, Burnett tried to get him fired. As one of rock's most valued honkers, Berlin placed a premium on capturing on record the live-wire intensity of the band, which he would soon join as a full-fledged member. "I like records that sound like they were played, not built or crafted," he told the *AV Club* in 2012. "I'd rather hear the sound of things crashing into each other." Burnett, as much as he strived for a live, spacious recorded sound, was very much a craftsman who recognized that songs which sound great onstage can sound terrible in the controlled environment of the recording studio.

With its rambunctious dance numbers, accordion-fueled Spanish-language laments, and rollicking cover of Ritchie Valens's "Come On Let's Go," Los Lobos' 1983 EP debut, *... and a Time to Dance*, did what it was supposed to: capture widespread attention. Who were these guys, and where the heck had this stuff come from? It was voted the year's top EP in the *Village Voice*'s Pazz & Jop critics' poll and won a Grammy as Best Mexican American recording. With its potent mix of bar band swagger, hard rock heroics, and social conscience, the full-length album *How Will the Wolf Survive?*, released a year later, had listeners who thought Los Lobos little more than a curiosity eat that opinion. Ranking ahead of Bruce Springsteen's *Born in the USA*, Prince's *Purple Rain*, and U2's *The Unforgettable Fire* on many Top 10 lists, the recording established them as one of America's great bands.

On *How Will the Wolf Survive?*, Los Lobos emerged as full-time songwriters, sometimes recording tunes even as they were being written. The songs could generally be divided between the ballads and traditional tunes of singer-guitarist-accordionist David Hidalgo and drummer-guitarist Louie Perez, which dealt with the plight of Mexican immigrants and the band's struggle to maintain its ethnic identity in their star-making city; and the funky, crunching rockers of singer-guitarist Rosas. "We would record something that didn't have the lyrics yet, and David and Cesar would almost scat over them," Burnett tells Morris. "They would just sing a melody over the band [track], and then they would go home and write lyrics."

"We were really burning the candle at both ends," Perez says in Paul Zollo's invaluable book *Songwriters on Songwriting*. "I was working on two things and they were doing a dance song. T Bone kept calling on the phone and saying, 'Do you have that other verse done yet?' And we'd say, 'No, not yet.' And finally he figured he would work on the part himself."

Burnett completed the slammin' opening tune, "Don't Worry Baby," which proved to be one of the band's most durable numbers. When Lobos bogged down with "The Breakdown," a song they had been playing live for a year, he got them going again by dropping the zydeco section that gave the song its title and transforming the tune into an acoustic, medium-tempo vehicle with laid-back accordion, warm baritone sax riffs, and neat percussion effects. "When you get into a rut, T Bone's good at getting things rolling again," Hidalgo tells Zollo. "Just because of his personality. He starts jumping around. He's a silly guy, you know. There were a couple of times we couldn't do anything, we just couldn't think anymore. So he'd go and buy a fifth of Scotch. And that helped a great deal. We got a couple songs out of that."

The most important song was Hidalgo's late-arriving "Will the Wolf Survive?," a gorgeous vehicle for his remarkable pop-operatic tenor and a perfect anthem to convey Los Lobos' heart and soul involvement in social causes. "[Previously] they'd been way more into a 'Don't Worry Baby' kind of mode, a blues kind of mode," Burnett tells Chris Morris. "I had thought for a long time that the Hispanics were the new soul men. There was a sense that there was something coming from the Hispanic community that was going to be unbelievably soulful. When they showed up, I thought, 'OK, this is *them*—these are the ones.' They just told the truth, but it was in the way a blues musician would tell the truth. But when they started getting into these high-consciousness songs, as I'd call them, they started telling the truth at a different level."

Not all ruts, as Los Lobos learned, are created equal. As is the case with many bands facing the challenge of following a breakthrough effort with something equally good or better, living up to people's grand expectations proved excruciatingly difficult for them. Two years after the release of *Wolf*—which, as good as it was, was not a commercial hit, topping out at No. 47 on the *Billboard* album chart and producing no Top 40 single—there was still no word on a follow-up. Had the pressure gotten to Hidalgo and company? Had touring to cash in on the success of *Wolf* worn the band out? Would the wolves survive?

During their extensive time on the road in support of *Wolf*, Los Lobos hadn't written any new songs. And when they did get around to working on songs for their next album, challenged by Burnett to go even deeper than before, they came up empty. "It was real hard," Hidalgo told the *Chicago Sun-Times* critic Don McLeese. "There were times we got pretty discouraged. We were trying to move forward, and to do that is hard. A lot of times we would rehearse a song until we thought it was right, and then go play it and put it down, and it wasn't right. So we'd have to start over and get the acoustic guitar, and that's usually when it came out the best. It was painful a lot of the times, because we really had to put our feelings aside, and think of the album itself, to make sure that we had it right."

To add to their burden, as well as the madness in the studio, a few weeks after they started recording music for the new album, *By the Light of the Moon*, they were approached by the filmmaker Taylor Hackford and the screenwriter Luis Valdez (of *Zoot Suit* fame) about recording songs for *La Bamba*, their biopic about the Latin rock hero Ritchie Valens. For Los Lobos, great admirers of Valens who had played and recorded some of his songs, the offer was impossible to turn down. They ended up working on both projects at the same time, in different parts of the Sunset Sound recording studio, with Berlin concentrating on the film score at one end and Burnett on the follow-up to *Wolf* at the other.

Inevitably, the differences between Burnett and Berlin became magnified. Berlin declined to comment on the sessions. "Having been pilloried for decades just for speaking the truth about Paul Simon, I'm not exactly looking for more dog shit to step into," he e-mailed, referring to his public attacks on Simon for claiming songwriting credits to "The Myth of Fingerprints," a tune Los Lobos wrote during the sessions for Simon's hallowed 1986 album *Graceland*. But one major bone of contention was Burnett's use of outside players—"a sensitive subject" for Los Lobos, Berlin later acknowledged in an interview with the Pennsylvania newspaper *The Morning Call*.

Accomplished drumming had never been a high priority for Lobos during the do-it-yourself punk era, when Perez added traps to his résumé with next to no experience playing them. Now, Perez's limitations, particularly his tendency to rush the beat, were causing problems. Burnett imported three different drummers for *By the Light of the Moon*: Anton Fier, formerly of the quasi-jazz group the Lounge Lizards; the Elvis Presley veteran Ron Tutt; and Mickey Curry, who had been playing with Hall and Oates. Though Burnett tells Morris that concerns about Perez came from inside the band, and he was only trying to satisfy them, it's difficult to imagine this most drummer-centric of producers being that passive about this issue.

For all the conflicts, complications, and looming deadlines, Los Lobos got things better than right. *By the Light of the Moon* is a great album. Assessing their early approach in a 1992 interview with the *Chicago Tribune* critic Greg Kot, Burnett remarked, "They play so many styles, and their idea of making a record was to do a blues song and a rockabilly song and a Tex-Mex song and so on. I just tried to get them to merge all that." In fighting for their "purity" as a band, he told *Musician*, he sometimes ended up "fighting against them." Judging by the glowing cohesiveness of *Moon*, the fight was worth it. As stylistically varied as the songs are, they add up to a soulful and gripping statement about life on America's margins during the Reagan era, when "tired souls with empty hands" were "searching for the promised land." Set against that backdrop, the trembling rockabilly number "Shakin' Shakin' Shakes," written with Burnett, is the purest kind of release.

As stirring a work as *By the Light of the Moon* was, though, it was Los Lobos' last-minute cover of "La Bamba"—not the version they recorded for the soundtrack, but a separate single produced by the Burnett protégé Mitchell Froom—that made them superstars. For Berlin and the band, who like everyone else hadn't expected much from the film or the recording, the freak hit was a godsend. For Burnett, as he lamented to John Milward of the *Philadelphia Inquirer*, "La Bamba" wiped out three years of developing Los Lobos "so that they wouldn't be perceived of as the token Mexican-American band."

Burnett would work again with Los Lobos on *La Pistola y El Corazón*, the 1988 EP that won a Grammy for Best Mexican American / Tejano Music Performance, and he has recorded frequently with David Hidalgo. But for other members of Los Lobos, sour memories of *By the Light of the Moon* linger, particularly Burnett's lengthy absences from the studio to deal with personal issues. In the end, Rosas tells Morris, he and Burnett's engineer Larry Hirsch were left to complete the album. "I leave people alone when they need to be left alone," Burnett tells Morris, while asserting that he did mix and master the record. "I don't think that's a bad thing."

Burnett admits to dictating to artists when he started out as a producer. He wrote out arrangements, told drummers what beats and fills to play (he still tells them to lay off the hi-hat, which he compared in

Modern Drummer to "a teacher tapping on the podium with a pointing stick"), and played parts himself. "To find a drummer who can play a completely unimportant part in a really important way is a rare thing," he told *Musician*. But as he grew as a producer, learning from his mistakes and putting greater faith in working from his instinct, he set himself apart with a less-is-more approach. "T Bone's not a control freak," said the veteran music publicist and A&R man Bill Bentley, who was at Warner and Slash during the Los Lobos years. "He'll never make you do something you don't want to do. He goes after shaping songs and helping a band discover the best side of itself to record."

In his 2010 memoir *Soul Mining*, the brilliant French Canadian producer Daniel Lanois writes that in preparing to produce Emmylou Harris's 1995 album *Wrecking Ball*, "I decided I was going to build a classic. The overwhelming sensation that I have felt at every moment of great decision rode over me like a wave; I was going in and I would not let up until we were there." He added, "I felt that I had a chance to make a record as spine-chilling as Phil Spector's production of the Crystals."

Every producer relates to his work differently, and in the case of *Wrecking Ball*, Lanois, "guided by Emmy's emotional makeup," did indeed create a classic—as he did with Dylan's *Time out of Mind* and the Neville Brothers' *Yellow Moon*. But it is difficult to imagine Burnett putting his ambitions for a recording first or discussing his intentions apart from that of the artist. "There are some producers who live through the artist they're working on, and they think of it in some way as their record, which it's not, really," he told *Musician*. "I much more like the feeling of sitting on this beach and this is the sand, and over there are the trees, and overhead are the birds . . . and I'm a creature made by God who's *part* of this thing going on." He sounded a lot like Ornette Coleman, who said about his role as leader, "I don't want them to follow me. I want them to follow themselves, but to be with me." (The similarities between Burnett and Coleman, who died in 2015, are intriguing: both were raised in Fort Worth, came of age artistically in Los Angeles, coined a personal approach to recording—Coleman called his "sound grammar," Burnett his a "world of sound for something to exist in"—and refused to compromise on the road to icon status.)

When Burnett produced fellow Takoma alumnus Leo Kottke's *Time Step* in 1983, Kottke was best known as a fingerstyle guitarist with a serviceable voice. Burnett showed him how appealing he could be as a singer, yet still do wonderful things on guitar, by having Emmylou Harris sing harmony with him on Kristofferson's "Here Comes That Rainbow Again." The nudge toward country broadened Kottke's appeal without compromising his artistic identity.

Marshall Crenshaw's 1985 album *Downtown* was a more difficult project. The whip smart retro-rocker had cut eight or nine songs before Burnett entered the picture and wasn't happy with any of them. In an interview with Bill Cochran of the Chicago alternative rock station WXRT in 1986, Cochran told me, Burnett confessed he wasn't familiar enough with Crenshaw and what he was going after to help him sufficiently: "All I was trying to do was get his voice present in the mix so people could hear what a good singer he was." (On Crenshaw's previous album, *Field Day*, his sophomore effort, Steve Lillywhite, who had produced U2, among many other bands, had turned him into a singing mannequin dressed up in a booming wardrobe of sound.)

But as disappointed as Burnett was with *Downtown*, songs like the rockabilly-tinged "Little Wild One (No. 5)" capture the Detroit native's uncanny ability to both celebrate and update vintage rock 'n' roll with his modern cool. Aided by Burnett's electric sitar and Jerry Marotta's bongos taking things into strange, enticing territory, "Terrifying Love" ranks among Crenshaw's aching masterpieces.

In contrast to Burnett's restorative efforts with Crenshaw, *Peter Case* (1986) was a surprising work of reinvention. Case was known for his stints with the LA new wave bands the Nerves and the Plimsouls. Unbeknownst to many of his fans, the Buffalo native started out as a blues buster. "I had these new songs, story songs based on blues and folk ballads, and a whole new way of working," Case told me. "But I didn't know where to go with them." Largely based on his admiration for *Truth Decay*, Case turned to Burnett, whom he knew from encounters on the LA music scene and related to as a Christian artist.

"T Bone has the kind of charisma that makes you feel like things can happen," Case told me in a 2007 *No Depression* interview. The 1985 project got underway in Fort Worth, where Case joined Burnett for two months to work on songs, demos, and recordings. Back in

Los Angeles, with Geffen Records dollars to spend, Burnett brought in a big-name cast for the album—Ry Cooder, Roger McGuinn, John Hiatt, guitarist Mike Campbell from Tom Petty and the Heartbreakers, and Jim Keltner. But it wasn't star voltage that made *Peter Case* special as much as the distinctive sound that Burnett, Case, and the co-producer Mitchell Froom crafted in the studio. "We put the songs, which we called 'tribal folk,' to a groove," "playing and singing live with a drum machine going—not a programmed drum machine, but one that was attacked by Jerry Marotta. He ripped up the instructions to it and played the thing with a screwdriver."

"Peter is a folk musician, but he never played with any sort of folk piety," Burnett told me. "I remember him assaulting that acoustic guitar, just playing the shit out of it, knocking out these unusual but completely happening chords. No one plays like him."

Boasting a Grammy-nominated song in the harp-driven "Old Blue Car" and three Burnett co-writes, *Peter Case* accomplished much of what *Truth Decay* did: it established an important, idiosyncratic artist on his own terms and drew attention-grabbing praise (for instance, the *New York Times* critic Robert Palmer named it the best pop/rock album of 1986). Unfortunately, *Peter Case* also linked up with *Truth Decay* by falling into a pile of "lost" recordings of the era. While Case has gone on to enjoy an active and interesting career, you can't help thinking that he was one star who got away.

No such fate awaited the BoDeans, four unknowns whose partnership with Burnett enabled them to live out the great rock 'n' roll dream of coming out of nowhere—in their case, beautiful Waukesha, Wisconsin—and becoming a big-time success. When Burnett first met with the band, according to the *Milwaukee Journal Sentinel*, he lectured them, telling them they needed to go home and learn how to play their instruments. In retrospect, that may have set the wrong tone, but it appears they took his words to heart. Few first albums achieve the instant liftoff that their 1986 Slash debut, *Love & Hope & Sex & Dreams*, did with its levitating melodies, ramble tamble attack (Buddy Holly to the rescue again), and alternating acoustic and electric currents. With their unusual vocal harmonies, Kurt Neumann and Sam Llanas (he of the whiney, asking-to-be-spanked voice) could be

Everly-like one moment and Louvin-like the next, but mostly they sounded like themselves.

How much did people love *Love & Hope*? Let us count the yays: *Rolling Stone* named the BoDeans Best New Band. The group was profiled at length in *Time*. The *Washington Post* deemed the album "one of the year's best." *Love & Hope* got them tons of airplay on college and alternative radio stations. And the song "Still the Night" was featured on the soundtrack of Martin Scorsese's *The Color of Money*. For all that, the BoDeans were unhappy with the album, which they said cramped their style and limited their audience. Neumann, Llanas told me in 2014, was upset that there wasn't enough time or budget for him to work on his guitar sound.

You would think that a band that went by Bob, Guy, Beau, and Sammy BoDean (after Jethro Bodine, the dim-witted character on the 1960s sitcom *The Beverly Hillbillies*) would be thrilled to score with alt-country listeners, but they were after bigger game. "They wrote these little songs, like 'Runaway,' about a woman whose husband beat her and she shot him, and then she took off in the car," Burnett told the *Chicago Tribune*. "They wanted to do it like it was all 'Apocalypse Now,' even when it didn't make sense for the songs. That was the fight on that record: How 'big' was it gonna be?"

To bulk up on their second album, *Outside Looking In*, the BoDeans hired the Milwaukee native Jerry Harrison, keyboardist in Talking Heads, to produce. "He trusted us a bit more," Llanas told me. "He let us steer." But with all the steerage they may have gained, the BoDeans lost their direction. The warm cohesion of their debut gave way to a piecemeal approach that aimed for the arena crowd with synthesizers and exploding drums and discarded their pop tunes for reggae workouts. The quality control of the songs was gone. By the time they overcame their misgivings about Burnett and had him executive produce their largely acoustic 1993 effort, *Closer to Free*, it was too late to recapture all that was lost, even if the title track did become their biggest hit. Burnett largely sifted through what they had already recorded and advised them what was and wasn't working. He also arbitrated when Neumann and Llanas didn't see eye to eye, which was often.

Another young artist who regretted falling out with Burnett was Tommy Keene. The guitar-playing indie rocker was knocking on the door of stardom following his acclaimed 1984 EP, *Places That Are Gone*, which had critics talking about him in the same tones as Alex Chilton, Matthew Sweet, and Paul Westerberg. But he and Burnett clashed in the studio, and Don Dixon, a gifted North Carolina singer-songwriter who went on to produce REM, was brought in to finish the sessions. That album never came out because Keene signed a deal with Geffen barring the release of any of the material. Four of the songs ended up on his Geffen album *Songs from the Film*, but they were given a commercial gloss by the producer Geoff Emerick. "They wanted me to be like Bryan Adams," Keene told *Rocker Magazine*.

You don't have to be a fan of Burnett as a producer to acknowledge that even when he encourages artists to hear themselves in a new way, he doesn't ask them to be anyone but themselves.

CHAPTER 7

Co-Conspirator

Taking a page from Ray Charles's *The Genius Hits the Road*, Burnett took his act east, north, and south, guitar in hand. In New York in October 1983, opening for Richard Thompson's "Big Band" at the Bottom Line, he called up Warren Zevon to play keyboard—and straight man—on an unruly encore of "Gloria." After rapping out a charming narrative about a girl who "used to be so full of hope and dreams" but now pees on the couch, passes out, and takes out her false teeth and eyeball, Burnett turned to Zevon and said promptingly, "You know her." And then again, when there was no response, "You know her," to which, reported a spectator, Zevon blurted out, "Yeah, I remember the bitch."

Headlining at Tuts in Chicago a few months later, dressed in suit and bow tie, Burnett opened on his knees, making grand stabs at a preprogrammed keyboard, appearing to be playing it himself. Then, with the stentorian chords still pouring out, he walked away to get his acoustic guitar. "Are you all a cult?" he asked the crowd. "I know I'm a cult artist—I've read it a thousand times." At show's end, he dashed into the crowd, Springsteen-style, to shake hands with audience members, and concluded the performance with an a cappella version of "There's No Business Like Show Business."

These shows proved to be a warm-up for a larger undertaking. Beginning in spring 1984, in one of the more significant developments in his not-a-career, Burnett went on the road as the opening act for Elvis Costello. Performed over three legs, in the United States, the UK, Japan, and Australia, the tour was Costello's first as a solo attraction—sans the Attractions, his often battling band. Burnett, who in 1977 had attended the first American concert by the brilliant, cutting, perturbable, impossibly prolific Brit but had not met him until they hit the road together, also performed solo. Not surprisingly, the two became fast friends and collaborators, bonded by their caustic wit, lofty intellectualism, devotion to music history, shared contempt for the ruling class, and love for Bob Dylan.

"A sort of Billy Bragg with an American accent, wider horizons, and the heritage of Bob Dylan and Hemingway, no one in Saturday night's crowd knew quite what to make of him," wrote the *Glasgow Herald*'s David Belcher of Burnett's set at the Playhouse in Edinburgh, which boasted what Edinburgh University critic Duncan McLean (future author of *Lone Star Swing: On the Trail of Bob Willis and His Texas Playboys*) called "first-class buffoonery." As in Chicago, Burnett opened his performances at the keyboard, making like a concert idol—only this time, he had a grand piano at his disposal and the jazz great Keith Jarrett's *Köln Concert* to pantomime to. Cole Porter was along for some tomfoolery as well: "Terrorists were once alarming / Now they're discreetly charming," Burnett sang. "On TV shows / Anything goes."

A highlight of the tour was the introduction of the Coward Brothers, Howard (Elvis) and Henry (T Bone), alleged long-lost sons of the great playwright and songwriter Noël Coward. In their "unscheduled" encore appearances, the duo informed audiences that they were determined to give the people what they wanted: "We're not like those other guys—we play all our hits." That translated into delirious covers of old favorites such as George Jones's "Ragged but Right," Bobby Charles's "Tennessee Blues," the Isley Brothers / Beatles hit "Twist and Shout," the Kingston Trio's signature cover "Tom Dooley," and an unlikely medley of Scott McKenzie's hippie anthem "San Francisco (Be Sure to Wear Some Flowers in Your Hair)" and Tony Bennett's chestnut "I Left My Heart in San Francisco." They added new covers as the weeks progressed, notably Los Lobos' "A Matter of Time" and the Hank Thompson hit "The Wild Side of Life," performed with a teasing splash of the Beatles' "She's a Woman."

The Cowards recorded one single, "The People's Limousine," a co-written original about a girl in crystal heels who becomes involved in some serious foreign intrigue. It features boisterous vocal harmonies and David Miner's slapping, Johnny Cash–style bass. The B-side was "They'll Never Take Her Love from Me," a Leon Payne composition that George Jones had covered. In an NPR interview, Burnett compared Jones's typically gripping reading to a John Steinbeck story; done up by the Cowards, however, the tune trades in emotional immediacy for cornpone, hold the grits.

During their travels, Costello played for Burnett solo demos he had recorded for his next album. Coming off *Punch the Clock* and *Goodbye, Cruel World*, a pair of mixed recordings that producers Clive Langer and Alan Winstanley had dressed in horns, strings, and synthesizers, Costello had a sparer production in mind. He especially wanted to get away from overpowering keyboard effects. Burnett encouraged him to record the new album with a close focus on voice and acoustic guitar—the best way, he said, to stay focused on the songs as originally written. While they were airborne between Japan and Australia, Burnett blueprinted what became *King of America* (released in the United States in 1986), matching up songs and musicians. As Costello recounts in his 2015 memoir, *Unfaithful Music and Disappearing Ink*, he planned on recording half of the Columbia album with the Attractions and the other half in acoustic settings with Burnett's LA regulars, among them three alumni of Elvis Presley's TCB Band of the 1970s, guitar hero James Burton, bassist Jerry Scheff, and drummer Ron Tutt. But Costello hit it off so well with the TCB men that, with Burnett producing, they recorded seven tracks, all live, in two days.

"Understandably, the Attractions' sessions for *King of America* were less good-humored and rather uneasy affairs," Costello writes in *Unfaithful Music.* "They all hated T Bone, casting him as the provocateur." Furthermore, the man also known as Declan MacManus writes in his extensive liner notes to Rykodisc's 2005 reissue of *King of America,* "After spending so much time together on the road, T Bone and I had a rapport based on a humour that unwittingly drove a wedge between the band and myself." By the time they arrived, the Attractions were so pissed that they delivered what Costello called in his liner notes "some of their worst performances" and ended up appearing on only one number. (All is well that ends well, sort of: the Attractions were back at full strength for Costello's next album, *Blood and Chocolate.*)

There was another reason the Attractions' participation on *King of America* was limited: the rarified presence of jazz bassist Ray Brown and R&B drummer Earl Palmer. Between them, they had played on countless classic recordings with the likes of Charlie Parker, Oscar Peterson, Little Richard, and Fats Domino. Now, having never played together during all their years in Los Angeles, they were teaming up in support of Costello. If he wasn't nervous enough when he entered the studio with these giants to record his country lament "Poisoned Rose," hearing Brown utter to the younger musicians, "Okay, just don't anybody play any ideas," put him even more on edge. (In the 2015 Showtime documentary *Elvis Costello: Mystery Dance*, Burnett calls Brown "one of the most intense musicians I have worked with.")

Neither of the songs featuring Brown and Palmer are magic, but Costello more than holds his own on "Poisoned Rose," which requires him to sing in tandem with the bassist known in the jazz world as "Father Time." And high spirits prevail on a loose, organ-dappled, cross-faded reading of the Chicago bluesman J. B. Lenoir's "Eisenhower Blues." Hearing Elvis thrive in such august company was rewarding for Burnett, who made a point of putting his un-cowardly partner in that situation. "At the time, everyone thought punk rockers were all bluffers," he told the *New Yorker* in 2010, alluding to the image still clinging to Costello from his raw early years. "Because there was a lot of bluff in it. So he had a lot to overcome."

Burnett, writes Costello in his memoir, "produced the album with a weightless, caring touch. He knew when to let the light and air in and when to pick up the pace." He also credits his friend with knowing "just when to introduce an instrumental counter point to the narrative," as with Cajun artist Jo-El Sonnier's French melodeon on "American without Tears" and Costello's own mandolin part on "Little Palaces." It was also a masterstroke to have David Hidalgo of Los Lobos sing harmony on "Brilliant Mistake," Costello's leading commentary about the "boulevard of broken dreams" called America.

In support of the album, Burnett performed some live dates as a rhythm guitarist with the Confederates, a band drawn from the *King of America* sessions that also featured bassist T-Bone Wolk. (The Rykodisc package includes a disc of cover versions from one of the shows, including Sonny Boy Williamson's "Your Funeral and My Trial" and the Dan Penn–Spooner Oldham classic "It Tears Me Up.") For all the deserved acclaim it got, *King of America* (officially credited in the United States to the Costello Show featuring Elvis Costello) didn't fare particularly well commercially. It peaked at No. 39 on the *Billboard* 200 (a significant drop from the No. 11 spot claimed by *Get Happy!!* six years earlier).

"Burning through Warner Brothers' money at top speed," as Costello writes in his book, he and Burnett teamed again a few years later on a very different project, *Spike*, the Brit's 1989 debut for Warner. Several albums in one, it was recorded in Dublin, London, New Orleans, and Los Angeles with different sets of musicians, during "the last couple of years when you were encouraged to make expensive experiments." Though Costello took charge this time, making extensive demos in England in the beginning and overdubbing a mess of instrumentals in the end, Burnett again played a key role. He influenced the direction of the music by encouraging Costello to continue in the same experimental vein he had been in when writing songs and producing the soundtrack for *The Courier*, a 1988 drug drama starring Costello's wife since 1986, former Pogue bassist Cait O'Riordan. And

Burnett's work as co-producer (aided by the engineer Kevin Killen) both sharpened and animated the album's spirited sound.

Burnett likened *Spike* to a hip-hop record: they put down a loop, Costello put down a vocal, and then the fun began. "I would jump into it like it was a playpen or a sandbox and splash around and see what I could come up with," says the guitarist Marc Ribot in Graham Johnson's 2013 Costello biography, *Complicated Shadows*. The percussionist Michael Blair, a partner of Ribot's in Tom Waits's band, threw in the bathroom as well as the kitchen sink with metal pipes, hubcaps, horns, glockenspiel, and assorted noisemakers—ultimately inspiring the album's title through his connection to the musical prankster Spike Jones. (The cover of *Spike* depicts Costello in antic clown face, in contrast to his sleepy-smirky pose on *King of America*.)

With such guest players as Paul McCartney, Roger McGuinn, Chrissie Hynde, the Dirty Dozen Brass Band, and Allen Toussaint, the album bursts with energy, emotion, wit, and improbable variety—here political, there romantic, here historical, there satiric. For Burnett, the opportunity to work with McCartney (in London, where he dubbed his bass part on "Veronica") was a major highlight. "He's probably the most musical person I've ever met," Burnett told *Vulture*. "Music comes out of his pores. He played bass on a couple of tunes, and it was completely effortless. He wasn't trying to do anything. From him, I learned something about ease and grace."

Spike didn't place much higher than *King of America* on the *Billboard* 200. But the luscious, glockenspiel-dappled "Veronica," a collaboration between Costello and McCartney, was an unlikely Top 20 hit—the straw that stirred the concoction. If this isn't Costello's greatest album, it is certainly his freest.

By the time Burnett next produced a Costello album, more than twenty years later—this time in Nashville—Costello was less rock's "Beloved Entertainer," as he self-mockingly proclaimed on the cover of *Spike*, than a seasoned art-rocker preaching to a somewhat diminished choir. Listening to *Secret, Profane and Sugarcane* (2009), a return to the spare roots setting of *King of America*, you wonder whether these brothers in arms needed a third party to nudge them out of their comfort zone. Points for the speed and spontaneity with which they cut this album (which did hit No. 13 on the *Billboard* chart, but in a weakened marketplace) and cheers for Jim Lauderdale's power harmonizing. But there is little on *Secret* and its successor, *National Ransom*, that can approach the thrills and immediacy of *Spike*. In an Elvis song death match, *Secret*'s wordy travelogue "Sulphur to Sugarcane" would have its lunch eaten by *Spike*'s uproarious, soul-baring "Deep Dark Truthful Mirror."

During the stretch of time during which *King of America* was completed, Burnett got his feet wet in TV. His previous experience in film and video consisted mainly of working on a short 1972 film about the inaugural gala of Fort Worth's Kimbell Art Museum. John Fleming and Bob Shaw, an East Coast photographer who became part of their Fort Worth circle, shot it, and Burnett—in his first feat of programming screen music—juxtaposed Nat King Cole's 1956 recording of "When I Fall in Love" over a montage of people walking through the museum. Now he took on the task of directing an odd 1985 TV drama that was, according to its leading man, John Doe, "way over our heads." A fantasy mystery shot for KABC's Saturday night local programming slot, *Legends of the Spanish Kitchen* was inspired by an actual LA restaurant called the Spanish Kitchen, which the owner's wife suddenly shuttered in 1961, with plates and silverware awaiting the dinner crowd on the red-and-white-checked tablecloths. The place had remained that way ever since. No one had set foot inside. Rumors of murder abounded. The story became such a source of fascination that tour buses stopped by and an episode of the popular TV series *Lou Grant* was based on it.

Legends boasted two fifteen-minute segments, both of which featured Los Lobos as house band. Burnett's segment starred Doe, cofounder of the punk rock trailblazers X, as a drifter who gets shot by a woman—spoiler alert!—who turns out to be his mother. (The other mini-feature starred former *Bonanza* patriarch Lorne Greene—as the devil—and Phil Hartman, later to star on *Saturday Night Live*.) Initially, Burnett thought he would be too busy with *King of America* to take on *Legends*. He asked video veteran Hudson Marquez if he wanted to shoot it. Marquez said yes and proceeded to do all the preproduction work, including rehearsing the actors.

"On the day of the shoot," Marquez told me, "T Bone calls up and says 'I wanna do this with you.' I say, 'T Bone, this is the *day* of the shoot. We busted our ass for ten days. You can't just show up like that.' He says 'I'll meet you there.'" He added, "T Bone was just the cheerleader. I was the director. They said trust the cameraman, but the guy was terrible. It was a complete mess, totally amateur night."

"Hudson knew lighting and T Bone was a great storyteller," said Doe, who went on to become a prolific character actor in Hollywood but had appeared in only one indie film at the time. "He definitely had an idea of how he wanted the thing to look. He and John Huston were cut from the same cloth—big, blustery types who speak softly when they ask you to do something and say, 'That won't be a problem, will it?'"

That same year, after reading about plans for a cartoon show that allegedly was going to make Elvis Presley "bigger than Mickey Mouse," Burnett was so "offended" (per the *Los Angeles Times*) that he concocted his own "brief Saturday morning scenario." In his script, published in the December 1985 issue of *Musician*, Colonel Tom Parker (to be played by the *Looney Tunes* character Foghorn Leghorn) confronts Presley's bodyguard Red West (Yosemite Sam) about the lateness of the truck carrying Elvis Lipsticks ("Always keep me on your lips, girls") to the arena at which Elvis will be performing. Elvis (the cartoon likeness of which "better be good," Burnett noted on the script), who has been practicing his bullfighting moves backstage, climbs a rope up into a magically appearing Blue Thunder helicopter and speeds across the city to wrest the truck from the Blue Meanies (the menaces from the Beatles' *Yellow Submarine*, here played by characters from TV's *The Smurfs*). After racing back to the venue in time to perform his concert, Elvis gets a call from *Air Force One*. "You've, uh, done it again," says President Reagan.

"Burning Love," as the piece was called, did not prompt *Mad* magazine to inquire about Burnett's availability, which was all for the better considering the rarified heights he was about to climb as a musician.

CHAPTER 8

Seeker

In May 1986, Burnett appeared as guest speaker at the annual retreat of the Chicago faith and arts group CHART. The event, held at a summer resort in Lake Geneva, Wisconsin, included various talks, music performances, and a 1960s-themed party (i.e., lots of head scarves). When the organizers invited Burnett, they didn't think he would be available. But he flew in from Los Angeles and fully involved himself in the proceedings. He spoke to the gathering and, dressed in a black suit and white shirt, showed off his modest twirling and windmilling moves on the dance floor. He also surprised one of the organizers, Chris Stacey, by performing not just one tune with Stacey's band, but fronting it on several surprisingly hard-edged covers ("The Letter," "Bad Moon Rising," "Subterranean Homesick Blues"). Burnett's guitar solos were worth the price of a donation.

"He was a hero to a lot of us," said CHART member and WXRT DJ Bill Cochran, with whom Burnett sat for an interview in a cottage at the resort. "We were sensible, intelligent Bible people, but edgy in our own ways, a kind of guerilla group of Christians. And he acted like he was one of us."

Burnett's "speech" consisted of a single line: "Generosity is the hallmark of the artist, any questions?" For those in attendance wanting advice on how to incorporate their Christian faith into their art "without being propagandistic," as Cochran put it, the remark had many shades of meaning. Sharing yourself through art, revealing yourself, availing yourself to other artists' sharing is surely what they should all be about. But that kind of generosity, Burnett said in a brief Q&A session that followed his opening/closing remark, is opposed by self-consciousness, which he deemed "the artist's enemy." How well you deal with doubt and fear will often determine what kind of artist you are. Sometimes, he said, the best solution is simply to drive through those insecurities. He acted out that strategy at the retreat by plowing through a section of empty chairs.

In recording his next album, *T Bone Burnett*, that summer, Burnett chased self-consciousness by acting out of character—by taking a vacation from high concepts, production effects, and star turns. Gazing at the album cover, you don't expect a stripping away of artistic guises. Wearing dark glasses and a fashion-statement jacket with wide, dotted lapels, his arms crossed meaningfully at the wrists, Burnett stares at us with an enigmatic, sub–*Mona Lisa* look, daring us to guess what he's thinking. But backed by an acoustic band including the Nashville wiz Jerry Douglas on Dobro, Byron Berline on fiddle, and David Hidalgo on acoustic guitar and accordion, Burnett made his deepest, purest, and most revelatory album—the one he started to make before *Proof through the Night* got hijacked by his producer.

Following his own advice to Elvis Costello, Burnett focused on voice and acoustic guitar and recorded the album quickly, live to two-track tape—a standard method before multitracking and digital editing became the norm and one that has long been his preferred approach because it produces a clean, punchy, natural sound. The band plays together in the room, feeding off one another's energy and ideas, as opposed to recording individually in isolation booths. Produced by Burnett's frequent sideman, David Miner, *T Bone Burnett* is frequently described as the closest Burnett has come to a traditional country album. Some reviewers praised it as a beautiful collection of love songs. It might also be regarded as a personal reckoning akin to Dylan's marital breakup masterpiece, *Blood on the Tracks*.

Burnett's rueful, plainspoken voice—that of "a man with a lot of oblivion behind him," as Howard Hampton memorably wrote in the *Village Voice*—is one we haven't heard before. Burnett's marriage was on the rocks—he would be divorced in December. You can hear the tears between the lines on "Little Daughter," a folk benediction for Angelina (now a successful TV writer) and Molly: "Little daughter, I pray the Lord will always bless you" and "When I'm not with you, little daughter / I pray the Lord surrounds you with his angels." You also get the sense that this was a last-gasp album by an artist who didn't know where his career was going—or if it was going anywhere.

"Art enables us to find ourselves and lose ourselves at the same time," wrote Thomas Merton, a twentieth-century Catholic mystic whose words have had a strong impact on Burnett. To find himself, the singer stripped away the defense mechanisms—the caustic wit, the irony, the posturing—and allowed himself to be vulnerable. The hymnlike masterpiece "River of Love" sets the tone: "I had to run before I knew how to crawl / The first step was hard but I've had trouble with them all," he sings, with Douglas's strings answering back in a sympathetic voice. Dogma is easy, belief is hard.

On the near-perfect "Shake Yourself Loose," one of Burnett's most generous expressions of humanity, he wrestles with resignation in addressing a lover or friend who is too far gone to help but not so far that he can't recognize in that person his own troubling state of dependence: "I believe that you believe, you're searching for the truth / I don't know what hold that rounder downtown has on you / But keep on shaking, baby, till you shake yourself loose."

"You're a garden in this God-forsaken land / And the only true love I have known," Burnett sings on "The Bird That I Held in My Hand," written with Bob Neuwirth and Billy Swan. This is not the judgment-rendering Jeremiah of earlier phases, but an inwardly directed artist, searching for solace and belief in the face of the most basic mortal struggles. What makes these songs so powerful is Burnett's self-effacement in giving himself over to musical expression with a spiritual commitment that, as Merton wrote, "lifts it above itself, takes it out of itself, and makes it present to itself on a level of being that it did not know it could ever achieve."

On secular tunes such as the Elmer Laird hillbilly chestnut "Poison Love" and Burnett's "I Remember," a riff on the country god Hank Williams's "I'm So Lonesome I Could Cry," Burnett's embrace of the religion of music is a seamless extension of the religion of religion. The only song to break free of the darkness is "Oh No Darling," an infectious skiffle-rockabilly hybrid boasting a superb harmony vocal by Swan. But with its underlying promise that spiritual striving is its own reward, the album pays heed to what Leonard Cohen calls the "crack in everything" that allows the light to get in—just enough light, in the vastness of time and space, to illuminate hope.

"I believe that if you believe Jesus is the light of the world, there are a couple of kinds of songs you can write about," Burnett told Robert Hilburn and Chris Willman. "You can write songs about the light or you can write songs about what you see by the light." In the acknowledgments for its 1991 album *Achtung Baby*, U2 thanks Burnett for "the truth in the dark"—for going where few pop artists were comfortable in going. "Nobody really wants to do that," Sam Phillips told Jeffrey Overstreet of the *Patheos* site. "Everybody wants to look cool. And to try to fight that is important."

(Burnett first met Bono face to face at London's Portobello Hotel in 1985, when they shared a manager. They co-wrote "Having a Wonderful Time, Wish You Were Her," which appears on Burnett's *Beyond the Trap Door.* Their friendship has endured the occasional jab from Burnett. Writes Bill Flanagan in his book *U2: At the End of the World*, "T Bone says he's decided U2 are a lot like [1920s evangelist] Aimee Semple McPherson . . . who began to think it was *her* power that was healing people and not God's.")

With its enveloping warmth, understated devotion to heroes past, and throwback countrypolitan lineup, *T Bone Burnett* also recalls Dylan's country departure *Nashville Skyline* (however chirpier that 1969 gem is). The irony is that Dot Records, the briefly revived label that released this one-shot, was home in the 1950s to Pat Boone, a blandly handsome TV host in white buck shoes whose success in covering hits by black R&B artists like Little Richard and Fats Domino should not be construed as early efforts in roots revivalism. Those recordings were soulless rip-offs—though viewed from a postmodern perspective, their thoroughgoing blandness may seem downright radical. With its heartfelt religious expression, though, *T Bone Burnett* might well have been a favorite of Boone, a born-again Christian.

If *T Bone Burnett* suggested that T Bone had traded in his wild card, his live performances a few months later suggested he had gotten a joker in return. His three-night gig in Fort Worth—at Caravan of Dreams, of all places—had audience members shaking their heads as much in disbelief as in amusement. Performing solo, he dedicated the first half of his epic thirty-seven-song performances to originals ("The People's Limousine," "Madison Avenue," "Monkey Dance") and covers (Johnny Cash's "Ring of Fire," Willie Nelson's "One in a Row," the Rolling Stones' "Lady Jane"). After intermission, things took a turn for the weird. His hair slicked back, Eddie Cochran–style, Burnett began with Johnny Carson's *Tonight Show* theme—*DA dot da da da!*—accompanied by a synthesizer player and noise effects man called Mr. Literal. He proceeded to demolish Cole Porter's "Anything Goes" again, this time inserting references to rock 'n' roll druggies and the Plasmatics, the punk band led by the rowdy and ribald Wendy O. Williams. Dancing on tabletops, Burnett encouraged people to clink their glasses "to get some polyrhythms going" and basked in the recorded applause played by Mr. Literal. A drink-server and lyric-sheet holder called Nurse Shot also joined the party.

"Why he isn't a star is anybody's guess," wrote the *Dallas Morning News* reviewer Dave Ferman. Less taken with the spectacle, the *Fort Worth Star-Telegram* critic Jeff Guinn felt no need to join in the guessing. Coming from someone with Burnett's discomfort as a performer, the crazy antics can be seen as his way of lunging—shades of Rolling Thunder—past self-consciousness and self-doubt. What better way to get over yourself than to take on an alternate identity? This lover of show tunes might also have been unleashing his inner Tommy Tune, another tall, high-stepping Texan, one of Broadway's most beloved stars. One thing was clear: there was, indeed, no business like the show business for which Burnett was becoming known.

CHAPTER 9

Svengali

On the second day of the *T Bone Burnett* sessions, Burnett received a visit from the woman who would become his next wife. The young Christian pop singer Leslie Phillips was brought to the studio by Tom Willett, the A&R director at her label, Myrrh. He thought that Burnett, with whom he had worked on rocker Tonio K's *Romeo Unchained*, might be just the man to produce her. After recording three albums for Myrrh and establishing a following in contemporary Christian music (or CCM), Phillips had had it with being told by label executives not only what kind of songs she could and couldn't record and how they should sound, but also what clothes she could and couldn't wear and what her evangelical responsibilities were before the public. (At the 1985 Gospel Music Association's Dove Awards, wearing a fluffy layered pink outfit with her hair seriously puffed, she looked like she was on an audition for the World War II generation's favorite TV bandleader, Lawrence Welk.)

When Phillips told Willett she was going to quit the label, he assured her that if she would record one more album for him, she could do whatever she wanted. The prospect of working with Burnett appealed to her. "I had *Trap Door*," she told me. "I loved his music but had no idea he was a producer. I didn't know about the Los Lobos record." She subsequently went with Willett to meet with Burnett at the historic Hollywood Roosevelt Hotel, which had just been redone. He was living there out of large steamer trunks. "He was such a character," Phillips told me. "I was so taken with him. I just sat there, just listening to him. Poor Tom thought it was a disaster, she's not saying anything."

"At that point," Phillips said, "it wasn't really, necessarily, about producing me. He had experience with fundamentalism, he had a brush with those people. I think he was willing to meet with me and just see if he could inspire me because he was sympathetic to what I had gone through."

Phillips played Burnett a new song she was working on. In a 1996 interview with the *Dallas Observer*'s Robert Wilonsky, Burnett said he told her it was "really sweet" but that she was "trying to be something [she was] not. [She was] dealing with these tough issues, but not honestly. I think she liked hearing that because, in retrospect, it was her struggle. She'd been incredibly sheltered in a world where you can't see R-rated movies or go to the ballet because the girls wear tutus. Seriously. Seriously. That's the world she was trying to work in." He described her albums as "diabolical"—drowned in syrupy arrangements and noisy production effects that sometimes had "the Christian Cyndi Lauper," as she was touted, screeching in a painful falsetto.

"We liked each other from the start," Phillips told me. "I had never met anyone like him before. He was very kind and loving and at the same time a complete pistol and eccentric. He was kind of doubtful about the record company. He said, 'I don't know that they'll pay me my fee.' And I said, 'Oh they'll pay you.' He liked that. I was so inspired by that meeting, I went home and wrote five or six songs."

Burnett had never met anyone like Phillips, either. A native of the LA suburb of Glendale, she had played jails, homeless shelters, and halfway houses as a teenage activist during the punk era, singing her songs of salvation. Her background was in dance and drama; she got into music to provide a spiritual alternative to what the mainstream culture was offering. Though at thirty-eight Burnett was considerably older than Phillips (he and his wife, Stephanie, were the same age), they were a good match with their shared interest in things spiritual and intellectual, their love of the Beatles, the Great American Songbook, and the power of melody—and their antagonism toward the burgeoning religious right.

During a follow-up meeting, she played him her songs. He agreed to produce what would, in fact, be her final Myrrh album (not counting a subsequent best-of collection he put together). The only catch was they had to record the album in Fort Worth, where Burnett was spending the rest of that summer to be near his daughters. That was fine with Phillips, who was happy to get out of Los Angeles. Plus, this would be a good way to mark her "starting over" as an artist. The analog studio they used, Eagle Audio, was a funky place that had mostly done commercials—a far cry from the state-of-the-art rooms Burnett used on the West Coast. "But T Bone said it had a good enough board and we could use our ingenuity to get the best out of it, do some experimenting," Phillips told me. "It was fun. Tom Willett was very supportive. We both felt a lot of freedom to do what we wanted."

"There was just a great amount of excitement both of us felt over what we could do, what music we could make," she told me. "I grew up sheltered. T Bone threw open the windows and doors and said look out there, look at the possibilities. I think he had a blast playing me things, saying how do you like this record, how do you like that record? There was drama in our personal lives, both of us coming out of relationships, there was that element, too. I felt so understood. I was open to changing and he was open to changing me. There was so much excitement over what we could do, what music we could make. We were dreaming our dream, we were together."

"His ideas were freeing," she said. "I was trying to find a way to be an artist and he made it easy. He helped me clarify what I wanted to do and who I was. If he hadn't shown me an alternative artistic path, I would have quit, stopped writing music, and gone back to school at twenty-four. I would have done something completely different."

With its twangy Burnett guitar solos, rockabilly energy, and soulful intensity, the music plugged into mid-1980s currents in Los Angeles, where alternative country acts like Lone Justice (featuring Phillips's high school friend Maria McKee), Green on Red, the Long Ryders, Peter Case, and his wife, Victoria Williams, were making a noise. At the same time, the melodic drum programming, girl group–style backing vocals, and other production touches on the album, aptly named *The Turning*, anticipate the music of Sam Phillips (she adopted her childhood nickname to formalize her break from CCM). And when it doesn't, as with her spare version of "River of Love" and "God Is Watching You," a folksy call-and-answer number she co-wrote with Burnett, it still shines a different kind of light. "T Bone said to me if I was going to make gospel music, why try to sound like someone on the Top 40 charts?" Phillips told me. "Why not make real gospel music, like Mahalia Jackson?"

For all its fetching touches, *The Turning* is no casual farewell note. A hard, probing voice and dark, searching perspective replace the blanket praise and unshakable faith of Phillips's earlier efforts. Aching questions about faith and trust—ones with which Burnett was intimately familiar—abound: "How long have I got / To answer a higher calling? / And how long have I got / To walk the line without falling?" and "Why do I run away / When I come face to face / With anything I need?" and "Have I lost it if I hope for something more / Than feeling fatalistic pain? / And if true love never did exist / How could we know its name?"

That *The Turning*, reissued in 1997, placed eighth in *CCM Magazine*'s 2001 selection of *The 100 Greatest Albums in Christian Music* tells you how much mainstream Christian tastes had changed. Recording these songs had been an open act of rebellion by Phillips against her bosses' directive to never question her faith in public. Now, the songs were part of a map for other Christian artists to follow.

Working with Phillips had a significant impact on Burnett as well. With the exception of Elvis Costello and possibly David Hidalgo, he had never produced anyone with her rarified melodic gift—or committed himself to the extent that he did, over the course of their four albums for Virgin Records, to the most meticulous, painstaking pop-craft. For Burnett, who married Phillips in 1989, it was a labor of love.

The cover of Phillips's 1988 Virgin debut, *The Indescribable Wow*, which took its title from a signboard at an alternative church in West Hollywood, seemed to promise another girl singer with attitude. Looking pretty through a hot pink filter, her arm wrapped beneath her chin, Phillips gazes directly at us through her one exposed eye as if issuing a dare, her name and the title circling her face like a crown of pop art thorns (it would seem you can take the contemporary Christian out of the Bible belt, but you can't take the Bible belt out of the contemporary Christian). But from the casual, strumming opening of "I Don't Want to Fall in Love"—our introduction to the comforting folk-meets-cabaret sound that helped brand *Gilmore Girls*—the album marks the arrival of a different kind of artist than the cover art was promoting.

Showing off his unalloyed affection for 1960s rock, Burnett dresses up the songs with organ and raga effects, guitars that emulate the Beatles' "Taxman" and edgy instrumental fades. "Out of Time" is fashioned after 1960s girl groups. "I Can't Stop Crying" combines an irresistible Turtles-like melody and big drums. "What Do I Do?" boasts doubled and divided voices (few singers have overdubbed themselves as winningly as Phillips) and a moody symphonic-style string arrangement by the gifted pop maestro Van Dyke Parks, celebrated for his work with Brian Wilson of the Beach Boys.

Making *The Indescribable Wow* was "a full-time job," Phillips told me. Pro Tools, the digital technology that made editing music dramatically easier by eliminating the need to cut and splice tape, was still around the corner. The basic technique was to start with the drum machine and then build songs around vocal and guitar. Each song was a major production in and of itself; Burnett obsessed on small details and experimented relentlessly to fit them together. According to Phillips, he could work on a guitar part for hours to get it right.

Though he has been known to call a musician back after a session—sometimes from out of town—to redo a part, Burnett says he doesn't tell anyone what to play or how to play it. "Usually the first thing a musician plays is the best thing he's going to come up with," Burnett told *Tape Op*. "So, if a guitarist comes in and the thing he's doing isn't working—I just say, 'Thank you. Fantastic. Thank you very much. We'll see you later.' I don't torture musicians. I take what they give me and I'm very grateful for it."

What would be the point of dictating to a creative wiz like the guitarist Marc Ribot, on whom you depend for his off-the-chart inventiveness? Or requiring a stylish pro like the drummer Mickey Curry to play licks for hours—as the big-time hard rock and Shania Twain producer Mutt Lange is known to have done—before him turning him loose in the studio? Trust is the key: "One of the things I learned from T Bone is if you're a smart casting director, you can sort of get out of the way," Joe Henry told me. A protégé of Burnett who became a coveted producer himself, he defined smart casting as bringing in musicians with "less thought to instrumentation than personhood."

To get the right musicians—in many cases the top players in their field, like the drummer Jim Keltner, who has recorded with three of the Beatles—Burnett is not shy about paying top dollar for them. That doesn't always sit well with budget-minded label executives when days go by with no noticeable accomplishments in the studio. "T Bone can sit in his office all day if he senses that's what's called for, if a band needs to work out things on its own, for example," the A&R man Bill Bentley told me. "And when he believes his time is not being well spent, he'll leave."

"What I won't do is sit around the studio for hours and hours while somebody practices," Burnett told the *Hollywood Reporter*. "Or while somebody tries to punch in a part or something like that. And that was a lot of recording for a long time—overdubbing." Executives also aren't endeared by what Phillips calls her ex-husband's "stubborn grace." "I remember people wanting to drop in on my sessions and hear what we had," she told me. "He wouldn't let them. He's very protective of artists, and the whole creative process."

Following their marriage in 1989, Burnett and Phillips moved to Texas for three years, a period that involved considerable back and forth between Fort Worth and Los Angeles. They recorded much of her next album, *Cruel Inventions*, at Eagle Audio. A more cohesive collection than *The Indescribable Wow*, it boasts luxuriant Chamberlin effects, drum choruses, Marc Ribot's jagged lyrical guitar, and a string quartet arrangement by Van Dyke Parks that is straight out of the Beatles' "Eleanor Rigby."

As he demonstrates on Phillips's agitpropping "Go Down" ("Break the code of death for profit, break the guns / Break the silence of money, break the greedy unison"), Burnett is not a producer who needs to devise all the solutions himself. Struggling to come up with finishing touches for the song, which is graced by a lilting Spanish guitar, he ran out of Ocean Way's prized Studio B and dragged in Elvis Costello from the next room. Costello listened to the song, grabbed a twelve-string guitar, and played it with pencils to produce the kind of texture Burnett liked. On another, much later occasion when Burnett was stumped in the studio, he left to attend a holiday concert at his daughter Simone's school. "Sitting in the quiet and dark among these beautiful fourth graders, he was able to clear his mind," said Phillips. "After the show, he went right back, picked up his guitar, and just started playing the feel and everyone followed him."

Along with their pair of postmillennial collaborations for Nonesuch (and not counting anthologies), Burnett produced seven Phillips albums. The runaway favorite among fans and critics is *Martinis and Bikinis*, the third Virgin release; its swooningly lovely "Strawberry Road," inspired by an American Indian parable that says the route to paradise is covered with fresh strawberries, is her best-loved song. The way that Burnett frames his wife's voice on the tune—those airy violins playing off that plucky strummed guitar, those overdubbed vocals circling with the delicacy of angels dancing on the head of a pin—is as powerful a statement of love as you can find in popular music. The arrangement keeps adding new details, the way the light keeps changing, "down between our longing and desire." (You can't help wondering how someone who once wailed with the Legendary Stardust Cowboy became capable of work as exquisite as this.)

Burnett's guitar is all over *Martinis and Bikinis*—and then there is that sitar lending the dreamy raga feel to "Baby I Can't Please You." But ultimately, when Phillips falls, "amazed by it all," she does so on her own passionate terms. If there were justice in the world, these three albums would have made her a star on the level of Tori Amos or Alanis Morissette. But at a time when hook-driven melodic pop was struggling to break through in the marketplace (see also Marshall Crenshaw, Elliott Smith, Matthew Sweet, Shoes, et al.), the personal and sometimes secretive feeling of her songs held her back. Her final Virgin album, the bold pop experiment *Omnipop (It's Only a Flesh Wound Lambchop)*, added a chilliness to that equation.

Released in 1996, the recording gave the lie to the stereotype of Burnett as a stripper-down of sounds. Here, we encounter his production style writ large: fuzz, wah-wah, and distorted guitar effects; a Tijuana Brass chorus, unison baritone saxes, and free jazz–wailing bass clarinet; Chamberlins, marimbas, and harmonium; doubled and tripled drums, bongos, maracas; loops, bicycle horns, and "interesting noises." Burnett even took the opportunity to engage in hip-hop with "Slapstick Heart," which Phillips wrote with members of REM.

Playing the role of art-rock ringmaster in this sonic circus, where "Animals on Wheels" (read: empty trends) go "faster all the time," Phillips does her best to invest cheery irony in lyrics steeped in disillusionment and dystopian alienation: "You watch my lips / Like a pair of wrists that have never been slit" and "Love doesn't pay attention to / The metal teeth of ugly rules" and "Painted smile but I don't feel the part / In dream I hold your knife over my heart." And her poetry has such scalpel-like authority, you are willing to go along for the ride most of the time. But for all of *Omnipop*'s musical activity, it is a bit stuck in place emotionally, leaving fans who were expecting more *Martinis and Bikinis* magic feeling like they were trapped on a Ferris wheel. Critics were unkind: the *Village Voice*'s Robert Christgau dropped a bomb on the album in his *Consumer Guide*; in a sophomoric dismissal, *Entertainment Weekly* said Phillips's lyrics "convey all the depth of a tortured graduate student."

Looking back, Phillips told me it is her least favorite of her albums: "At that point, we were under way too much pressure. I knew something was coming to an end, that this was the last record I was going to make [for Virgin]. I wish I had taken more time; it came out way too quickly."

Virgin was in a state of flux; executives were jumping ship. Though she had survived four regimes there, she said, "No one at Virgin seemed to know who I was." The label quickly shelved *Omnipop*. Her final release for them, *Zero Zero Zero* (1998), was a retrospective designed to preserve some of the best songs she and Burnett had recorded while asserting its own identity. Things being as they were, they feared that all their music would fall off the edge of the earth. (At this writing, all of her Virgin albums were available as MP3s, but with the exception of *Martinis and Bikinis*, reissued in 2012, the recordings were available on CD only from third-party online sellers.)

Done up Burnett-style, *Zero Zero Zero* included alternate mixes and remixes of selected songs, plus an eerie Ribot interlude and a timely new song, "Disappearing Act." "I'm not sure I agreed with T Bone about going back and correcting things," Phillips told me. "Maybe it's better to leave a snapshot of what you did at the time alone. So it's really his anthology."

Following her unceremonious departure from Virgin, Phillips took an extended break. Freed from the pressures of making records, she laid low—and, oh yes, had a daughter. She spent her time raising baby Simone with Burnett, reading books, and enjoying time with friends—some of whom would prove crucial collaborators with her and her husband on two masterpieces yet to come.

CHAPTER 10

Imagist

Signed by Columbia Records, Bob Dylan's longtime label, following *T Bone Burnett*—and, notably, his production of the rapturously received Roy Orbison cable tribute *A Black and White Night*, more on which in the next chapter—Burnett was determined to make an album that would break the commercial ice. Abandoning the austere settings and low-key performances of *T Bone Burnett*, he returned on 1988's *The Talking Animals* to the edgy narratives and thematic ambitions of *Proof through the Night*, while consciously trying to avoid slipping into the "bad mood" he said he was in when he recorded that album. "I was being real hard on myself on that record, and I decided I wasn't going to do that on this record," he told the *Los Angeles Times*.

His co-producer on *The Talking Animals* was David Rhodes, Peter Gabriel's regular guitarist. As you might guess from titles such as

"Dance Dance Dance," "Euromad," and "The Wild Truth," Burnett is in a frisky mood on this record. James Thurber trumps Keats and Byron on "Monkey Dance" (a way to "become advanced"); the *Great Gatsby* femme Daisy Buchanan is linked to Lauren Bacall on "You Could Look It Up"; and what could be more disarming than a song with words by five-year-old Molly Burnett, "The Killer Moon" (what it's called when it's "so big and yellow"). Never mind that; as delivered by her father, the lyrics, in which "we seem like we're being followed," produce the dark shivers of a Maurice Sendak story.

But for this committed exposer of big lies, playing things loose doesn't mean letting up on the attack. Behind its bouncy beat and *Playboy* comic book setting—an exotic South American island populated by Hollywood starlets—"Dance Dance Dance" tells of a cold-blooded military intervention. (In a slightly biased review of *The Talking Animals* in *Musician*, Elvis Costello called it "the smartest song about American foreign policy since Randy Newman's 'Political Science.'") "We don't need no voodoo stories / From no magic president," Burnett sings on the ferociously rocking "Wild Truth," a scathing indictment of greed, lies, miscarriages of justice, and torture that ends on a searching note and an understanding of the injustice in the world with a line drawn from Thomas Merton's 1964 essay on "the beautiful inconsistency of mercy," "To Each His Darkness."

"Mercy is not consistent, it's like the wind," pronounces Burnett. "It goes where it will." "Mercy is comic, and it's the only / Thing worth taking seriously." Wrote Merton, "Mercy breaks into the world of magic and justice and overturns its apparent consistency. Mercy is inconsistent. It is therefore comic. It liberates us from the tragic seriousness of the obsessive world which we have 'made up' for ourselves by yielding to our obsessions."

If anything defined Burnett's writing at this juncture, it was his embrace of dualities and opposites, whether in the form of paradox ("It's a funny thing about humility / As soon as you know you're being humble / You're no longer humble") or the steady push-pull of reality and illusion. "Image," the most abused song on *The Talking Animals*, is not one of Burnett's most successful efforts. On it, four vocalists, each speaking a different language, repeat the same brief lines in which they relate how their images of one another entered into conversation: "And somewhere along the way / Our image sort of let each other down." Burnett speaks in English, Cait O'Riordan in French, Ruben Blades in Spanish, and the mystery singer Ludmila (who Burnett said he found in a Russian bar on Sunset Avenue) in Russian. As a vocal art installation, "Image" is flat in affect; as a statement on universal misunderstanding, it is awkward.

Still, set against Van Dyke Parks' gorgeous tango arrangement for strings and *bandoneons*, or button accordions, "Image" exerts a stubborn attraction. "None of us is what he thinks he is, or what other people think he is, still less what his passport says he is," Merton wrote in *The Waters of Siloe*. "And it is fortunate for most of us that we are mistaken. We do not generally know what is good for us. That is because, in St. Bernard's language, our true personality has been concealed under the 'disguise' of a false self, the *ego*, whom we tend to worship in place of God." As on "House of Mirrors" from the *Truth Decay* album, Burnett reveals a fascination with those false selves even as he rejects them. What is, in the end, the true self? And what do we do if we don't like it?

"The Strange Case of Frank Cash and the Morning Paper," the album's other outré item, is a very different kind of head-scratcher. The Beat-style spoken narrative relates the experiences of a lonely hustler who makes a fortune betting on football games after the newspaper that is delivered to his doorstep every day starts listing scores ahead of time. You don't have to be a seasoned *Twilight Zone* watcher to know that tabloid is suddenly going to run out of magic. But even Rod Serling would be surprised by the meta-fictional turn "Strange Case" takes after the bitterly disappointed Frank returns to his old digs looking for the day's sports section, tussles with the occupant, and shoots him dead. In his defense, Frank—a handy stand-in for some critics?—blames "this guy" T Bone Burnett for making everything up and says he doesn't believe in him or his existence. Song over. Except then, Frank's creator—now speaking in the first person—befriends him, gets him back the money he'd lost, and sees him marry a soulful woman who gives birth to a future president.

Burnett wrote "Strange Case" with Tonio K (an unlikely future collaborator of Burt Bacharach), whom he met in the late 1970s through the actress Mary Kay Place, then a recording artist cashing in her popularity on the mock soap opera *Mary Hartman, Mary Hartman.* In exploring the idea of a character discovering he is being manipulated by someone or something assuming divine powers, "Strange Case" was a decade ahead of Peter Weir's film *The Truman Show.* Judging by the *AV Club*'s inclusion of it on a 2007 list of songs "that are just as good as short stories," it may have been ahead of its time. But its studied abstractions, on top of the chilly conceptual trappings of "Image," invested *The Talking Animals* with more of a curiosity factor than it could bear.

In its review of the album, *People* said that Burnett "tends to err on the side of the precious." In its album guide, *Trouser Press* wished "this talented jerk weren't so impressed with himself." Half of its songs, *TP* said, were guilty of "scaling new heights of pretension." The *Chicago Tribune* pronounced the album "wildly uneven." In what passed for a rave, *New York Times* critic Stephen Holden called it "a fascinating oddity."

You couldn't help noticing a pattern developing with Burnett. When working quickly, on a tight budget, in a controlled setting, he came up with three exceptional efforts: *Truth Decay*, *Trap Door*, and *T Bone Burnett.* Given major label money and too much time to tinker in the studio, he recorded the inconsistent and less easily approachable *Proof through the Night* and *The Talking Animals.* What makes these tendencies fascinating is that as much as Burnett may have craved commercial approval, he never compromised his art to attain it. On the contrary, unlike most artists who have the good fortune to land on a major label, he dug down deeper into his identity as an artist and embraced his eccentricities. He also accepted the risk of making political statements he needed to make—a commercial kiss of death on the marketplace if your name isn't Dylan or, later on, Springsteen. In the face of what had to have been considerable pressure, he remained true to himself on *The Talking Animals*—believing, beneath his self-doubts, that that was his ticket to stardom.

CHAPTER 11

Native Son

With its broad expanses, high sky, and thunderstorms that Burnett said he could see coming from two hundred miles away as a kid, Texas has nurtured some of the boldest and most capacious musical voices. Would Illinois Jacquet, King Curtis, and Dewey Redman have developed their brawny, high-flying tenor saxophone sounds in, say, Ohio? Would Van Cliburn have had the bullets in his piano to conquer the Russians had he grown up in Count Basie's hustling, bustling Kansas City? And would Roy Orbison and Jimmie Dale Gilmore, two of the most idiosyncratic singers of the rock era, have developed their soaring vocal styles anywhere but in Texas?

Orbison, who was born outside of Wichita Falls and spent much of his childhood in Fort Worth, was for Burnett nothing less than "the greatest singer of the twentieth century." His vocals had a transcendent beauty and power. Even as he embodied romantic desire on songs such as "Only the Lonely" and "Oh, Pretty Woman"—which, a half century after hitting the charts, have lost none of their unearthly appeal—he lifted himself and his listeners above mortal concerns with his refusal to hold anything back. Indeed, his compositional style required him to go for broke. "He didn't write songs in a form like verse, verse, chorus, verse," Burnett told Terry Gross. "He wrote songs that would start on his lowest note and go to his highest note. And he would just find a way to arrive—to leave the one and arrive at the other. 'In Dreams' is a good example of that . . . There are no parts that repeat themselves. It's like a little aria, like a little pop aria."

Burnett first went into the studio with Orbison in April 1987 to record a new version of "In Dreams," which the director David Lynch had made spectacular use of in his film *Blue Velvet.* (Dean Stockwell's character lip-syncs to the song in a supremely creepy scene.) The remake, and the collection of redone Orbison classics on which it was included, was designed to capitalize on both the success of the 1986 film and Orbison's induction into the Rock and Roll Hall of Fame in May 1987, and to show the world that this artist was anything but a 1960s relic.

Serving Orbison's outsize talent, Burnett flashed his own Texas sense of proportion as musical supervisor of the 1987 Cinemax tribute, *Roy Orbison and Friends: A Black and White Night*, for which he convened an adoring all-star band featuring Bruce Springsteen, Elvis Costello, Tom Waits, and two sets of backup vocalists: Bonnie Raitt, k. d. lang, and Jennifer Warnes, and Jackson Browne and J. D. Souther. Burnett himself strums away self-effacingly on acoustic guitar in the back row, head tilted down, cutting quite a different figure than he did in the Rolling Thunder Revue.

Shot at the Cocoanut Grove in Los Angeles in wispy black and white, with a generous amount of haze effects, the salute has an uncommonly relaxed feel to it, reflecting Orbison's cool likability. What could have been a collection of star turns instead became another celebration of community. Even as the tribute elevates a single voice in honoring its lasting influence, the gathered congregation exuberantly shares in the glorious traditions that produced "In Dreams," "Oh, Pretty Woman," and "Only the Lonely." Orbison's beaming smile beneath his trademark dark shades assures you that, less than a year before he died, he knew his place in history was secure.

Put into rotation as a public television pledge-drive special, *A Black and White Night* took up permanent residence in the pop culture zeitgeist. With each airing, Orbison's stature was further polished—and so was Burnett's. By the time the Burnett-produced live album from the special was released in early 1989, Orbison was in posthumous orbit thanks to the astonishing success of *The Traveling Wilburys, Vol. 1*, the super session he recorded with Bob Dylan, George Harrison, Tom Petty, and ELO's Jeff Lynne. The release of the 1989 hit album *Mystery Girl*, for which Burnett produced two songs as part of a Valley creative consortium to which the Wilburys, Dave Stewart, Randy Newman, and Roger McGuinn contributed, was icing on the cake.

Jimmie Dale Gilmore grew up idolizing Orbison in the West Texas town of Lubbock, where he formed the legendarily unlegendary Flatlanders with Joe Ely and Butch Hancock. His 1991 album *"After Awhile,"* the most acclaimed offering in Elektra's short-lived American Explorers Series, introduced to mainstream listeners an "alt-country" singer with his own mystical values—part Irish, part Native American, full-time Buddhist.

Like Burnett, Gilmore had strong memories of gazing in wonder across Texas's wide-open spaces. He knew that in this producer, he had someone who understood his need to avoid being confined by genre any more than geography—someone who would help him, he told me in a 1999 *Chicago Sun-Times* interview, "get unshackled from the country label." Elmore James's distorted, screaming electric guitar, he said, meant every bit as much to him as "any Hank Williams thing." So did Chuck Berry, *Mad* magazine, and Bobby Darin's "Mack the Knife."

"I told T Bone I didn't want to make a Roy Orbison album," Gilmore says in the liner notes to *Braver Newer World*, their 1996 collaboration, "but I wanted to go in with the attitude Orbison, his producers and his musicians did, more of an anything-goes attitude. And T Bone knew what I was talking about, and maybe even took it further than I understood was possible."

The challenge, Burnett told Geoffrey Himes, writing for *Texas Music* in 2008, was "How do you capture that high consciousness thing without it becoming New Age? How do we keep the music on the ground but make it much deeper? How do you make a country record in an imaginary world where Roy Orbison had done this rather than that?" One answer was to use as a reference point those storms young Burnett saw heading toward Fort Worth. In the album's liner notes, Gilmore said they "would start off like a little black thumb sticking up on the horizon. And as it would come closer the sky would get darker and darker, and then it would be black, and then there'd be lightning, and then it would be all purple and orange and gold, just a blurred mass of beauty all around. And then there'd be these beautiful blue skies . . . I wanted to make a record like that."

Burnett steered Gilmore through sonic weather neither of them had experienced before. Though Burnett, rather curiously, said he saw Gilmore, he of the slow-moving drawl and soulful pinched delivery, as a "classic" singer who ranked up there with Tony Bennett and Frank Sinatra (a more apt analogy might be the idiosyncratic ballad singer Jimmy Scott), he recast him as a psychedelic rock and blues fiend. Wasting no time announcing its stylistic intentions, the album opens, on the title cut, by taking the listener into the realm of art rock with a mix of electric "Bombay" sitar, twanged notes, and dramatic slabs of sound. Gilmore sounds as if he is singing from the eye of a weird, temperamental storm—or, complicating his Buddhist beliefs, preparing for the Rapture. He assures us, however, that "there's still time for heaven, though we're already there."

Backing him with a full flank of guitarists, Burnett has Gilmore change stripes to vastly different effect on "Black Snake Moan," a Blind Lemon Jefferson song Gilmore had performed in the Flatlanders as "Long Snake Moan" in the early 1970s. Dogged by the drummer Jim Keltner's relentless, rock-steady attack, his voice dripping in reverb, Gilmore sounds like he is singing from an alternate dimension—one of dead reckonings. Typical of Burnett's production are the rivulets of organ streaming below the sound. Like the action on the margins in *Mad*, you may not become aware of it until after several listens.

The Orbison factor certainly is in play in Gilmore's yearning delivery of Sam Phillips's lovely ode to Oliver Twist, "Where Is Love Now." Dressed with twanging bass notes, Moog fills, and beatbox effects, it is the kind of production that shows off Burnett's willingness to challenge artists he respects and admires. (Gilmore said the only way he could master the melody was by imitating Phillips.) So does Darrell Leonard's French horn arrangement on the Texas songwriting hero Al Strehli's dreamy "Come Fly Away." Gilmore sums up the risky moves he and Burnett made on *Braver Newer World* on "Outside the Lines": "I painted myself into a corner / But footprints / Are just about to become part of my design." "I caught a lot of grief for that album in Texas," Burnett told me. "Some of our homeboys thought he sounded pretty strange."

On the upside, the *Austin Chronicle* pronounced *Braver Newer World* "a minor masterpiece"; the *Texas Monthly* declared, "There are moments when—for the first time ever—[Gilmore] rocks as effortlessly as he rolls." Heard all these years later, when genre demands are more forgiving, *Braver Newer World* sounds even braver, its footprints even deeper. There is the distinct possibility that, ultimately, this will be the Jimmie Dale Gilmore album prized above all the others.

"I listened to that record for the first time in a long while recently," Gilmore told Himes, "and I was struck by the ethereal vibe of the music. Sometimes in the process of doing the record, it felt like we were pushing the boundaries too far, but I always ended up loving the end product. That's what experimentation is all about—overcoming your own boundaries. It wasn't about, 'You play this part on this instrument and you play that part on that instrument.' It was more, 'Let's get together and play and see where it goes.'"

CHAPTER 12

Mentor

As an aspiring artist living in Ann Arbor, Michigan, circa 1980, Joe Henry mailed his first demos to record companies using addresses he found on the back of album jackets. His first response was a letter from T Bone Burnett. The big-time producer encouraged him to keep at it, saying he was a talented songwriter—the only indication from the outside world, Henry told me, that he should take himself seriously as an artist.

Flash-forward to 1989. While attending a business meeting, Burnett overheard the A&R director of A&M Records, which that year had released Henry's second effort, *Murder of Crows*, talking discouragingly about the singer-songwriter's ambitious plans for his next album. He said there was no market for the moody songs and atmospheric production Henry had in mind, and that there was no way the label would let him make that album. According to Henry, "T Bone piped up and told the A&R man that the musician he was talking about was really talented and that A&M should just let him do what he did." And then, though Burnett had never met or spoken to Henry—who was upset with the way *Murder of Crows* had been produced—he offered to help him record the new album. Trusting that a producer of Burnett's savvy and experience would keep the young artist's ambitions in check, the A&R man gave his approval. Chalk up another victory in Burnett's campaign against the corporate oppressors.

Henry, who was then living in Brooklyn, flew to Los Angeles to meet with Burnett—not in an office or boardroom or recording studio, but on a golf course, where business was the furthest thing from the producer's mind. "It wasn't until he was putting on the last green that he brought up possibilities regarding the album," Henry told me. "And it wasn't until we were in the middle of a conversation about something else a while later that he said, 'Let's make a record together.'"

A singer of soulful tones and pensive, prophet-like phrasing, Henry had the songs for his album, *Shuffletown*, and its overall concept in place. He wanted to expand folk forms in the elastic, jazz-inflected way Van Morrison had on his 1968 masterwork *Astral Weeks*. To do so, he had lined up a pair of distinguished jazz artists, the bassist Cecil McBee, who had accompanied the likes of Charles Lloyd, Wayne Shorter, and Pharoah Sanders, and the cornetist Don Cherry, a member of Ornette Coleman's history-making 1960s quartet. McBee would provide the deep, resonant heartbeat that Richard Davis did on *Astral Weeks*. Adding to the all-acoustic unit, Burnett brought in the string man David Mansfield and the percussionist Michael Blair.

Shuffletown was recorded in three days in New York. Per usual, Burnett had the band perform the music live, a new and nervous-making approach for Henry. Burnett assured him it was the way to go by explaining that recording the music as a whole on two tracks of analog tape instead of dividing it into pieces on multiple digital tracks would ensure that no one at A&M would be able to "fuck with it" later.

"It was an intensely focused way to work, but also very freeing," Henry told me. He recalled everyone playing a percussive role, "poking the air in the room, moving it around," while the suggestion of richer and wider orchestral sounds radiated up from the deep pulse. ("I watched [Burnett] walk around the studio with his hands out like a blind man," Stephen Bruton told *Los Angeles Magazine*. "And he was going, 'Okay, put a mike here. Put a mike there, because that's where the air is moving.' He picked that up from some old engineer at the radio station in Fort Worth.")

Henry contrasted Burnett's open methods in the studio with the closed, set-in-stone approach of other producers. "I get the sense," he told me, "that the way Prince [Nelson] approaches the studio is, 'I already know everything about how this goes, and if you can't get me what I need, I'll get someone else in here or do it for myself, but I know the one way it works.' I observed in T Bone the idea that you're engaging something that's already in play and you're trying to abide it, very much like jumping into the ocean, and learning sort of how to swim or, on a good day, surf on top of it, but you didn't create that momentum and you're not going to control it." He continued, "You're going to learn to be grateful within it, and when you get together with musicians in a room, there's a notion that there's all kinds of ways that a song might work. Our job is to find what it is and be fully committed to it, which liberates you from thinking, did I guess right? The question is have we authentically engaged something that's alive?" (Folk-rocker Freedy Johnston, whose beautiful, subdued 1999 gem, *Blue Days Black Nights*, was produced by Burnett, felt as liberated in the studio as Henry did: "I've always wanted to control things in the studio and this time I was advised to stop trying so much and to let it happen," he told *Triste Magazine*, adding, "I never thought in the past that I could do a live vocal on demand.")

Like *Astral Weeks*, *Shuffletown*, which was released in 1990, is less an album of songs than a streaming reverie—just the kind of effort that A&M was primed to dump. On the day the album came out, the label dropped Henry, telling him he had no future with them. This "cult artist waiting for his cult to discover him," as the critic Don McLeese described him, would have to wait some more—much like his mentor. Some young artists who found themselves in Henry's painful and precarious position might have thought that Burnett had led them down the wrong path. Henry had uprooted his family and moved to Los Angeles. Now he was without a recording deal or any prospects. He didn't fit into the LA scene any better than Burnett had as a singer-songwriter. But he felt only gratitude for all that Burnett had done for him: "T Bone allowed me to see myself as a professional musician, even though I felt cast off. The world he invited me into has remained open to me ever since."

Burnett invited Henry to hit some more golf balls (or watch him hit them, at any rate) and offered him a job as a production assistant. That required Henry to run errands. During the making of Sam Phillips's *Cruel Inventions*, he found himself picking up her dry cleaning. But the gig also gave him the opportunity to learn all aspects of recording music from one of the top men in the field, and to be around great musicians such as Bruce Cockburn, Booker T, Jim Keltner, and Edgar Meyer during the making of Cockburn's *Nothing but a Burning Light*. There's little doubt that an artist as deep and original as Henry would have made his mark as a singer and songwriter had he not had the good fortune to cross Burnett's path. But would he have become the prolific, wide-ranging producer he is (with clients ranging from Solomon Burke and Rodney Crowell to Aaron Neville and Bonnie Raitt) had Burnett not taken him under his wing during those scuffling days following *Shuffletown*? Not only did Burnett show him the ropes of production, he instilled in Henry the notion that producing was a way of expanding his artistic base, making a wider mark on the world—and providing himself with a regular source of income to offset the financial sacrifices that artists of his individuality and refined taste usually must make.

Burnett and Henry share many of the same standout session players, notably the drummer Jay Bellerose (whom Henry introduced to Burnett), the keyboardist Keefus Ciancia, and the guitarist Marc Ribot. "I've never felt in competition with him," Henry said to me. "I feel like we're a community. Anytime T Bone has a session going, he invites me, and I never miss a chance to stick my head in. I always come away having something affirmed. And with projects he doesn't think he's suited for or doesn't have time for, he recommends me."

Following *Shuffletown*, Burnett produced other emerging artists with mixed results. *A. J. Croce* (1993), co-produced by John Simon of the Band fame, was the nonstarting large-scale debut by the late Jim Croce's son, a bluesy-jazzy artist striving after Dr. John–like authenticity. *David Poe*, the tantalizing 1997 debut by a folk-oriented singer and guitarist with strong eclectic tastes and quietly unsettling songs, was also a commercial bust. And perhaps most frustratingly, there was *Sweetie*, the 1996 debut of a nineteen-year-old LA phenom named Daniel Tashian, son of the singer-guitarist Barry Tashian, whose much-liked Boston band the Remains opened for the Beatles on their final North American tour and who teamed with his wife in the folk duo Barry and Holly Tashian.

Daniel, also a singer and guitarist, had fashioned a unique blend of country-rock and power-pop (a hybrid that found expression in Nashville much later in groups such as Sugarland and the Band Perry). He was supported by the guitarist and future producer of note Jay Joyce and his band. And as his ace in the hole, he had the extravagantly gifted pedal steel player Bucky Baxter, a Bob Dylan regular. The sessions, at Groove Masters in Santa Monica, went well. The songs were solid. Burnett played some guitar and brought in Booker T and the Wrecking Crew veteran Larry Knechtel to play keyboards on one track each. Baxter was in top form. And during one moment when Burnett seemed to lose interest ("He's got ADD to a pretty extensive degree, so he gets bored quite easily," Tashian said in an online interview), the band captured his fancy with a spontaneous pop experiment on which Daniel played an old mandolin he said had been left in a storage room by Jackson Browne.

Burnett, Tashian told me, "let me run the show and do my thing" in the early going "to get me focused on the music." But the pressure became too intense for the quintessentially sensitive young artist, who was going through a lot of upheaval in his personal life. Burnett, he told me, "stepped in and took the reins and sort of held my hand. He has wonderful ways of nudging you in the right direction. Like if I wasn't singing in tune, he'd say, 'You're like me, you don't like singing with headphones.' Or if he didn't like a song or think it was up to caliber, instead of saying it wasn't good enough, he'd say that in order to get it right, it would take a week, which we didn't have, so we should concentrate on other songs."

To Tashian's dismay, the people in control at Elektra, which was in a state of flux following the sudden exit of the label head Bob Krasnow, stripped Baxter's steel guitar from the recording. They wanted something trendier, he said, "more Pearl Jam than Byrds. T Bone asked me if I wanted him to jump on someone's desk and make a big stink. But because we thought we were going to do another album together pretty soon, we let it pass. In the end, it's really up to the artist to stand up—the producer can stand up only so much—and I just wasn't confident enough to do that." However much standing up Burnett did, here was a rare instance of record execs holding serve on one of his productions.

As it is, *Sweetie* is a strong album with a great guitar sound and standout tunes, including a flawless Byrds-style number, "Where Have You Gone." But the production, notwithstanding some edgy effects, is slicker than anything Pearl Jam would have gone for, leaving you thinking the label did more than remove the steel. Elektra quickly buried *Sweetie* in its distribution slush pile, effectively ending Tashian's big-time pop career before it started. Now based in Nashville, where he has done well for himself as a songwriter and leader of the band Silver Seas, he has good memories of working with Burnett—and not only because the producer took him to Barney's and bought him a $4,000 Comme des Garçons suit. "He was very kind," Tashian told me. "It was like having a magician for an uncle."

CHAPTER 13

Hit Man

Even as far as we have come with musical technology, many people still think that producers are the dudes who twist knobs and push buttons. It's an image reinforced by cultural artifacts like Dave Grohl's *Sonic Highways* documentary series, in which the nerdy, bespectacled Butch Vig (producer of Nirvana and Garbage) sits by the board waiting for all the joking around to stop, and TV's late and lamented *Parenthood*, in which Dax Sheperd's Crosby gazes unhappily through the glass at the temperamental bands causing problems in his Luncheonette studio.

There are certainly plenty of producers, like Burnett, who do their share of knob turning. Some standouts in the field, among them Daniel Lanois, believe no producer is worth his or her salt unless the person has superior, all-encompassing skills at the board and knows how to apply them in every situation. But that is called audio or sound engineering. The history of producers reveals a wide range of methods and approaches that have little to do with mixing and mastering.

John Hammond's reputation rests more on his "discovery," support, and promotion of great artists such as Count Basie, Billie Holiday, Bob Dylan, and Bruce Springsteen than his skills in recording them. He basically put young Dylan in front of a microphone and pushed the record button, occasionally telling him to stand back a bit. As Dylan wrote in *Chronicles: Volume One*, Hammond also had a profound impact on him by introducing him to Robert Johnson via a copy of *King of the Delta Blues Singers*.

The Atlantic Records legend Jerry Wexler was unmatched in bringing out the best of Aretha Franklin, Dusty Springfield, Wilson Pickett, and many other artists by matching them up with particular musicians and treating them with certain instrumental combinations while remaining open to new ideas. In his 1993 memoir *Rhythm and the Blues*, Wexler freely acknowledges learning from the great Muscle Shoals Rhythm Section "a new way of making records spontaneously, synergistically" through a numbering system that made it easy to change keys and left room for other variations.

Tom Wilson, the first black staff producer at Columbia Records, was a brilliant "out of the box" conceptualist—he's credited with electrifying Dylan and rescuing the folk duo Simon and Garfunkel from navel-gazing obscurity by redoing "The Sounds of Silence" with instrumental overdubs. A native of Waco, Texas, Wilson also lifted artists with his "ebullient spirit," Van Dyke Parks told *Texas Monthly*. He was "charismatic, statuesque, and curiously empowering for those in his orbit."

Bob Johnston, the producer of such Dylan masterpieces as *Highway 61 Revisited* and *Blonde on Blonde*, was willing to go many extra miles to prop up his artists. After Leonard Cohen, unhappy with his attempts at "The Partisan" (included on the poet's 1969 album *Songs from a Room*), remarked that it would sound good with French voices, Johnston flew to Paris and brought back three female singers—and an accordion player. Secretly, he had them overdub their parts and then sprang the results on a pleased Cohen—revealing a thoughtful side to his personality that those who remember Johnston only for his brashness need to know.

George Martin, the "fifth Beatle," was known for his spontaneity and experimentation. He introduced a new level of sophistication to cutting and splicing different takes together and broke new ground with sound effects and orchestrations—the double string quartet on "Eleanor Rigby" is one of pop music's monuments.

And among Burnett's peers, Rick Rubin, who has played guru for artists as varied as Slayer, the Beastie Boys, and Johnny Cash, is known to employ meditation methods to put artists in the right frame of mind. "One of the main things I always try to do is to create an environment where the artist feels pretty comfortable being naked," he told *Forbes*.

What has made T Bone Burnett special as a producer—and, indeed, what has enabled him to transcend that status like no one else—is his incorporation of the aforementioned methods and practices, plus the special insight he brings to the studio as an artist himself. "He doesn't do what he does without being a great songwriter, deeply invested in craft, at a level most producers couldn't dream of," Joe Henry told me. Burnett's curatorial skills are unsurpassed. Using his encyclopedic knowledge of recorded music, he puts together voluminous playlists of songs from all stylistic precincts to expose artists to songs they have forgotten or never heard before—songs that, if not used, might suggest other cover material or inspire other directions.

In terms of a producing style, Burnett was developing from an enabler—a neutral presence dedicated to concentrating on the music before him and "listening it into existence"—to a catalyst who gets out on the floor with a guitar or bass or exotic instrument to help guide artists. But as his longtime engineer Mike Piersante told me, "I don't know if we've ever consciously gone after a particular sound. The goal has always been to capture the artist in the best possible light, without being gimmicky."

When you ask someone Burnett has produced what makes the experience so rewarding, he or she will typically begin by discussing how at ease he puts them in the studio, how laid back the atmosphere he creates is, and how well he treats them. "T Bone is a deep soul with an artist's mind," Rosanne Cash told me. "He has tremendous respect for musicians and never acts like he is the authority figure. He's interested in the conversation, in the process. He's very attuned to what is happening *in the moment* and is able to switch courses, make a left turn, find a completely new idea, and let go of the old without regret."

None of which is to suggest there aren't artists he has rubbed the wrong way, industry peers who see him as a prima donna, listeners who believe he does a disservice to artists by bottling up their sound. In 1997, Burnett worked for weeks on an album by the E Street Band singer Patti Scialfa for which he summoned Marc Ribot (of course), the keyboardist John Medeski of the progressive jazz-funk group Medeski Martin & Wood, and the experimental guitarist David Torn. All he had to show for the sessions in the end was a single song. Grace Potter, leader of the Nocturnals, didn't like Burnett's mixes for her 2009 solo album—about which she recently had great things to say—and shelved it. (The record may well have been doomed from the start when Burnett, who has no compunction about swapping an underachieving player for a top-level pro, replaced the drummer Mark Barr, Potter's boyfriend, with Jim Keltner). Another young and overconfident artist who shall remain nameless was so displeased with Burnett's production that he put out his own demo instead. It got little attention.

Ironically, as with BoDeans, Burnett has been spanked by artists who recorded their best albums with him. Discussing the making of his resplendent *Nothing but a Burning Light* in his 2014 memoir *Rumours of Glory*, the Canadian legend (and Christian music hero) Bruce Cockburn chafes over Burnett's sense of control: "If a song doesn't come out the way he thinks it should, he'll insist on re-doing it or throwing it out. He would call me on the music and even the lyrics." He continued, "T Bone spoke with Texan courtliness but projected a clear assumption that he was in command of his environment. He had about him an intriguing intensity and a penetrating intelligence, along with the faintest whiff of a cruel streak held in check by moral resolve." This while acknowledging the producer's "taste, discernment and instinct" and recognizing that "with him at the helm, everything rolled into place like the ball in a roulette wheel."

Cockburn also had positive things to say about the experience in an interview with Paul Zollo. He began the project, he said, looking to take a break from what he called "the droning effect" in his lyrics—to simplify his songs and make his melodies more singable. From Burnett, he "picked up an understanding . . . of how to focus on the essence of a song without screwing it up in the process of adding instruments to it." That understanding is reflected in lovely, shimmering songs such as "Great Big Love" and "A Dream Like Mine," which brought out winning qualities in the usually sober singer-songwriter that we hadn't heard before.

If, as Cockburn said in a 1991 radio interview, Burnett got "sort of fed up" with how long it was taking Cockburn and band to record "Indian Wars," his decision to have Cockburn, the violinist Mark O'Connor, and Jackson Browne (on Dobro and low harmony vocals) break apart from the full band and do the song live off the floor resulted in another of the album's standout tracks. The session, a rare one for Cockburn outside his hometown of Toronto, ended on an up note when Burnett asked Cockburn if he had any songs he had been wanting to record and Cockburn picked Blind Willie Johnson's "Soul of a Man"—a tune close to Burnett's heart that Cockburn awakened on resonator guitar. But relations between the artists were off from start to finish during the making of *Dart to the Heart* (1993). In his book, Cockburn puts the onus for the album's mixed results on "T Bone's gift for running up expenses" while admitting he (Cockburn) was off his game because an affair with a woman he had met in Los Angeles had ended badly.

As for the would've-could've-should'ves in Burnett's producing life, we can only imagine what John Fogerty's 2009 album *The Blue Ridge Rangers Rides Again* would have amounted to had not an unhappy encounter with the high-strung singer caused Burnett to walk away from the project. And what about the 2013 Jerry Lee Lewis album that was in the works until the Hall of Fame rocker rejected the songs and musicians Burnett had lined up for it? Plans were to hold the sessions in the basement of Memphis's historic Peabody Hotel—where Memphis Minnie, among others, cut tracks in temporary studios during the 1920s. Lewis decided to go the safer, all-star route instead on *Rock &*

Roll Time, the solid but less than ear-opening effort co-produced by Jim Keltner at Sun Studios, Jerry Lee's old home away from home.

Well, maybe the Killer remembered Burnett disarming him on the set of the 1989 biopic *Great Balls of Fire!* Burnett was producing him on new versions of his songs for the film's star Dennis Quaid to lip-sync along with. Recalled Burnett's ex-wife Sam Phillips, "Jerry Lee came in with a gun the day before the sessions started and T Bone kind of looked at it and said, 'Hey, that's a really nice piece, can I see it?' And Jerry Lee said, 'Sure,' and handed it over. T Bone took out the bullets and put them in his pocket."

The sessions went well—better than the Jim McBride film, which, for all its Memphis color and sneering grins by Quaid, soft-peddled the Jerry Lee myth. But killers do have such long memories.

CHAPTER 14

Reluctant Artist

As the eighties turned into the nineties, Burnett was performing very little and touring not at all, but the shows he did play were memorable. After a solo acoustic set in June 1989 at McCabe's Guitar Shop, he strolled onto Pico Boulevard and led the people standing in line for the late show in a sing-along of "Kumbaya." Two years later at the same Santa Monica landmark, he hosted a series of offbeat Friday night variety shows that were recorded for an NPR Christmas Eve special. Among the "surprise" guests were the actor Jeff Bridges, the satirist and *Simpsons* voice artist Harry Shearer, and an exotic dancer billing himself (and, perhaps, his invisible partners) as the Zen Nude Dancers. According to the *Los Angeles Times*, Burnett handed out paper-bag masks for audience members to slip on in case they were planning "to run for office someday."

As for "the recording thing," as he put it, "I hated the whole deal," he told me. The failure of *The Talking Animals* had deepened his self-doubts. More than ever, he feared that he didn't have what it took to be a successful recording artist—success being defined by record sales and exposure, not artistic achievement. Though he had no problem working with other artists on their songs (as tiring as working on so many outside projects could be), he was stymied by his own efforts to negotiate words and music. He thought his lyrics were pretentious and marked by "silly schoolboy attitudes." He told me, "I had reached a point where I couldn't tell why one note should be there and another shouldn't. I think John Cage found himself in the same place when he began experimenting with silence."

During his long stretch with Phillips in Fort Worth, where he could be "a part of ordinary life again," he spent time with his daughters, read a lot of books, and listened to a lot of recorded music, including his own. "I tend to write really well in Fort Worth," he told the *Los Angeles Times*. "There's something about seeing the horizon all the way around you, all 360 degrees, for hundreds of miles. It lets you look a long way off. It gives you room to think."

"I tried to pick out what I do well," he told *Pulse!* in the early 1990s, as quoted by *Musician Guide*. "I noticed that the more simple stuff, the stuff which comes more naturally to me, is generally the stuff that works best, so I tried to work within that vein." Who better to school him in the art of simplicity than Lead Belly, with whose works (such as "Goodnight, Irene" and "Cotton Fields") he spent many hours.

With the mushrooming of Operation Desert Storm, Anita Hill's harassment charges against Clarence Thomas, the continuing fallout from Iran-Contra, and the rise of the religious right, there was no lack of bad stuff going on in the world to fire up his writing. In an article in the November 1992 issue of *Spin*, "25 Things to Remember about George Bush When You Go to the Polls," he ripped the president for "kissing the ring of Pat Robertson, as power-mad a religious figure as we've been afflicted with since Rasputin," and for declaring "the system has worked" after the acquittal of the Los Angeles police officers charged with using excessive force in arresting black motorist Rodney King—a verdict that led to widespread rioting.

But Burnett shied away from returning to the studio, conscious of what happened the last time he flexed his politics on record. In a meeting with Donnie Ienner, the new president of Columbia Records, he said he didn't feel like he fit into the label's plans as a recording artist and offered to stick to producing. Ienner assured him he was an important artist and wanted him to continue making albums. Only when Bob Neuwirth signed on as Burnett's co-producer did the reluctant artist's resistance weaken.

Neuwirth convinced his friend to concentrate on his songs and not worry about the things over which he had no control. He also prodded Burnett into stepping more into his own spotlight. "I generally try to put the person I'm recording with very big in the frame, and make it a good, close, intimate record," Burnett said in a 1992 *Billboard* article. "A few times in the past, I've lost my nerve and obscured myself on my own records, stayed hidden so to speak, and Neuwirth just didn't let me hide." (In the *Billboard* piece, Sam Phillips remarked on her husband's tendency to "shoot himself in the foot" when it came to recording his own work.)

As the title of his 1992 album, *The Criminal under My Own Hat*, makes clear, Burnett wasn't letting himself off any hooks regarding the sorry state of the world. The day of reckoning he invokes—"The big heat is coming down / Like hail from the sky" and "We live in an age lit by lightning / After the flash we're blind again"—is coming for him as much as anyone. In the CD booklet, he is seen, as on *Proof through the Night*, in Sherlockian attire—in one photograph with his hands cuffed and his head bowed down, and in another in prayerful repose, his eyes closed and his hands clasped in front of him. Returning to his theme of dual identity, the images tell us that each of us must investigate and answer to our own misdeeds—to the criminal inside us—before we can point fingers at anyone or anything else.

Inside the CD booklet is an unsettling collage by his friend John "Flex" Fleming, a troubled soul who committed suicide in 2004. Embedded in the collage is a small photo of a tattooed man whose head is etched with the likeness of a suffering Christ—shades of the tormented soul in Flannery O'Connor's blistering "Parker's Back." As Burnett described this favorite short story of his, it is "about a wife who is very religious, and her husband gets a tattoo of Jesus on his back, and she screams, 'Blasphemy!' That, to me, is the South in a nutshell."

With their acts of defilement, the Fleming work and "Parker's Back" address the meeting of the spirit and the flesh that informs *Criminal* songs such as "Primitives" ("The frightening thing is not dying / The frightening thing is not living") and previous Burnett songs, such as "River of Love." Without pain in our lives, without sins to atone for, these songs tell us, there would be no need for belief in a higher power. That there is no freedom from pain is, in the end, a kind of blessing.

However bleak Burnett's vision is on *Criminal*, however lethal the atmosphere, the melodies are so strong, the rockabilly currents so alive, the singer so relaxed in his element, that it is one of his most appealing albums. On "It's Not Too Late," a jaunty Euro cabaret-style number written with Neuwirth and Elvis Costello, Burnett offers hope even with "the weather crashing down." Riding over Burnett's vocal and percussive acoustic guitar playing on "Over You," Roy Huskey Jr.'s slapped bass bounds in good feeling. "Any Time at All" is a heartfelt pledge of undying love.

The album, half of which was recorded with drummerless acoustic units and half with spatially oriented electric trios, is not without its oddball features. "Humans from Earth," Burnett says in his *Twenty Twenty* liner notes, dates back to the 1960s, when during the height of the military-industrial complex he founded the Interplanetary Real Estate Agency to sell deeds to lots on "hospitable" planets. But listening to him scathingly sing, "We're out here in the universe buying real estate / Hope we haven't gotten here too late," you can't help but think of Ed Bass and Biosphere 2 and the friendly(?) planet of Mars.

On two versions of "I Can Explain Everything," which works over lying TV preachers and politicians, Burnett employs a jarring theatrical falsetto to deliver pithy Ogden Nash–like lyrics ("The genius of France can be seen at a glance / And it's not their fabled fashion scene

/ It's not that they're mean or their wine or cuisine / I refer of course to the guillotine"). "For years, my hotel name was 'Ogden Nashville,'" he told *Vulture*. "I spent a tremendous amount of time studying the way he played with words, made up words, with a light touch, like a twinkle in his eye. I look at most of my songs as musical versions of what Ogden Nash did."

It could be that people had trouble finding the Nash in his nightmares. *Criminal* was nominated for a Grammy for Best Contemporary Folk Album ("Kumbaya," indeed) and was awarded an A grade in *Entertainment Weekly*. "Burnett's highly moralistic, deeply religious compositions—especially the intimate, disarming acoustic tracks—tilt nobly at the windmills of human weakness, both global and personal," wrote Billy Altman. "Of such honest, cathartic communications are masterpieces made." But for all that, *Criminal* was, excuse the expression, criminally overlooked commercially and was the last recording he would make for nearly a decade and a half.

"I got behind the scenes as far as I could," he told me. When you're T Bone Burnett, though, being "behind" the scenes, however far, hardly keeps you out of the frame. Just ask the next band he would launch for proof of that.

Paschal High senior yearbook photo.
Courtesy of Don Duca.

Burnett leading the Shadows, circa 1964.
Courtesy of David Graves.

Burnett with David Graves at Sound City, 1965. Photo by Phil York; courtesy of David Graves.

Burnett in ten-gallon hat at the Lodge, in Tujunga, California, 1973. © Bob Shaw. Courtesy of BobShaw.com.

Burnett with Bob Dylan at the Houston Astrodome, during the Rolling Thunder Revue, 1976. © Bob Shaw. Courtesy of BobShaw.com.

Publicity shot for the Alpha Band's *Spark in the Dark* (1977). Arista handout.

Burnett opening for the Who, Chicago Amphitheatre, 1982. Photo by Paul Natkin.

Burnett performing with Jennifer Warnes, Jackson Browne, Warren Zevon, and Richard Thompson at McCabe's Guitar Shop, 1984. Photo by Sherry Rayn Barnett.

Burnett with Elvis Costello at McCabe's Guitar Shop, Santa Monica, California, 1984. Photo by Sherry Rayn Barnett.

Burnett posed at Tuts, Chicago, 1984.
Photo by Paul Natkin.

Left: Burnett at CHART conference, Lake Geneva, Wisconsin, 1986. Courtesy of Chris Stacey (taken from VHS tape).

Right: Publicity shot for *The Talking Animals* (Columbia Records, 1987). Photo provided by Columbia/Legacy.

Polaroid of Burnett at a Fort Worth graveyard, circa 1989. Photographer unknown; photo provided by T Bone Burnett.

Burnett and Sam Phillips, 1992. Photo by Frank Ockenfels.

Burnett with Stephen Bruton on the set of *Crazy Heart*, 2008. Photo by Jeff Bridges.

Burnett in the studio with Elton John, Bernie Taupin, and Davey Johnstone during the summer of 2015. Photo by Joseph Guay; photo provided by T Bone Burnett.

Studio shot of Burnett at the sound board. Photographer unknown; photo provided by T Bone Burnett.

Publicity still for the *New Basement Tapes*, 2014. Photo provided by Big Hassle Media.

Burnett performing at the Hardly Strictly Bluegrass Festival, San Francisco, 2015. Photograph by Peter Dervin.

CHAPTER 15

Starmaker

In 1993, a demo by a highly touted but still-unknown San Francisco band landed on Burnett's desk. Containing not just a few songs, as was the norm, but more than a dozen, and sounding ten times better than the average demo, the tape had set off a major bidding war. The Geffen executive Gary Gersh—the man who had signed Nirvana—was the winner. After considering other top producers, Counting Crows chose Burnett.

If they had known what kind of state he was in, they might have gone with someone else. "I was tired of studios," Burnett told the *San Francisco Chronicle* pop critic Joel Selvin in 1994. "They reek of despair. It sinks into the walls." Unswayed by their cheering section, he told the Crows that they needed to come up with a more distinctive sound—"something that sounds just like you," the keyboardist Charles Gillingham recalled in an interview with the *Vancouver Province*. And, Gillingham told *Musician*, "T Bone said you've made a demo that sounds like an album, now you've got to make an album that sounds like a demo."

When Gersh set up the Crows in a rented old mansion in the hills above Los Angeles to rehearse and record, that was fine with Burnett. Dylan and the Band and Big Pink came to mind. Why not think big? When it comes to reekage, great memories beat despair every time. But a small problem arose with one of the more promising songs, "Mr. Jones." The drummer Steve Bowman, widely considered the most talented member of the band—lead singer and songwriter Adam Duritz included—refused to play on it because he didn't like the beat. He thought it was too square and too country. Weary or not, Burnett pulled one of his all-time savviest and most audacious moves in the studio—one that anyone with inside knowledge of his methods would have seen coming from ten miles away. He replaced Bowman with the top-notch studio drummer Denny Fongheiser. With Fongheiser at the traps, the Crows nailed the song—the number that made their career—in a single take.

How distinctive Counting Crows sounded on their debut, *August and Everything After*, remains up for debate. Duritz's too-close approximation of Van Morrison's vocal style drew criticism. Other reviewers heard too much of a debt to Bruce Springsteen and the Band. But thanks to the roaringly infectious "Mr. Jones," which wasn't a single until listener demand made it one, and the nearly-as-irresistible "Round Here," the album overcame its artistic debts, and a pokey start out of the gate, to soar up the charts. And with *August*, Burnett did some soaring himself—from the ranks of rock's top producers into an elite group of hitmakers.

For him, this proved to be not an entirely good thing. After *August* attained multiple-platinum success, Burnett received an avalanche of demos from bands hoping he would work his magic on them as well. Some producers would have eagerly turned to the next band in line, but he had no desire to babysit undeveloped talent. "A lot of songs that came to me as producer were like 12th generation," Burnett told *Mix*.

"The kids hadn't heard of Led Zeppelin, much less Willie Dixon." However indisposed he was toward working with any more artists who were still wet behind the ears, he was no more able to resist being pulled back into the fold than was Michael Corleone in *Godfather III*. When Bob Dylan's twenty-two-year-old son asks you to help him out, there are few circumstances under which you say no. Rescuing Jakob Dylan, labeled a Julian Lennon–type wannabe after his band the Wallflowers' 1992 debut tanked, wasn't one of them.

Burnett, who has known Jakob since he was four, has maintained close ties to the Dylan family; another of Bob's sons, Jesse, did the photography for Burnett's 2006 comeback album, *The True False Identity*. Burnett has covered many of Dylan's songs and commissioned him to write new ones or provide old ones for film and album projects. While Burnett has never gotten to produce his now self-producing hero (though there has been talk in recent years of him assuming such a role, playing guitar on 1986's *Knocked Out Loaded* was the most he's been involved with a Dylan album), Dylan celebrated their close-knit connection after all these years by letting Burnett produce an album of previously unrecorded lyrics from *The Basement Tapes*.

And so, in 1994, Burnett accepted the assignment of helping Jakob bounce back from the failure of *The Wallflowers*, and Virgin's dumping of the group, amid reports that Dylan was difficult to work with. There was, indeed, strife within the band as they pursued another label. When Jakob Dylan asked Burnett to produce what in effect would be a second debut—one that would show what he was *really* capable of as a leader—he did so knowing that with Burnett's high standards, the band would be upgraded. Sure enough, by the time Jakob and company entered the studio, the keyboardist Rami Jaffee was the only holdover. ("Groups are more difficult to work with, with all the conflicts within the group," Burnett told Bill Cochran in his 1986 WXRT interview. "Usually there are one or two really good guys and three or four not so good guys. It's frustrating because you think how good the record could be if there weren't these guys.")

Recorded mostly live in the studio over two years in Los Angeles, *Bringing Down the Horse* boasted what Burnett called a "hyper-modern folk" sound by strongly featuring mandolin, Dobro, and pedal steel (and Sam Phillips, Stephen Bruton, Gary Louris, and Michael Penn among the backup singers). Working with the gifted young engineer Mike Piersante, who has been his right-hand man in the studio ever since, and Tom Lord-Alge, one of the most creative mixers in the industry, Burnett gave the music a big, vibrant, room-shaking presence. "One Headlight," a Springsteen-like escape-to-daylight narrative told from the downbeat fringe, made the biggest splash. A No. 1 hit on three *Billboard* Top 40 charts, it was named by *Rolling Stone* and MTV as one of "The 100 Greatest Pop Songs since the Beatles." And the rest of the album, a Top 5 achiever on the *Billboard* 200, is nearly as good—particularly the rest of the near-perfect A-side, which includes "6th Avenue Heartache," a churning leftover from the Wallflowers' first album featuring a corrosive slide guitar solo by Mike Campbell, and the sly, enigmatic "Three Marlenas," which combines the literate quality of Dylan Sr. and the power-pop storytelling of Penn—whose narrative-rich 1989 debut, *March*, provided a kind of template for *Bringing Down the Horse*.

Burnett challenged Dylan to up the ante on his songwriting—to make all the tunes on the album equally strong, a standard few young bands set for themselves. While the lyrics on *Bringing Down the Horse* sometimes smack of dorm room writing ("The only difference that I see / Is you are exactly the same as you used to be"), the album's melodic intensity and the sneaky urgency of Jakob's groggy vocals overcome that shortcoming. One of the wonders of *Horse* is how well it sustains that urgency, even in the quieter moments. Years later, when Burnett and Dylan teamed up on the latter's country-leaning solo debut, *Women and Country* (2010), the results were not so great. Even with the sublime duo of Neko Case and Kelly Hogan singing backup—a genius stroke by the producer—this is a pretty sleepy affair. But with its depth of sound—the stage it sets for the singer—the production helped Dylan see himself, as he told the *Huffington Post*, "as kind of a player amongst other players with the role of narrator . . . a unique way for me to tell stories again."

Burnett has always been drawn to storytellers, the darker and more primal the better. Perhaps knowing that, Daniel Tashian urged him to see Gillian Welch, a young songwriter who was beginning to make a noise on the folk and bluegrass circuit with her haunted tales and heartfelt sound. Emmylou Harris had introduced Welch's gifts to the record-buying public with her beautiful cover of "Orphan Girl" on *Wrecking Ball* (1995). During a break from recording *Bringing Down the Horse*, Burnett caught Welch in Nashville, opening for Peter Rowan at the Station Inn, a popular bluegrass venue. In much the same way that Los Lobos turned people's heads with their unique sound, Welch seemed hatched from mysterious beginnings. Burnett liked Welch and her musical (and life) partner David Rawlings so much, he went backstage and told them he wanted to produce them, ultimately beating out Mark Knopfler for the job.

Like Jakob Dylan, Welch grew up in Los Angeles, and like him she came from a well-off musical family. But if Dylan's literate songs could be heard as an extension of his old man's poetry, Welch's Appalachian-style originals represented quite a departure from the music her parents wrote for *The Carol Burnett Show*. Welch, who had signed with Almo, the new label of the former A&M heads Herb Alpert and Jerry Moss, was part of a unique duo with Rawlings, a brilliant guitarist and harmony vocalist who had been a classmate of hers at Boston's Berklee College of Music.

Understandably, as artists who thrived on what they call a "tiny" sound that highlights their nuanced interactions, they felt a bit uneasy subjecting themselves to the designs of a man who made arena stars out of Counting Crows. Burnett quickly put them at ease. During their first week of recording, the only person present, aside from the artists and producer, was the engineer Rik Pekkonen. "We got so inside our little world," Welch told Bill Friskics-Warren, writing for *No Depression*. "There was very little distance between our singing and playing. The sound was very immediate. It was so light and small." Within a few days, they had recorded a series of duets.

Burnett, Welch told the *New York Times* contributor Billy Altman, "had a deep and abiding concern that I find my way as an artist, that my first record should show the world what I wanted to talk about and what I wanted to sound like. He wants the records he produces to be what the songs want to be. It's a very transparent production style and very changing from artist to artist. I think it's one of the reasons he's so great at making first records on people. He has this crazy knack, even if you don't know yourself what your core material is, he does."

Revival was recorded in Nashville at Woodland Sound, which owed its place on the map to such 1970s albums as the Nitty Gritty Dirt Band's *Will the Circle Be Unbroken*, Neil Young's *Comes a Time*, and Kansas' *Dust in the Wind*. Burnett's original plan was to record Welch and Rawlings on an old Wollensak machine he had found—the kind once used for Hank Williams. But problems with the recording heads forced him to use equipment that was a bit more modern. To heighten the agelessness of their sound, he recorded four songs in mono, including "Orphan Girl," on which Welch's rapt vision sails forth on the strength of her strumming. But the song does not go quietly into the acoustic night, undergoing an eerie transformation via optigan (an electronic keyboard originally developed by Mattel) and buzzing electric guitar.

On future albums, Welch and Rawlings would dispense with electro-acoustic experiments. But *Revival* is full of such arresting moments. On "Tear My Stillhouse Down," boasting Welch's hardest-edged vocal ever, James Burton rips ribbons on guitar and Jim Keltner is at sweeping high tide on drums. On "Paper Wings," her vocal is treated to the startling, overarching wail of Jay Joyce's electric guitar. And in what is the most thrilling moment of the album, "Pass You By," the duo hooks up on fully charged electric guitars with Roy Huskey Jr.'s upright bass. Huskey's sound was so powerful in a room-filling way that Burnett had to remove his bass microphone and record him through Welch's vocal mike, about six feet away. "After the take, I remember him putting his bass down and saying, 'I gotta go outside for awhile,'" Burnett told *Tape Op*. "And he just put his bass down and walked outside. He walked around for about fifteen minutes—he'd put out so much." Sadly, it proved to be one of the last recordings by the forty-year-old Huskey, who died of cancer the following year.

In the end, Welch and Rawlings were left to master *Revival* themselves. And Burnett, who produced their second album, *Hell among the Yearlings* (1998), actually didn't hear finished versions of some of its songs until it was released. If the partners were put out by his early exits, they weren't saying. "Oftentimes, he is working on a lot of things, and he had a lot more energy at the beginning of these projects than he did at the end," Rawlings told *Tape Op*. In an interview with the *Huffington Post*, Welch said, "When he's working with someone, he just puts everything into it, and then I think he necessarily has to move on."

In the case of artists, like Welch, who have a strong sense of who they are and what they want to achieve in the studio, setting up the recording, getting it going, and then moving on is sometimes the best thing Burnett can do. There are no set rules of conduct to adhere to, simply because different creative types, for better and for worse, have different needs. We certainly shouldn't overlook Burnett's efforts to get Welch and Rawlings to think about producing themselves. He talked them into acquiring a recording apparatus for their home. In 2001, they purchased Woodland Sound and converted it into a dedicated analog center. "I kind of learned how to make records from him," said Welch—when he was there, and then when he wasn't.

CHAPTER 16

Company Man

Whatever strange vibes existed between them during Rolling Thunder, Burnett and Sam Shepard seemed made for each other as creative partners, not least because they could relate as musicians. Shepard played drums with the counterculture folk duo the Holy Modal Rounders in the 1960s. In a way, he continued pounding the skins as a playwright. "If you take the rhythm out of [Sam's] plays, there's nothing left," Burnett told the *Chicago Sun-Times* writer Dave Hoekstra. "His dialog is very much like drum solos."

In 1996, knowing of his friend's artistic struggles, Shepard invited him to write new words and music for an extensive reworking of his ripping rock opus *The Tooth of Crime*. Things had changed in the twenty-five years since the play's premiere. "It seemed to me that rock and roll, as we had known it up till then, was being transformed into a river of sameness," Shepard wrote in his preface to the revised edition. "It was beginning to lose its original fire and brass balls." He admired the way Burnett "went for the throat" as a songwriter. What better way to help him get his songwriting juices going again than with *Tooth*, a dystopian dissertation on the soul-sucking effects of fame featuring a verbal duel to the death between a fading rock star and a gangbanging punk rocker?

Burnett could relate to Shepard's vision as much as Shepard could relate to his. Two of the staunchest disassemblers of American myth, the artists operate on surrealistic common ground. Shepard's eruptive plays are seated on psychological plates whose seismic shifts tear through commonly held values relating to family, social class, and freedom. Burnett's scabrous, free-associating commentaries shake up our cozy acceptance of false promises and empty values. Burnett, who loves Shepard's knack for smudging the line between the horrific and the hilarious, deftly plugged into the special language of *The Tooth of Crime* with his jiving reversals ("Anything I Say Can and Will Be Used against You"), image-conscious themes ("You've changed your face you've changed you're scent / You've even changed your fingerprint"), and cyber-punk poetry ("I see blowdown damage / Static kill / Mean square displacement baby / Just for a thrill"). When he became stuck, worried that he was losing a handle on his songwriting, Shepard told him, "When you do it, that's what it is." The remark freed up Burnett to do some of his best work.

Burnett recorded the songs for the cast and crew as he wrote them. Only a half dozen of them ended up being used in the play—not enough for a cast album. But long after the Off Broadway run of *The Tooth of Crime: Second Dance* ended, he returned to the recordings and discovered they included songs he forgot he had captured. Ultimately, all of the *Crime* tunes came together, he said, "like a broken mirror"—reflecting, like so much of his work, the many and varied dimensions of myth and reality, dreams lived and dreams misspent. An album of ten of the songs was released on Nonesuch in 2008 under the title *Tooth of Crime*.

Despite its sci-fi/noirish song titles ("The Rat Age," "Dope Island," "Kill Zone"), bleak scenarios, and sardonic humor ("I'm sober on the grapes of wrath / While running down the psycho path"; "Swizzle stick / And lace your faith with cyanide"), the album contains some of Burnett's most accessible and even radio-friendly songs. "Kill Zone," written with Bob Neuwirth, is set to a soaring, never-recorded Roy Orbison melody that Burnett had carried around with him for years. "How much grief and sin / Till a heart caves in," he sings in stirring, uncharacteristically open, Orbison-style fashion, filling the melody with as much love as hurt.

On the jazz-influenced "The Slowdown," Burnett's electronically treated vocal and Darrell Leonard's nifty juxtaposition of buttery brass over dissonant reeds impart an unexpected lyricism. And "Dope Island," featuring a rare vocal duet by Burnett and Sam Phillips, layers Brazilian and Indian melodies over a dense drum sound. You can't help thinking that outfitting a third dance of *The Tooth of Crime* with these evolved songs would result in a dreamier but no less biting production.

The Tooth of Crime: Second Dance opened in December 1996, starring Vincent D'Onofrio (best known as Detective Goren on *Law & Order: Criminal Intent*) as Hoss, the fading rock star, and Kirk Acevedo (famous for playing the harried cop Charlie Francis on *Fringe*), as Crow, the punk. The *New York Times*' Vincent Canby wasn't crazy about the music or the revival as a whole. "Not having seen the original production, I have no idea if the T Bone Burnett score is better than Mr. Shepard's," he wrote, "but it doesn't give much resonance to these proceedings, which depend more on language, style and presence than on music." Well, maybe Canby, a lapsed film critic who was a bit out of his element on the theater beat, wasn't ready to be led into "an unexpected shamanistic world of sound in the dark conjure of the blues," as Burnett described the musical setting in the album acknowledgments. "The best thing about the production was T Bone Burnett's score, a vast improvement over Shepard's original music," wrote the Shepard biographer Don Shewey in *American Theater*. "Burnett's witty, spring-loaded lyrics meshed well with Shepard's made-up argot."

In May 1999, Burnett teamed with Shepard again, appearing with him in an evening of spoken words and songs (some from *The Tooth of Crime*) at Chicago's Steppenwolf Theater. Once again, the existential visions of the playwright and the songwriter couldn't have matched up better. "Can you speak with one who is no one?" said Shepard, portraying a poor, star-stricken soul. "I am not important, I am a broken man," sang Burnett, providing a preview of "Earlier Baghdad (The Bounce)," which surfaced years later on *The True False Identity*.

Back at Steppenwolf in October of that year, Burnett introduced a newfangled, old-style revue featuring Sam Phillips, Marc Ribot, Gillian Welch, David Rawlings, and a pair of Nashville aces, the mandolinist Mike Compton and the bassist Barry Bales. "I ripped up everything and started in on something that has nothing to do with rock 'n' roll," Burnett told me before the show. He added, "I realize this is completely insane, but at this stage of my life, if I'm not doing something to change the world, to at least attempt to hold back the tide a split second, what am I doing? Show biz has nothing left for me at all. I don't need anything from culture. If I got it, it would be like, where were you when I needed you?"

Void, as Burnett dubbed the company, was spread out on couches and chairs. He sat in a straight-back chair in the middle, his vintage guitar plugged into a small old amp that gave his instrument a distinctive rumble and buzz. As prolific a guitarist as Burnett is—and as well-known a collector of old guitars, like the maple-topped Kay Thin Twin, Jimmy Reed's "ax" of choice, and the Gibson J-45 acoustic model—his extravagant skills on the instrument aren't often discussed. Perhaps that is because his guitar playing is about tone and what Joe Henry calls "the authority of rhythm" rather than attention-grabbing solos. "I never had the desire to be the lead guitarist or the hot instrumentalist," Burnett told *Performing Songwriter*. "I've always just gone for the groove."

The songs, all Burnett originals, were performed as a kind of cycle. He told me he had been going through "huge shifts" in his life since the birth of Simone—who, he joked, was "hilariously funny but also makes you jump out of your skin." ("Being a parent is not the most natural thing for him," Simone Burnett lightly remarked. "It stresses him to be patient.") Whatever those shifts may have been, much of the material on this occasion was bleak: "You are my darkness / I crawl through you / Feeling my way / To no light"; "People tell me

I look like hell / I am hell"; "Strike a match so I can see if I've been down here before / Where is the floor? / What is it for?"

In 2000, Burnett moved on to another Shepard play, *The Late Henry Moss*, which opened that December at San Francisco's Magic Theater. Like other Shepard works, notably *True West*, this one features battling brothers (played at the Magic by Nick Nolte and Sean Penn) and is set in a mythic American West. The work concerns the secrets left behind by a boozing father (played by James Gammon of *Major League* fame) following his death and the anguished efforts of his sons to come to terms with them and each other. The big-time Hollywood cast also included Woody Harrelson and Cheech Marin.

As Burnett explains in *This So-Called Disaster*, noted indie director Michael Almereyda's 2003 documentary about the making of *The Late Henry Moss*, he set out to write a score in which the rhythms and tones of the music would go under the rhythms and tones of the dialog. "As soon as you do that, it actually becomes a song," he says in the film. In an unusual bit of staging, he and fellow guitarist Jerry Hannan performed the music, much of which has a meditative, droning quality, from the side of the stage during each performance. With all those movie stars shouting and making faces and getting physically hurled through space, there was little likelihood that the audience paid much attention to the music. (Burnett's way-inside joke was that was that everything was in D minor except for the guttural major chord howl Gammons lets out when he makes his entrance.)

The best the *San Francisco Chronicle* could say about the "murmurous" music was that it "burnishes the scene." *Variety* reported that "Burnett's sporadic guitar strummings seem hardly worth the bother." Reviewers were not terribly kind to the onstage action, either, in San Francisco or New York. And revivals of *Henry Moss* haven't done anything to correct its standing as one of Shepard's lesser efforts. However, not yet done with theater, Burnett traveled to Galway, Ireland, with the Steppenwolf cast members John Mahoney and Martha Lavey in the summer of 2001 to perform *True America: The Work of Sam Shepard*, a basic restaging of the Chicago show, without Shepard. And that September, Steppenwolf's revival of *Mother Courage and*

Her Children was staged with an original score by Burnett and Darrell Leonard, still close collaborators after all those years.

As originally written, the music for *Mother Courage* (as well as *The Late Henry Moss*) was influenced by Delta blues great Skip James's unusual use of a guitar tuned to an open E-minor chord. The composers also borrowed liberally from the traditional sounds of New Orleans and eastern Europe. But as rehearsals proceeded—uneasily, in the aftermath of 9/11—and rewrites piled up, the singing actors grew less and less comfortable with the score. Sam Phillips recorded demos of the songs to guide them, but they didn't help. Finally, the cast started singing whatever it felt like singing and the production shed much of the original music.

Whatever the outcome of such efforts, Burnett was artistically renewed by his involvement in the theater. In an interview with Mark Guarino of the *Chicago Daily Herald*, he said that writing for characters in a play freed him up creatively and got him out of the singer-songwriter trap, which is "always about you." He added, "When I started performing, there was a very, very strong tide that ran toward being louder and more treble, and there was this whole aural assault. And after working in the theater you begin to see that there are many, many, many other ways to approach music. Because you're essentially underscoring this story that's being told. And that's what music is at its core: Storytelling. It opened up pure universes of sound to me."

As reported in *Variety*, for the purpose of recording all the music he wrote for *The Late Henry Moss*, *Mother Courage*, and *The Tooth of Crime* in his home Electromagnetic Studio, Burnett purchased the soundboard used at Sunset Sound to record such albums as the Doors' *LA Woman*, Janis Joplin's *Pearl*, and Led Zeppelin's *II* and *III* and to mix the Rolling Stones' *Exile on Main Street.* (According to engineer Mike Piersante, Burnett loved the console's "big fat tone.") That promising project failed to materialize. But by then, thanks to an impulsive call he made to the filmmaker Joel Coen, Burnett's world was expanding in yet another new and compelling direction.

CHAPTER 17

Coen Brother

From the start, Burnett was a big fan of the Coen Brothers. He liked the bold visual style of their 1984 debut, *Blood Simple*, a postmodern noir shot in Texas (some of his friends worked on it). He was even more knocked out by their fevered 1987 farce, *Raising Arizona*, in which they made a baby crawling across the screen "look like the apocalypse" and had the cinematic chops to quote *Dr. Strangelove* (see the scene in which John Goodman's jailbird sees a reflection of the acronym POE, for Peace on Earth, in his bathroom mirror). He thought so much of those scenes that he called the director Joel Coen out of the blue and arranged to meet him.

"T Bone was tickled by the fact that we used a banjo to play Beethoven on the soundtrack, a version of 'Ode to Joy' which we'd heard Pete Seeger do on a record from the '50s," Joel Coen told Richard

Harrington of the *Washington Post* in 2004, referring to *Goofing Off Suite* (1954). Burnett and the brothers, who had a mutual friend in Tom Waits, discovered they shared many film and music favorites and talked about working together in the future.

That future arrived in the spring of 1996, when Burnett was in New York working on *The Tooth of Crime*. He ran into Joel Coen and his actress wife, Frances McDormand, at the Broadway opening of a simultaneous Shepard revival, *Buried Child*. The Coens were in the planning stages for *The Big Lebowski*, the ripping farce that foisted the Dude, Jeff Bridges's pot-smoking 1970s superslacker, on the uptight 1990s. They had already settled on a few songs for the film, including Kenny Rogers & the First Edition's psychedelic novelty "Just Dropped in (To See What Condition My Condition Was In)," and the Gipsy Kings' endearingly overheated flamenco-style cover of the Eagles' "Hotel California" ("such a luvva place"). They invited Burnett (who was known to substitute the name Don Henley when he sang the folk classic "John Henry") to put together the rest of the soundtrack. The rest is doper movie history.

Burnett's previous involvements in feature films included contributing a version of "Humans from Earth" to the German director Wim Wenders's *Until the End of the World* (1991), working on songs with the actor River Phoenix for Peter Bogdanovich's underrated Nashville rom-com *The Thing Called Love* (1993), and producing the soundtrack albums for Robert Altman's *Prêt-à-Porter* (1995) and Bernardo Bertolucci's *Stealing Beauty* (1996).

"I didn't really mean to get into the film business," he told the *Hollywood Reporter*. But after listening to the first Beatles albums to come out on CD, he said, he realized he had to "diversify" because "anybody could have made one of those CDs. It wasn't like a vinyl album where you had to go out and press it. Anybody could go buy a CD and press it at a workstation. So it was obvious they had released a master of a CD master, and that they were out of their minds. In the short term, record companies raked in a lot of money because of the CD replacement cycle. But it was obvious that they had let the cat out of the bag." He added, "It was clear even back then that the digital thing was gonna come down like hail on the musicians."

More on the perils of digital and the plight of musicians later. *The Big Lebowski*, about a stoned-out guy named Lebowski who is mistreated by thugs mistaking him for a millionaire with the same name, afforded Burnett the rare opportunity to float through time and memory to come up with cool tunes. Slipping into the Dude's substance-altered consciousness like Raquel Welch shooting the coronary rapids in *Fantastic Voyage*, Burnett dialed up the dog-frequency spectacularist Yma Sumac, the misfit blues-rocker Captain Beefheart, and that smoldering genre to herself, Nina Simone. He turned to the 1960s Hollywood songbook for the lush "Lujon," from Henry Mancini's album *Mr. Lucky Goes Latin*, and obscure 1960s Italian spy movies for Piero Piccioni's faux-funky "Traffic Boom"—the theme of the porno video in which the millionaire Lebowski's wife, Bunny, cavorts with the cable repair guy.

And then there is the Texas legend Townes Van Zandt's cover of the Rolling Stones' "Dead Flowers," which Burnett secured for the closing credits after some creative wrangling with Allen Klein. The former Rolling Stones manager owned the rights to the song and reportedly wanted $150,000 for its use. The Coens arranged a private screening of *The Big Lebowski* for him. As Burnett recounted the viewing for *Rolling Stone*, "It got to the part where the Dude says, 'I hate the fuckin' Eagles, man!' Klein stands up and says, 'That's it, you can have the song!'" Even if that's not exactly how things transpired—Alex Belth, the Coens' young personal assistant at the time, writes in his 2014 Kindle single *The Dudes Abide: The Coen Brothers & the Making of The Big Lebowski* that "it didn't seem as if anything had been resolved with Klein" at the screening—it makes for a good story.

What makes the soundtrack so good and fresh is Burnett's (and the Coens') refusal to program songs that comment directly on the characters or explicitly evoke the era. "I don't have a lot of desire to sort of reinvent the '70s, as a lot of these soundtracks are doing, or to republicize them," Burnett told *Entertainment Weekly*, alluding to the films of Quentin Tarantino and Wes Anderson. Rather, he lets his imagination run free, using the trippy, larkish vibe of the film as a thematic umbrella for his selections. "Everything sounds the same now, but everyone's looking for something different," he told *Spin* a few years later. "When you have a choice between *NSYNC and the Backstreet Boys, it's not like having a choice between Johnny Cash and Duke Ellington."

No one could have expected *The Big Lebowski*, which drew mixed reviews and did middling box office, to become a cultural touchstone. Bridges's ultra-convincing stoner performance certainly is central to the film's appeal; part of the fun is wondering how much Dude there is in Bridges, Cal-tanned son of the 1960s, and vice versa. But the songs opened up the film to repeated viewings. Foreshadowing the intense scrutiny of Burnett's soundtrack for the 2014 HBO sensation *True Detective*, *Lebowski* heads pored over the musical choices like treasure hunters examining a rare map.

Gabriel Rissa, contributing to the *LA Weekly*'s 2013 "Definitive Guide to the Music of *The Big Lebowski*," wrote that Captain Beefheart's "Her Eyes Are a Blue Million Miles" is "an homage to a rug in the film bearing a blue diamond within an oval." (The rug, as all Lebowski fans know, is "the impetus for Maude and the Dude's initial meeting.") Young grooms of Generation Dude adopted Bob Dylan's "The Man in Me" (a minor tune from *New Morning* that plays over the opening credits) as their wedding theme. "One summer a few years ago," wrote Paul T. Bradley in the *LA Weekly*, "I attended eight weddings, from New England to Alabama to Southern California, and all but one featured 'The Man in Me.'"

Largely because *The Big Lebowski* lasted such a short time in theaters, the soundtrack album didn't sell well. But that curse proved to be a blessing. Had there been a second volume of *Lebowski* tunes, it would have included the Stanley Brothers' recording of "Man of Constant Sorrow." Instead, via a thrilling new recording by Dan Tyminski of Alison Krauss's band Union Station, the aged folk standard became one of the centerpieces of the Coens' next film, *O Brother, Where Art Thou?*, the soundtrack album of which sold an astonishing eight million copies, introduced millions of Americans to native sounds they had never heard, and laid the groundwork for the sweeping musical movement called Americana.

A loose retelling of Homer's *Odyssey* set in late-1930s Mississippi, *O Brother* stars George Clooney as a chain gang escapee in desperate search of hidden loot. For all the history and tradition embodied in the songs, which reach back to England, Ireland, and Wales and the mountain communities of Kentucky, Virginia, and North Carolina—where, unbeknownst to most of America, powerful musical narratives were being passed around during the early years of the twentieth century—this was no archival project. "In recording period music," Burnett told me, "people usually are so focused on getting the form right that they miss the content. They use the latest digital technology, with a lot of echo and separation, and record the music like it's by an old-timey band. With *O Brother*, we used '30s technology, but we recorded it like a rock 'n' roll band."

This was one film for which the music came first. To enable the Coen Brothers to build their tableaux-like scenes around the songs, the soundtrack had to be completed months before filming commenced. The tracks were recorded at Nashville's Sound Emporium, Burnett's favorite place to capture acoustic music. But before a single dial on the soundboard was turned, he and his crew needed to make it known among local musicians that though *O Brother* was a high-spirited Hollywood comedy, the music would be treated with respect. As a welcoming gesture, the city's old guard players were invited to a gathering at the Ocean Way Nashville studio, built in a hundred-year-old Gothic revival graystone church on Music Row. With the venerated Ralph Stanley at her side, Gillian Welch played the assuring host. Musicians who wanted to audition for the soundtrack did so in a big room Burnett had set up for that purpose.

Located on the edge of a residential community facing busy Belmont Avenue, away from Music Row, Sound Emporium is the house built by one of the town's beloved figures, Cowboy Jack Clement. A great producer in his own right who broke into the field as a young hand at famed hitmaker Sam Phillips's Sun Studios in Memphis, he was, in Burnett's estimation, "a sonic genius," as well as a much-admired singer, songwriter, and raconteur. When designing the studio in the 1960s, Clement, who died in 2013, aggressively departed from the Nashville norm by eliminating anything that interfered with a true live sound. He didn't even like having a control room. Stepping into Sound Emporium's Studio A, with its thick fringes of dark wood baffling, high ceiling, and open space, you might think you walked into a converted barn.

An acolyte of Cowboy Jack's who executive-produced his final album, *For Once and for All*, Burnett follows suit in not allowing synthetic surfaces into his sound field—no vinyl road cases, no laminated guitars, no plastic drum heads. "You can take a plastic head and process it for nine million years and it will never sound as good as if you had just gotten a calfskin head and hit it once," Burnett told *Tape Op*, no doubt thinking fondly of the sideman David Kemper's thirty-inch double calfskin–headed bass drum—an instrument he credits with propelling him toward his low-end concept.

As Burnett always does when he records at Sound Emporium, he had Studio A turned into a warmly lit living room space with couches, love seat, lamps, and tables—and burning Palo Santo wood sticks, used for centuries by the Incas for their healing properties. "Musicians all want it because it ties all of the senses together, it's part of the community, you know, everybody smelling the same thing," Burnett told the British site *Bring the Noise*.

Things got off to a roaring start with Dan Tyminski's recording of "Man of Constant Sorrow," based on the call-and-response version recorded by the Stanley Brothers (featuring Ralph's sibling Carter) in the late 1950s. Tyminski established himself as a force to contend with thanks to his full-tilt take on this centuries-old folk tune (here credited to Dick Burnett, a blind Kentucky fiddler T Bone said he likes to imagine he's related to). It's no slap at George Clooney's vocal talent to say a piece of musical history would have been lost had the star sung "Man of Constant Sorrow" himself—as was briefly considered—instead of lip-syncing it to wide-eyed comic effect as Ulysses Everett McGill, impromptu leader of the Soggy Bottom Boys. With its cranked guitar and bass, Tyminski's rendition of the song has gale-force emotional power—klezmer-like in its simultaneous expression of intense joy and bottomless regret. "It ranks with 'My Sharona,' 'Whole Lotta Shakin' Goin' On,' and 'She Loves You' in its immediacy," Rodney Crowell told me.

In a second stroke of genius, Burnett had Ralph Stanley record "O Death." The bluegrass legend had previously played the song, on which a lowly doomed man pleads for more time on earth—"Won't you spare me over till another year?" But he had never heard the seminal 1929 version by Dock Boggs, a perennially rediscovered figure who has had a significant impact on contemporary artists ranging from Bob Dylan to the jazz/Americana guitarist Bill Frisell. Initially, Stanley wrote in his 2009 memoir, *Man of Constant Sorrow*, Burnett "wanted me to play it solo and real backwoods. Just me and my banjo, the way Dock Boggs done it back in the twenties. . . . He don't care for bluegrass-style banjo, except the way I play it." Burnett ended up using an a cappella recording of the song because, he told NPR's Terry Gross, "it was much more terrifying that way." Boggs's hardscrabble version has the brusque resignation of someone with one foot already in hell. Stanley's intense, showstopping performance—an aria, really—is directed at eternity.

Burnett, Stanley wrote, "hears things regular people don't hear, the way dogs hear sounds we can't hear." One day at Sound Emporium, the producer was unable to elicit a particular sound he heard in his head but had trouble describing to the musicians. What he was after, he said, was the sound of an old pair of scissors. The studio manager Juanita Copeland and her staff turned the place upside down until someone found the kind of scissors he had in mind. Recording accomplished. Burnett, wrote Stanley, "wanted to re-create the feel of the old-time music, same as when you make a piece of antique-style furniture using all the materials and tools and techniques from bygone days. It's new but done the old way."

The *O Brother* soundtrack was completed in three weeks. The musicians recorded alongside one another, unseparated by booths or panels, facing a single microphone from about twelve feet away. Using one mike goes a long way toward controlling bleed and eliminating anomalies in the stereo mix because everything is perfectly in phase. (Mike Piersante told me that Burnett's approach to control and separation was beyond anything the engineer had been taught.) Burnett also miked the cozy area where the musicians relaxed between takes because, he told *Tape Op*, "the casual thing that you're doing when you're running a song down is actually the thing." To capture the natural ambience of the room, Piersante set up old-fashioned ribbon mikes on the three points of a Decca Tree, an apparatus designed in the 1950s to record orchestral music.

Burnett, who prefers the term "balancing" to "mixing," is no sound purist. He likes tape hiss and in fact has added sounds to a recording situation to enhance the sense of being in a particular place at a particular moment. "When we were in Sun Studios, one of the great parts of that sound there was an air conditioner up on that wall that just ran all the time," he told *Huffington Post.* "It was just one of those old wall units, and all those Elvis Presley records were recorded with that going. So, that's part of the world of sound."

As great as the individual performances on the *O Brother* soundtrack are—the other artists include Gillian Welch, Alison Krauss, Emmylou Harris, the Fairfield Four gospel group, the Peasall Sisters country trio, the folk legend John Hartford, and the young bluesman Chris Thomas King—the collective power of the music and its transmission of deeply held American values is what made the album such a cultural event. In the aftermath of 9/11, the collection provided comfort food even for many people who never listened to this kind of music. Elvis Costello was widely quoted as saying that when Stanley sang "O Death" at the 2002 Grammy Awards presentation from a pedestal in the middle of the audience, "that was the truest American response to the 9/11 attacks."

If only the film absorbed more of the humanity embodied in the songs. Farce is farce and satire is satire, but Preston Sturges, one of the Coens' acknowledged influences, never condescended to his characters the way the filmmakers condescend to theirs—in this case Clooney's leering McGill, John Turturro's gawping ninny Pete Hogwallop, and Tim Blake Nelson's tagalong Delmar. For *New York Times* film critic A. O. Scott, "the real brutalities of poverty and racism are magically dissolved by the power of song" in *O Brother.* The film's angelic Sirens—Welch, Krauss and Harris—certainly do a heavenly job of distracting us from said brutalities with the lullaby magic of "Didn't Leave Nobody but the Baby." Though it may have seemed like a great stroke of postmodern irony to have Stanley's "O Death" emanate from a Ku Klux Klansman presiding over a hellish grand finale, there is an unsettling disconnection between the grandeur of the singer and the cheap spectacle of the scene.

It is easy to understand Burnett's affinity for the Coens. Like him, they are card-carrying absurdists who take great delight in exposing our idiocies and self-delusions (though the Coens take aim at hapless individuals, whereas Burnett prefers to have demagogues in his sights). And Burnett admires what he sees as their Dylan-like ability to pull together strains of twentieth-century American culture into provocative modern statements. (He also relates to their refusal to tell actors how to read a line or act a scene.) But it is hard to figure how Burnett the born-again moralist (and reformed pronouncer of easy judgments) would forge such close ties with filmmakers who are most comfortable gazing down at we poor earthlings like superior beings from a distant planet.

Ultimately, the story behind "Po Lazarus," the prison work song that opens *O Brother*, dwarfs the Coens' Homerian concoction. James Carter recorded the song for the musicologist Alan Lomax in 1959, when he was serving time at the Mississippi State Penitentiary. A group of inmates backed him on the tune, about a poor soul who is hunted and gunned down by a sheriff. Burnett had discovered the song several years before the making of *O Brother* in the Lomax archives in New York. For all anyone knew, Carter was dead. But just to be sure, when the soundtrack started climbing the charts Burnett and the Lomax Foundation launched a labyrinthine search for the singer. They enlisted a Florida newspaper reporter who was working on a project about Lomax. After more than a year of poring over databases, public documents, prison and death records, and such, they found Carter, alive and well, married to a minister in Chicago.

Carter, who barely remembered recording the song, was given a check for $20,000, his first royalty payment. A week later, the seventy-six-year-old boarded a plane for the first time in his life and flew to Los Angeles to attend the Grammy Awards. He died the following year but left his family with many more royalty checks to come.

Spirits were high following the completion of *O Brother*. Plans came together to stage a benefit concert for the Country Music Hall of Fame featuring musical contributors to the film at Nashville's Ryman Auditorium, the "Mother Church of Country Music." The documentarian D. A. Pennebaker (best known for Dylan's *Don't Look Back*) was lined up to shoot the event, which would be emceed by John Hartford. Holly Hunter, who played Clooney's wife in *O Brother*, would introduce Hartford. The problem was, the concert took place nine months before the release of *O Brother*—"a crazy idea," said Burnett. Tickets didn't go on sale until two weeks before the show. Sales were slow. But thanks to a record number of walk-ups following an eleventh-hour promotional blitz by Burnett and others, the Ryman was packed. The concert, held on May 24, 2000, went off without a hitch. In his last public appearance, the ailing Hartford, who died within a month, drew heartfelt cheers from the audience with songs such as "Big Rock Candy Mountain."

After the show, rather ominously, a tornado blew through Nashville, causing extensive damage. *O Brother* opened to a meager turnout in a handful of theaters on Christmas Day, 2000, and though it turned out to be the Coens' best-grossing picture, it fell way short of a smash. Still, without a lick of radio exposure—its only "airplay" came in movie theaters and then on home systems—its unfashionable mountain music stormed the charts, bucking trends, popular tastes, music biz conventions, and Hollywood wisdom. The soundtrack album cleaned up at the Grammys, winning five awards, including Album of the Year, Best Producer for Burnett, and Best Male Country Vocal for Stanley—his first. As Burnett had predicted from the start—"He never had any doubt about it," Juanita Copeland told me—"O Death" made a star out of the seventy-five-year-old Stanley. It bought him a house and led to his stark, self-titled solo album on DMZ Records, the short-lived label Burnett, the Coens, and Columbia Records formed in the wake of *O Brother*. Stanley also was featured on an *O Brother* concert tour, "Down from the Mountain," and in the Pennebaker documentary.

"There was something T Bone told me I've never forgot," wrote Stanley in *Man of Constant Sorrow*. "He said he understood what I'd been doing all these years, sticking with my old-time mountain music when everybody else was going uptown. I told him it wasn't a strategy. More like an instinct." He continued, "It was just the way I felt I had to go after Carter died. I didn't want to follow the herd. I said I felt like an old moonshiner who heads way back up the creek to the head of the hollow. Where there ain't nobody to bother him. 'I think you were right to do that,' said T Bone. 'You had to go backward to go forward.' When I heard him say that, I knew we were going to get along fine."

In analyzing the soundtrack's success, Burnett credited the greater availability of historical sounds in the computer age. "Now two clicks and you have Charlie Patton's complete recorded history," he told the *Chicago Daily Herald.* "So the audience, because they have so much more to draw from, they are much more savvy than they are given credit for."

The *O Brother* soundtrack (which was reissued in a two-disc tenth-anniversary edition containing extra tracks) certainly had a galvanizing effect on a generation of pickers. "A New Wave of Musicians Updates That Old-Time Sound" was the headline for a 2006 Sunday *New York Times* feature on the rise of "newgrass" groups. "A lot of venues that would never book a string band five years ago are open to us now," said Ruth Ungar, then the fiddler and singer for the Mammals. And while her group, along with Nickel Creek, Crooked Still, the Duhks, the Yonder Mountain String Band, Uncle Earl, and Old Crow Medicine Show, carried the newgrass torch in the States, the Grammy-winning British band Mumford & Sons broadened the meaning and reach of Americana.

Burnett wasn't crazy about the term "old-time sound," which seems to belong to 1930s and 1940s vocal groups like the Mills Brothers (not that there is anything wrong with that). But he surely was pleased by all the young musicians engaging the mountain music tradition, finding fresh ways to push it forward—and being rewarded for their efforts. "The thing about this music, this ancient, old music is you can reinvent it at any time," he told *Uncut*, lauding the new crop of players for being "so much better than any of us when we were reinventing it."

"I thought he might weary of that kind of music, coming from a blues background and a rock 'n' roll lifestyle," Bob Neuwirth told me. "Turns out, he became more interested."

CHAPTER 18

Soundtrack Auteur

As a film fan who came of age in what is now widely regarded as the golden era for American cinema, Burnett was exposed to pop soundtrack masters like Martin Scorsese, whose jukebox fantasies permeate the working-class struggles of his characters in *Mean Streets*; Robert Altman, who brilliantly matches song to narrative in *Nashville*; Altman's protégé Alan Rudolph, whose use of Marianne Faithfull on the title song of *Trouble in Mind* epitomizes his skill at thickening atmosphere; and Jonathan Demme, who mixed ethnic and rock tunes in *Something Wild*. Here were filmmakers who were not looking to pump up the commercial potential of a project by stuffing the soundtrack with marketable songs—as so many were asked to do in the wake of the Bee Gees' mega-selling *Saturday Night Fever* score.

They saw the music as an integral part of the film, a cog in the storytelling process.

With his soundtracks for *The Big Lebowski* and *O Brother*, Burnett served the Coen Brothers' surrealistic vision. *Divine Secrets of the Ya-Ya Sisterhood* (2002), the *Steel Magnolias*–style southern dramedy based on Rebecca Wells's beloved novel and stories, presented him with different challenges and opportunities. The film was the directorial debut of Callie Khouri, Burnett's future wife, who won an Academy Award in 1992 for writing Ridley Scott's iconic female buddy movie *Thelma and Louise*. *Divine Secrets* cuts between 1990s New York, where the successful playwright played by Sandra Bullock reveals that her miserable upbringing in the South was her greatest source of inspiration, and 1930s Louisiana, where we witness what the playwright's mother (played by Ellen Burstyn) insists was an ideal childhood.

Divine Secrets did well at the box office but was not well received by critics. There is an awful lot of talk in it but, wrote Roger Ebert in the *Chicago Sun-Times*, "not a character in the movie with a shred of plausibility, not an event that is believable, not a confrontation that is not staged, not a moment that is not false." But as phony-sounding as the southern-fried chatter of the sisterhood is, listen to the words of womanly wisdom, beauty, and resolve that anoint the film courtesy of Mahalia Jackson ("Walk in Jerusalem"), Macy Gray (a spiffy new version of Billie Holiday's "Your Mother's Son-in-Law," Linda Thompson (rebuking her estranged spouse Richard with his own heartbreaking composition "Dimming of the Day"), and Ann Savoy (lending Cajun flavor to "Lulu's Back in Town").

In the hands of a programmer with Burnett's superior taste and instincts, a mediocre film can be a good excuse for an enriching soundtrack, as further demonstrated here by Tony Bennett's eloquent, first-time-ever recording of Nat King Cole's 1940s favorite "If Yesterday Could Only Be Tomorrow"; Taj Mahal's rollicking, genre-crossing version of Fats Waller's "Keepin' Out of Mischief Now"; and Bob Dylan's newly written Cajun waltz "Waitin' for You." This lackluster film also occasioned the restoration of landmark roots recordings—something that doesn't happen every day in Hollywood, particularly if the subject isn't a roots artist.

While working on *Divine Secrets*, Burnett discovered that the Jimmy Reed songs he had chosen for the soundtrack were going to be heard via shoddy second- or third-generation CD versions. Moviegoers and soundtrack consumers who had never heard Reed were going to be treated to a pale digital reflection of his larger-than-life self. Going back to the original 1950s source recordings, which had been engineered by the legendary Bill Putnam, a hero of his, Burnett treated "Ain't That Lovin' You Baby," "Little Rain," and "Found Love" to state-of-the-art upgrades. As lousy as *Divine Secrets* is, it deserves credit for making available to the world three, count 'em three, Jimmy Reed tunes in new and improved condition.

Back in Mississippi (fictionally speaking) with the Coens for their 2004 adaptation of *The Ladykillers*, the beloved British farce from the 1950s starring Alec Guinness and Peter Sellers, Burnett shifted his focus to gospel. The remake stars Tom Hanks as the fancy-talking "professor" Goldthwaite Higginson Dorr, leader of a misfit gang of bank robbers who plan on tunneling from the basement of a churchgoing widow into the vault of an adjacent riverboat casino. Taking his cue from her lively disdain for "hippity hop," Burnett turns the film into an exercise of cultural activism. Merging gospel and hip-hop, he exposes the links between them while demonstrating how songs from decades ago can be every bit as vital and relevant as the hippest new sounds.

The key number is "Trouble of This World," which is heard in multiple versions: Bill Landford and the Landfordaires' gorgeously harmonized 1949 recording; the southern rap group Nappy Roots' sampling of that recording; a rousing live version performed by Rose Stone of Sly and the Family Stone; and a sprightly, faux-baroque take on "Trouble" by the Coens' house composer, Carter Burwell, who seems to have in mind the guitarist Mason Williams's hit instrumental from 1968, "Classical Gas." If "O Death" expresses a down-and-out soul's desperation to avoid the next life, "Trouble" bubbles over with acceptance: "There'll be no more weeping and wailing / I'm going home to live with God my Lord / Soon I will be done with the trouble of this world."

"I'm Jonah," Burnett told the *Los Angeles Times*. "I'm this guy who said he was going to follow God, but I wasn't going to have anything to do with Christian music because it's doctrinaire and a poor imitation of pop music. And I find myself all these years later, and everything I'm working on is gospel. The curtain has been ripped back from the tabernacle and we all are in the reality of the modern world. I no longer can recognize the distinction between secular and sacred."

Boasting a sixty-three-member Alabama church choir among its musical contributors, his next film, the Civil War epic *Cold Mountain*, eased that vision problem. His biggest challenge was living up to the expectations of the Miramax film mogul Harvey Weinstein, who had spent more money on this $80-million-plus Christmas release than on any of his other films and was looking for *O Brother*–like dollars in the soundtrack. Like *O Brother*, oddly enough, *Cold Mountain* (based on Charles Frazier's best-selling, National Book Award–winning novel) was inspired by *The Odyssey*. But if the Coen Brothers film was the ultimate in shaggy Depression comedies, carried and ultimately outrun by its soundtrack, Weinstein's expensive baby was an attempt by Miramax to create nothing less than a *Gone with the Wind* for the new millennium. The film starred the Hollywood actress of the moment, Nicole Kidman, as Ada, the love-struck North Carolina belle waiting for her Inman (Jude Law) to return from the shell-shocking atrocities of battle. It was adapted and directed by the classy British filmmaker Anthony Minghella, who deservedly won a Best Director Oscar for the Best Picture–winning *The English Patient* (1996)—another historical romantic epic based on a prized book.

Burnett liked working with Minghella, who took a meticulous approach to film scoring. *The English Patient* is rich in popular music of the 1930s and 1940s. His 1999 film, *The Talented Mr. Ripley*, featured atmospheric 1950s jazz. For *Cold Mountain*, Minghella was determined to avoid making "a middle-aged record" by using young artists who could breathe new life into traditional songs.

Burnett's casting coup, on the face of it, was recruiting Jack White. Though the young singer and guitarist was best known as the leader of the enormously popular, garage-rocking White Stripes, he was passionate about roots forms. He grew up in Detroit, in a predominantly Mexican neighborhood, but became involved in Delta blues and bluegrass at an early age. He first played "Sittin' on Top of the World" (one of the tunes he recorded for *Cold Mountain*) when he was fifteen and covered "Wayfaring Stranger" (another of the film's featured songs) in a previous band, 2 Star Tabernacle.

Burnett spent hours discussing music with White and playing him old songs by Blind Willie Johnson, Dock Boggs, the Delta blues master Son House, and the early country legend Jimmie Rodgers. "Of all the young singers out there, he has done the most homework," Burnett told me. "It's not easy to do those songs, to make them new. You have to really metabolize them somehow. They have to mean something to you. Like all storytelling, you have to believe them, believe in what you're singing."

Playing the character Georgia, a mandolin player who captures the fancy of Renée Zellweger's mountain woman, White has a likable enough screen presence, in a poor man's Johnny Depp kind of way, but there is something secondhand about his vocals, too. Fortunately, Burnett had plenty of other musical weapons at his disposal. With the help of the musicologist, filmmaker, and photographer John Cohen, a founding member of the New Lost City Ramblers, he recruited an expansive cast of brilliant young players specializing in early American music. They included the banjo virtuoso Dirk Powell, the Reeltime Travelers (Ralph Stanley's bus driver tipped Burnett off to the Tennessee band), and Tim Eriksen, whose eclectic world music band Cordelia's Dad had worked with the celebrated Chicago punk producer Steve Albini—just the kind of unlikely connection Burnett loves. Eriksen was an expert in shape-note, or "Sacred Harp," vocals. A community-based form with deep roots in the South, this vocal style attains unusual power through full-throated, four-part harmonies that are at once earthy and otherworldly. Eriksen's crucial contribution to the film was to turn Burnett on to the Sacred Harp Singers.

The original plan was to record them at Sound Emporium. The *Cold Mountain* sessions there had a warmly glowing, churchlike feel, with the gathered artists feeding off one another's presence, raptly watching one another when not performing. But it became obvious that to capture the Sacred Harp Singers' soul-stirring essence, the chorus needed to be recorded at home, in the Liberty Baptist Church in Henagar, Alabama. There, Burnett and Minghella experienced firsthand the wonders of the massed voices, which anointed the film's excruciating battle scenes. Among those voices was that of Cassie Franklin, a remarkable twenty-year-old who had never been in front of a microphone when she recorded her heart-stopping, unaccompanied version of the traditional tune "Lady Margret." Had the recording not been left out of the film, relegated to the soundtrack album, it might have served as an emotional center for *Cold Mountain* the way "O Death" did for *O Brother*. (Burnett and Frazier, in whose novel music plays a major role, fought with limited success to get more songs into the film.)

In the end, two British rock veterans who seemed out of place on the soundtrack gave *Cold Mountain* its greatest musical boost: Sting, who composed the string-sweetened "You Will Be My Ain True Love," on which Alison Krauss sings backup; and Elvis Costello, with whom Burnett co-wrote "The Scarlet Tide," which Krauss sings over the end credits in a cello arrangement. Both songs were nominated for the Best Original Song Oscar and the Best Song Written for the Visual Media Grammy. The Sting song also was nominated for a Golden Globe. And Burnett and Gabriel Yared won for Best Film Music at the British Academy of Film and Television Awards.

For all that, most reviews of *Cold Mountain*, which were not great—"I can't say I was deeply moved by one minute of it," wrote Owen Gleiberman in *Entertainment Weekly*—didn't even mention the music. And the soundtrack album, which was bottom-loaded with orchestral excerpts, peaked at No. 51 on the *Billboard* 200. A concert documentary featuring most of the contributing musicians that was shot around the time of the film's release was included as an extra on the *Cold Mountain* DVD, but unlike the *O Brother* doc *Down from the Mountain*, it was not shown in theaters. For all that, Burnett told me, overseeing the music for *Cold Mountain* "taught me a tremendous amount. I learned that a good song doesn't need anything, not even drums or chords or a beat. A great song is a great song."

A decade later, he returned to the Civil War battlefield as a singer when he recorded the old classic "The Battle of Antietam" for *Divided & United: Songs of the American Civil War*. Supervised by Randall Poster, best known as the film director Wes Anderson's musical right-hand man, the two-disc set, released in late 2013 to mark the 150th anniversary of the war, featured Loretta Lynn, Dolly Parton, Sam Amidon, Jamey Johnson, Vince Gill, Shovels & Rope, and Chris Thile among its contributors.

Singing about the single bloodiest day of the war like a man scorched by fate—"And as I lay there musing, I heard a bitter cry / It was, 'Lord Jesus, save me, and take me home to die'"—Burnett turns in his rawest and most powerful vocal ever. "The darkness of that story, the brokenness, the sadness, the violence, it's all in that track," said Joe Henry, who produced "The Battle of Antietam" and several other songs for the album in his home studio. What made the session especially meaningful for Burnett was the presence of Henry's son Levon, whose free-spirited clarinet playing gives "The Battle of Antietam" an up-to-the-minute chill. As friends of Henry and his wife, Melanie, Burnett and Sam Phillips raced to the hospital the night Levon was born. "To sit there on the floor of the studio, with T Bone in my booth looking out watching Levon getting wilder and wilder in an Ornetteish way—T Bone had a look of delight you rarely see in a person," said Henry. (In early 2015 at the hip LA club Largo, he and Phillips performed a special show that featured appearances by both Levon Henry and the budding rocker Simone Burnett, a fan of punk and industrial music. "I don't have much use for Nashville or the neo-folk thing," she told me.)

If *Cold Mountain* was right up Burnett's alley, a subsequent pair of movies about country singers, *Walk the Line* (2005) and *Crazy Heart* (2009), put him in the driver's seat. Burnett said he took on *Walk the Line*, James Mangold's disappointingly formulaic film about Johnny Cash, to ensure that the Man in Black wouldn't get "Hollywoodized"—like Hank Williams was in *Your Cheatin' Heart*, the 1964 film starring George Hamilton. No less an authority than Rosanne Cash, Johnny's daughter, said that *Walk the Line* did, in fact, give her father the Hollywood treatment. Without casting any aspersions on the filmmakers, she told me that Joaquin Phoenix, Reese Witherspoon, and Ginnifer Goodwin—as her father, stepmother June Carter Cash, and mother Vivian Liberto, respectively—"were not recognizable to me as my parents in any way."

That said, Burnett got more out of Phoenix and Witherspoon than could have been expected, especially considering these were their first-ever singing performances on film—and considering the close scrutiny they knew their impersonations would be given. During weeks of practice and rehearsal in Burnett's home studio in Los Angeles, both stars struggled with the music. Witherspoon had an especially rough time with "Wildwood Flower," the Carter Family classic. But Burnett got her on the right track by sitting with her in the quiet living room setting and accompanying her on the song. Vocally, Reese is no June and Joaquin is no Johnny, but backed by such players as the picker extraordinaire Norman Blake, who had appeared with Cash on record and played on his TV show, and Jack Clement, whose most famous move as a producer was adding the mariachi horns to Cash's "Ring of Fire," the actors were close enough to impress most critics. "Knowing Cash's albums more or less by heart, I closed my eyes to focus on the soundtrack and decided that, yes, that was the voice of Johnny Cash I was listening to," wrote Roger Ebert in the *Chicago Sun-Times*, pointing out that the preview audience he was in had not been informed about who did what. "The closing credits make it clear it's Joaquin Phoenix doing the singing, and I was gob-smacked."

Jeff Bridges, who did his own singing in *Crazy Heart* as the scuffling, boozing, vocally spent country singer Bad Blake—a made-up character—didn't have to worry about measuring up to anyone as a vocalist. His challenge was doing justice to the real-life artists whose stories he drew on in creating Blake. While Waylon Jennings, Merle Haggard, and Kris Kristofferson were mentioned as likely inspirations, no one contributed more to the character than the hard-living road warrior par excellence Stephen Bruton, whose participation in *Crazy Heart* proved to be a crowning moment in his shortened life. He was on a downward swing in his long battle with throat cancer when Burnett, one of the producers of the $7 million film, sensing an opportunity to improve his friend's spirits and possibly his physical state, had him flown with a nurse from Texas to Los Angeles to work on the independent production (which was released by Fox Searchlight Pictures). For several months, Burnett and Bruton listened to old recordings and, with Bridges and the writer-director Scott Cooper, figured out who Bad Blake was—and had been. "I used to be somebody, now I'm somebody else," Bridges/Blake sings.

Crazy Heart has its soft spots, but it exposes the underside of the country music life with more gritty insight than any work since *Tender Mercies*, the 1983 film for which Robert Duvall won an Oscar. It was disappointing to see "The Weary Kind," a so-so tune written by Ryan Bingham and Burnett and sung by Bingham, get nominated for an Oscar over Bruton's superior songs—and win. But awards can't measure what *Crazy Heart* did for Bruton, who died just before its release. Burnett called his friend "the soul of Texas music." *Crazy Heart* is a testament to how close Texas soul brothers can be.

CHAPTER 19

Minimalist

Had T Bone Burnett retired from music following *O Brother*, he would have earned serious consideration as one of the most formidable contributors to post-1960s culture. While not attaining the prominence he wanted to as a recording artist, his body of work as a singer and songwriter was strikingly original (there haven't been all that many covers of his songs, but one of the best was Kelly Willis and Bruce Robison's treatment of "Shake Yourself Loose" on their 2014 album *Our Year*). Burnett's success rate as a producer established him as *the* go-to man for artists in search of roots (and other kinds of) authenticity. In reviving and returning Roy Orbison to a place of honor, he set a high standard for such tributes. And with his soundtrack for *O Brother*, he opened a window on tradition that had been frozen shut.

But as he moved forward, Burnett wasn't out of ideas—or, as worn out as he was by the production wars, the energy to pursue them. And in Sam Phillips he had someone who was equally attuned to taking challenging next steps. During the five years since she recorded *Omnipop*, she had pulled back from the recording world to raise her daughter and recharge her creative battery. An inveterate reader who had turned Burnett on to Pablo Neruda (a fair exchange for him turning her on to Rainer Maria Rilke), she was reading a lot of books about performers, such as Colette's *Vagabond* and a biography of Louise Brooks. When she started writing songs again, she was in a different place than she had been. Tersely lyrical and sharply focused, the tunes owed as much to poetry as pop.

Burnett urged her to get the songs on tape. The couple invited musician friends over to their home and, over a period of time, recorded the new compositions in their comfy Electromagnetic Studio, surrounded by Larry Poons paintings and sound baffles designed by baby Simone (at some point, a life-size cardboard replica of Ralph Stanley became part of the décor). Phillips told me she initially had no thoughts of releasing the music, on which she experimented (and fell in love) with a brusque dual drum sound. But after Burnett gave several of the song demos to their friend David Bither, an executive at Nonesuch, Bither liked them so much that he signed Phillips to the boutique label, which boasted such artists as the jazz pianist Fred Hersch, the new music luminary Steve Reich, and the Brazilian pop superstar Caetano Veloso. She wrote more songs to fill out an album and, with Burnett producing and "Mikey" Piersante engineering, recorded *Fan Dance*.

Released in 2001, the album proved to be a breakthrough for both Phillips and Burnett. It reintroduced Phillips as a kind of lo-fi pop chanteuse who breathed hard-won wisdom through spare melodies and arrangements that made a strength of her essential shyness. Existentialism has never been catchier than in lines such as "I'm not falling going down / Dreaming and singing without a sound" and "When we open our eyes and dream we open our eyes." The words hang in the air, held adrift by the angularity of a guitar or the shimmer of the drums, waiting for resolution.

The album was just as much of a milestone for Burnett, who does wonders with its austere setting. You can listen to these songs a thousand times and still not quite figure out how they achieve such immediacy. (Was it the Palo Santo wood sticks?) "He was fatigued making records, working so hard to come up with new sounds, layering things," Phillips told me. "He was tired, I was tired, so he made a turn toward a little more performance-oriented, sonically different thing. This is when he began getting into the bottom end, the big bass drums and bass heavy sound."

Nowhere else in his work has Burnett revealed his painterly sensibility as boldly as he does here. The album opener, "The Fan Dance," is tantamount to musical cubism, with Phillips's assertive folk-style strumming occupying one plane; avant-garde rocker Carla Azar's trap drumming and Jim Keltner's hand drumming staking out another; and Marc Ribot's specially designed banjo guitar practicing an exotic math on yet another. The effect is heightened by the addition of Keltner's mild distortions on banjo and various twanging, scratching, swooshing, and tinkling sounds. "I'm firecracker lightning / I burn with no trace up in the cold sky," sings Phillips, floating through space. Exactly.

On other songs, Burnett engages in manipulated light: refracted tones on "Taking Pictures," which finds him on piano and Van Dyke Parks on harpsichord; chiaroscuro effects on "Wasting My Time," with Martin Tillman's charged lines on cello providing the heavy shadows; and action painting on "Edge of the World," with its splashy piano chords and eerily cool sustaining tone. *Fan Dance* validates Burnett's efforts to get Phillips to play guitar. "My guitar playing is very crude, I don't even play with a pick," she told me. "But he says he loves the way my hand dances on the strings. It does give the music a certain heart."

During the making of their next album, *A Boot and a Shoe* (2004), their hearts were hurting—they were in the process of breaking up. "It was a fiery relationship, I guess," Phillips said when I asked about the fire images in so many of her recent songs. "It was one of those things where you love who you love and you do the best you can at the time. It was tumultuous in the sense that we were constantly on the road, always around a lot of people. He didn't get married to settle down. That is coming more now to him."

As difficult as it was to spend all those hours together recording *A Boot and a Shoe*, Phillips told me, doing anything else didn't make sense: "In T Bone fashion, there was method to his madness. At that point, we had worked together so long. As luck would have it, we were growing apart, but he felt we should get out there and try. You go and record, that's what we did. Though he did stay out for a lot of the recording, which was unusual."

Phillips's emotional state comes through measured and clear on songs such as "How to Quit" ("Can't get free from freedom / When I refuse to choose"), "Open the World" ("My life went on without me till pain brought the house down"), and "Infiltration" ("If you're a dead man then stick to being dead"). But in the end, *A Boot and a Shoe* was a remarkably civil affair—nothing like the trading of shots that was Richard and Linda Thompson's splitsville masterpiece *Shoot Out the Lights*, or the open expression of marital discord on Rosanne Cash and Rodney Crowell's "divorce albums."

"I can't remember once having an argument with [Sam] in the studio, even during this last record," Burnett told *Chicago Tribune* critic Greg Kot. "That's been the easiest part of our life together." Now the question was, how would he fare in the studio alone, applying what he learned making *Fan Dance* and *A Boot and a Shoe* to his first solo recording since he dared to look under his hat?

CHAPTER 20

Lead Actor

In early 2005, Burnett retreated to the woods of Big Sur in northern California to "disconnect." Living alone in a tent, he said, without a guitar or any other instrument, he spent a month listening to blues, New Orleans soul, Appalachian folk, and Haitian music. He wrote down anything that came into his head, mostly in the form of couplets and verses. Back home in Los Angeles, he sifted through his jottings, devising song lyrics from them, and set them to music. He was finally ready after fourteen years—a stretch of time in which sports dynasties rise and fall and rise, Jewish boys attain manhood, and three leap years occur—to make a T Bone Burnett album.

Artists "disappear" for different reasons. The blues singer Alberta Hunter, considered the equal of Bessie Smith, left music at the height of her powers in 1950 to become a nurse and remained in "hiding" for nearly three decades. The British film director Michael Powell was blackballed by the film industry after audiences were scandalized by his final major work, the creepy 1960 masterpiece *Peeping Tom*. The comedian Dave Chappelle quit Comedy Central over creative differences, reportedly walking away from a $50 million deal, and dropped out of sight in South Africa. It is reasonable to think that Burnett disappeared from his own recording career because he was tired of rejection and weary of competing for attention, convinced he wasn't cut out to join the Elvis Costellos, Warren Zevons, and Jackson Brownes of the world. And, of course, he was so busy producing other people, it was difficult to find time to devote to his own work.

But it is also important to consider that in producing exceptional albums by such artists as Costello, Los Lobos, Gillian Welch, Sam Phillips, and the company of *O Brother*, he was making artistic statements that were as personal as the ones he made under his own name. He hadn't disappeared, he was just using those outside projects as conduits for his artistic voice. "I think he sees less and less separation between what it means to be the producer and the singer-songwriter," Joe Henry told me. "He's a record-maker. He's in the business of conjuring."

As an artist who, like his mentor, has mastered the art of sublimating his personal vision in the work of others, Henry knows something about this duality. He takes great satisfaction in knowing that, even if it is not immediately evident to listeners, his exceptional touch made gems like Allen Toussaint's 2009 piano masterpiece *The Bright Mississippi* what they are. Without Henry imagining that album—the New Orleans R&B great's first and only foray into jazz—into existence and steering it down the right paths, we likely would never have been exposed to this side of Toussaint's extraordinary talent. But unlike Burnett, Henry thrives on whatever opportunities he gets to perform and make contact with his devoted fan base. He learned long ago to stop worrying about making a commercial mark; he wouldn't be the artist he is if he did. (He had no illusion that the boost he got from his sister-in-law Madonna's recording of his song "Stop" was more than a single strike of lightning.) In the end, it is a question of constitution.

"Fran McDormand said an extraordinary thing when we were doing this movie, [the Coen Brothers'] *Inside Llewyn Davis*," Burnett told the *Hollywood Reporter*. "She said, 'The reason so few great actors make great musicians, and so few great musicians make great actors, is they're completely opposite disciplines. The actor submerges his own personality and projects another personality, and the musician projects his personality. So while the musician is projecting his personality, the actor is suppressing his.' It's difficult to do both things at once. It's like rubbing your stomach and patting someone else's head—in a different country. I'm not comfortable getting out in front of people and making the great gesture or anything. So maybe I'm more of an actor!"

When you factor in Burnett's comments about self-consciousness being the enemy of the artist, and the act of self-revelation being so difficult, the idea that this man, who once described himself to me as "the most embarrassed person I've ever met in my whole life," is more of an "actor" certainly rings true. For Burnett, being a "musician" unavoidably takes him to a dark place. That is where he finds his artistic voice, but it is also where he struggles with doubt. How much can he safely reveal? When is he being honest and when is he evading emotional truth, dancing away from it with irony and sarcasm and other writerly tricks? Does safety matter? Being an "actor," he assumes another identity, moves into the light of helping others, bringing out their best, facilitating their grand gestures. And yet few singer-songwriters in pop music who double as producers have compiled a body of work of their own that is as impressive as Burnett's.

Burnett tipped that scale when he returned from Big Sur and recorded his boldest, bravest, and most bewitching effort, *The True False Identity* (2006). With its massed percussion, tribal rhythms, and subterranean tones, this is jungle music for the ambient crowd, recasting the blues somewhere between Tom Waits's *Bone Machine* and King Sunny Ade's *Juju Music*. It is an album on which he catches up to his radical sound vision as it catches up to him. Good music should be "dense and booming and stomping and perplexing," Burnett told *Texas Music*. Judging by the free improvising that took place during the recording, and the cutting and pasting of recording tape that followed, à la *Bitches Brew*–era Miles Davis, good music should also be able to redefine itself on the run.

"I told my three drummers, Carla Azar, Jim Keltner, and Jay Bellerose, 'We've already heard every beat, so let's not have *any* beats,'" Burnett told *Sound & Vision*. "Let's just rumble, let's just all create a big thing that's too much to hear . . . make it so we and all the people out there listening are like beads inside a maraca and let's just shake it like that!"

With its depth charge tones—heavy acoustic bass plus heavier bass drums—and spooky effects, "Fear Country" is a searing State of the Union address. "I gotta tell on you," he sings, in a sly homage to Screamin' Jay Hawkins, warning us that "nobody knows what's going down, but it's going down." The religious right gets it in the chin on "Palestine, Texas," a spoken word commentary with jiving rhymes ("Phyllis" and "bacillus") and references to the Rat Pack (Frank, Dean, Sam, and Peter). "When you come out of this self-delusion / You're gonna need a soul transfusion," Burnett says over a crunching, Beefheart-like beat and wailing psychedelic guitar. He saves his greatest cynical ripostes for the place he works, "Hollywood Mecca of the Movies," where crime, drugs, cheating, and spying are proof that "Honesty is the most subversive of all disguises," and targets the opportunistic "black mass media" on "Zombieland." "Accentuate the positive / Destroy all the negatives," he sings, riding a click-clacking dub/reggae groove like a wave.

In vivid contrast is "Earlier Baghdad (The Bounce)," a darkly glowing, blues-based reverie by a broken man who "lost sight of the light." With its lovely melodic riff, it is Burnett's most affecting tune since "Madison Avenue." He finds solace and security in the shuffling "I'm Going on a Long Journey Never to Return" and the elegant Johnny Cash / Sun Records tribute "Shaken Rattled and Rolled" (the album is dedicated to the legendary Cash bassist Roy Huskey Jr.).

It wouldn't be long before Burnett was telling interviewers he didn't like recording or processing music, but coming off *The True False Identity*, he exulted in the possibilities of the studio. "I love sound and being able to bend it with precision, or imprecision if you like," he told the *Los Angeles Times* in 2006. He added, "The idea of going out and doing that live now is very exciting. There's some kind of focus I have now regarding playing live that I never had before."

His nearly two-hour performance at Chicago's Vic Theater, attended by a modest but demonstrative crowd, was rough around the edges. The band hadn't had much time to rehearse, but the looseness of the performance proved liberating. Rapping for all he was worth on the spoken material and tearing into "Blinded by the Darkness," his account of the unholy turf war in which the laws of man go up against the laws of God, Burnett sounded rejuvenated, his evangelical self returning in style. For once, the musician in him trumped the actor and had everyone singing his song. However quickly it fell from view, *The True False Identity* went a long way toward capturing his true true self. But it was, indeed, back in the studio, as an "actor" working with one of the most unusual star pairings in pop history, that he went on to make one of his greatest statements.

CHAPTER 21

Alchemist

Such a tight lid was kept on the recording of *Raising Sand*, according to the Sound Emporium studio manager Juanita Copeland, that no one in the outside world knew that Robert Plant and Alison Krauss were there making a record together. Even people on the inside were kept in the dark. The drummer Jay Bellerose thought he had come to Nashville to record separate Alison Krauss and Robert Plant albums. And there was no guarantee the right kind of chemistry would exist between the singers—or between them and the producer. When the trio descended on the studio from Krauss's Nashville-area home, where they chose songs and came up with basic arrangements for them, the plan was to cut a few tunes and see how things went. "People were muttering things to each other," Copeland told me. "They didn't see it working."

When Burnett's gear started arriving from Los Angeles in huge crates—one giant, coffin-like container held no fewer than forty of his guitars and assorted string instruments—it was clear that the game was on. But as these things went, it was a rather quiet game. Burnett had gone to school on Roy Orbison's remarkable ability to attain maximum power on record through minimal exertion. Orbison sang so softly in the studio that you could barely hear him from a few feet away, but captured on mike and turned up in the engineering, his vocals came through in all their strength and tonal richness. Based on the same principle, Burnett had his drummers play softly. "The more quietly you play, the less attack and more tone there is," he told *Performing Songwriter.* "If you hit a guitar too hard, it chokes the note off; the volume of sound that's attempting to escape from the box turns in on itself and cancels itself out, so the sound just collapses. The same with a drum: If you hit it too hard and leave the stick there, nothing happens. But if you tap it softly, you actually get a much fuller sound."

For Burnett, *Raising Sand* was a watershed project in fully realizing the promise of his low-end vision. To create "a new dimension in sound" he had experimented in creating "volume by depth"—increasing and expanding the infinite overtones down at the bottom rather than cranking up the decibels. A high percentage of modern music wastes the dynamic range of a CD and cripples the sound by pushing everything, including the lower/softer parts, into the upper dB range, to make it as loud as possible. "It's a question of finding how much low tone you can put on, at what volume, and at what relationship to the high tones," Burnett told *Tape Op.*

"If you've ever been to a football stadium and heard a marching band . . . there can be 25 tubas blowing their brains out, but at the top all you can hear is the one guy playing a triangle." He added, "Those triangle sounds go fast. In the time it takes a single 100-cycle tone to complete, 100 ten-cycle tones have completed. So it's *zoom*, the high sounds go. You can put them way, way back there and they're still effective. It's a question of now, in this new medium, of looking for the new balance. What makes sense in this medium as a balance? We're experimenting all the time—it's all completely experimental."

Raising Sand was recorded live to tape, but in a departure from *O Brother's* on-the-floor vocalizing, Plant and Krauss sat in a booth, half-facing each other at a 45-degree angle. As if guided by a harmonic divining rod, they gravitated toward the sweet spots of Burnett's resonant chamber sound—those overtones, in constant, reverberant bloom, those guitars gloriously a-tremble. A number of songs were cut in one take, immediately after the singers ran through the arrangement with the band, though there were occasional vocal retakes and a good deal of overdubbing. Marc Ribot would return to Sound Emporium at night, sometimes working on his ideas with the audio engineer Mike Piersante until the early morning hours.

One of Burnett's most string-centric productions—keyboards are absent on all but one of the songs—*Raising Sand* is an album of emotional extremes. At one end are the pure longing of Sam Phillips's Kurt Weill–inspired number "Sister Rosetta Goes before Us," on which Krauss speaks with piercing clarity to the "echoes of light that shine like stars after they're gone," and "Please Read the Letter," a sepia-toned lament Plant wrote and recorded with Jimmy Page during their post-Zep partnership. (His brief interjection of mentholated blues moans—"Well, well, well, well, well, *well*"—only serves to remind us what a different singer he is here.) At the other end of the spectrum are the stark denial of Townes Van Zandt's "Nothin'," which receives a swarming, fuzz-toned, psychedelic treatment on which Krauss cuts loose on violin, and a theatrical reading of Tom Waits's "Trampled Rose." The mood is subdued throughout: Not until the irresistible fifth song on the album, the Everly Brothers' "Gone Gone Gone (Done Moved On)," on which Burnett and Dennis Crouch double up on bass to give extra oomph to the beat, does the tempo quicken.

Bellerose, among others, was struck by the sheer range of the music. "It covered every moment of my life, every influence," he told me. "Watching [drummer] Paul Humphrey on Lawrence Welk, my brother's influence in turning me on to Gene Krupa, my band director with his Chick Corea charts, and T Bone referencing Sandy Nelson [of "Teen Beat" fame] on 'Gone Gone Gone.'" The drummer was equally impressed by the opportunity to plug into those sounds, and respond to them, in his own idiosyncratic, spontaneous way: "I had started to give up hope. I mean, I was ready to start making records at the end of an empty room with a click track. I had these weird dreams before that first session with T Bone and decided that I was just gonna be myself, playing the way I think. His first response was, 'That's great.' I felt like I had found home."

Raising Sand, the album some people thought had little chance of succeeding, found many homes. Released on October 23, 2007, on Rounder, an independent, roots-oriented label not accustomed to making such a loud noise, it opened at No. 2 on the *Billboard* charts, the highest Plant or Krauss had placed as a solo act and Krauss's first showing in the Top 10. It received a big boost fifteen months later when it shook up the Grammy Awards by winning Album of the Year (beating out efforts by Coldplay, Lil' Wayne, Radiohead, and Ne-Yo) and Best Contemporary Folk/Americana Album and trophies for three of its songs. "Please Read the Letter" won Record of the Year, "Rich Woman" Best Pop Collaboration with Vocals, and "Killing the Blues" Best Country Collaboration with Vocals. Burnett, an equal partner whose name deserves to be on the cover of the album along with those of Plant and Krauss, did not win Producer of the Year (in the nonclassical field). That award went to Rick Rubin, largely because he worked on five different albums (including Jakob Dylan's first solo effort, *Seeing Things*), though none of them in the same class as *Raising Sand.*

When Plant and Krauss toured in support of the album, Burnett accompanied them on rhythm guitar. As with Rolling Thunder, albeit in a very different guise, he got to sing a couple of his own songs. There were widespread hopes for a sequel to *Raising Sand.* In 2009, following the Grammy sweep, Burnett did in fact return to the studio with Plant and Krauss, but not surprisingly in the case of such a special undertaking—and one involving such sizable egos and delicate balances—the magic wasn't there the second time around. Neither was the fun. "There was this sense that there were too many cooks in the kitchen," Bellerose told me. "The first time, the whole thing was a bit of a mystery. T Bone was in command. But after being on the road with the album and having been through it, Robert and Alison and everyone all had an idea of how things should go. That clogged the process up, slowed it down."

Plans for a follow-up were dropped—or so it seemed. In a May 2014 chat with *Rolling Stone*, characterizing Burnett as "very elusive and incredibly hard to find," Plant said that he and Krauss had gone into a California studio with Daniel Lanois after the *Raising Sand* tour, but the new songs he and Lanois had written together "didn't really lend themselves to a vocal collaboration." Regardless of whether subsequent talks about a *Raising Sand* redux will lead to anything, the trio will always have Nashville—and Los Angeles, where during a break from adding final touches to the album at Electromagnetic Studio, Krauss started playing "Whole Lotta Love" and an impromptu Led Zeppelin hoedown broke out. Talk about a song never remaining the same.

CHAPTER 22

Jazz Man

Burnett's 2014 commencement speech at USC's Annenberg School for Communications—whose Innovation Lab was headed by his friend Jonathan Taplin, the former tour manager for Bob Dylan, film producer, and the investment adviser who helped the Bass Brothers defend Walt Disney Studios from a corporate raid—was pretty scattered. Like a zookeeper running after escaping animals, he was too busy chasing the next big thought to stay on the current one. But as a collection of impassioned statements, the talk hit its mark, none more squarely than with his declaration that "Louis Armstrong did more to communicate our message of freedom and innovation than any single person in the last 100 years."

In the 1920s, with such three-minute masterpieces as "West End Blues," Armstrong single-handedly changed the course of popular music through his invention of the improvised jazz solo (until then, bands played collectively). The trumpeter and cornetist went on to shake up convention with his extraordinary vocal style and brilliance as an entertainer. But at the same time, the man called Satchmo continued to honor the New Orleans and Chicago traditions from which he emerged. It is that sense of connection between present and past, between upholding tradition and rewriting it, that defines much of Burnett's work as an artist.

In 2002, Burnett took advantage of the opportunity to indulge his love of Satchmo by producing *A Wonderful World*, a collection of Armstrong favorites as sung by Tony Bennett and k. d. lang. Burnett and Bennett had hit it off during their session for *Divine Secrets of the Ya-Ya Sisterhood.* "T Bone is very intuitive and he looks to capture the moment of the performance very much like one would take a photograph," Bennett told me. "He concentrates on keeping it spontaneous rather than getting overly caught up in the technical aspects."

If the *O Brother* soundtrack was comfort food for Americans following the attacks of 9/11, *A Wonderful World*'s embrace of the Great American Songbook was a red, white, and blue cake. For once as a producer, Burnett did not get to shape the album with a free hand. The backing musicians were Bennett's, including the pianist-arranger Lee Musiker (who had replaced the singer's longtime accompanist, Ralph Sharon) and the zippy drummer Clayton Cameron. The veteran orchestrator Peter Matz was in place for three lushly arranged songs, and the distinguished tenor saxophonist Scott Hamilton was on hand as a guest soloist. Plus, *A Wonderful World* was recorded not in the friendly confines of one of Burnett's regular haunts, but over three days at Bennett Studios, a new facility in Englewood, New Jersey, built on the site of an old railroad station by Tony and his son Dae Bennett, an engineer. Actually, the music was performed live on the stage of the adjacent Harms Theater and piped into the control room through a sixty-four-channel fiber-optic cable. (For Burnett, this was a precursor to the cross-country concert he performed in 2013 with the singer-guitarist Chuck Mead of the band BR5-49 over a broadband connection. He was in an LA studio, Mead at an outdoor park in Chattanooga, Tennessee.)

Even as a "visiting" player, though, Burnett left his mark on the relaxed, elegantly understated performances. It has been one of the unspoken rules of marquee duets that the singing partners indulge in showbizzy mannerisms to create the illusion of intimacy. In sharp contrast, Bennett and lang, reflecting the congenial atmosphere Burnett created for them, connect with unforced ease across styles and generations (Bennett was seventy-six, lang forty-one). "What a Wonderful World," a 1967 hit for Armstrong, is rife with sentimentality, but Burnett draws genuine feeling from Bennett and lang—whose lungpower is one of her calling cards—by having them play it close to the vest.

Neither Bennett nor lang can be considered a jazz artist. But like the popular artists he idolized—namely, Bing Crosby and Frank Sinatra—Bennett can swing with the best of them. And lang, an eclectic singer whose career has encompassed country-punk and chanteuse-style pop, has learned from her heroes—notably Peggy Lee and Rosemary Clooney (to whom Burnett and Sam Phillips paid tribute at a memorial concert in December 2002)—how to inhabit a jazz sensibility. For Burnett, of course, treating jazz as something apart from other genres of American music is an exercise in artificiality. The sounds of jazz, he declared in his USC speech, are of a piece with all the other sounds with which this country has defined its character, going back to "Johnny Is Gone for a Soldier," "John Brown's Body," and "The Battle Hymn of the Republic."

As the producer of singer Cassandra Wilson's 2006 album *Thunderbird*, Burnett found himself working with an artist who played a significant role in expanding the meaning of jazz. Beginning with her striking 1993 album *Blue Light 'til Dawn*, she made a specialty of crossing genres with her dusky contralto, covering artists ranging from Van Morrison and Hank Williams to the Monkees and, most spectacularly, Robert Johnson. With her resistance to basic swing—hers is a luxuriant approach to melody that blurs time and stretches lines—she alienated some mainstream critics for whom her music didn't mean a thing. And yet, in saying he wanted to make "an honest to goodness, real life jazz record" with the then forty-nine-year-old Wilson, hailing her as "the premier jazz singer of the day," Burnett compared her to the sweetly swinging, bebop-charged Ella Fitzgerald—her polar opposite, stylistically.

What did he mean by "real life jazz"? Did he want to return Wilson to the mainstream approach of her one and only standards album, *Blue Skies* (1988)? Did he want to record her live in a hallowed jazz club like New York's Village Vanguard? Having been introduced to her music through her haunting recording of Billie Holiday's "Strange Fruit" (he met her during the recording of the 2003 soundtrack album he executive-produced for TV's *Crossing Jordan*), did he want to produce an album of songs associated with Lady Day? All Wilson knew when she showed up at Capitol Studios in Los Angeles to record *Thunderbird* was that, with the exception of her longtime bassist Reginald Veal, she would be playing without her regular accompanists. "Maybe I said I was interested in the new methodology, the whole sampling thing, maybe I didn't," she told me in 2006 for a *No Depression* profile. "I only know I wanted to experiment with that stuff, and that's what happened."

Burnett, as it turned out, wasn't interested in channeling Ella. He wanted to come up with songs that would "penetrate the zeitgeist" for Wilson the way "O Death" had for Ralph Stanley. *Time* magazine may have named her "America's Best Singer" in 2001, but she was still much less widely known than jazz's perennial "It" girl, Diana Krall. And she was nowhere near the commercial force of her labelmate Norah Jones. Venturing into new territory, Burnett backed her with members of his "kill squad" band, then doing double duty on *The True False Identity*, plus the bassist-programmer Mike Elizondo, who had produced Fiona Apple's *Extraordinary Machine*, a handy point of reference.

From the start, Wilson found herself participating in a novel kind of group collaboration. The wistful, backbeat-style groove number "It Would Be So Easy" and the bumptious lead track "Go to Mexico" began as wide-open jams that went on as long as thirty minutes. The latter song, which became the album's featured cut, started out with a brief vocal sample of "Hey Pocky A-Way" by the Wild Tchoupitoulas, New Orleans' beloved Mardi Gras Indians. Isolated in a booth with her acoustic guitar, Wilson sang spontaneous lyrics she said were influenced by the Robert Rodriguez *Mariachi* movies she had been watching and thoughts of a vacation south of the border. She orchestrated her own overdubbed vocals like horns, in some cases singing the words backwards. "There's some really crazy stuff in there," she said.

The heart of *Thunderbird*, however, is the blues, which in Wilson's close embrace shares a profound intimacy with jazz. On "Easy Rider," the Blind Lemon Jefferson staple, Burnett cagily matched her up with the Canadian blues guitarist (and *O Brother* contributor) Colin Linden. What begins as a slow-burning, prefeminist soliloquy—"There's gonna be a time when a woman don't need no man / So hush your mouth, stop raisin' sand"—breaks out into an incendiary seven-minute epic of alternating hope and despair. Wilson and company also transform Willie Dixon's "I Want to Be Loved" from an upbeat rouser into a leisurely but powerfully plainspoken statement. Linden and the Delta blues guitarist Keb' Mo' extend the melody with alternately stinging and trembling effects while dual drummers Jim Keltner and Bill Maxwell (another old Fort Worth crony) surround it.

Burnett and Wilson did record one tune from the jazz songbook, "The Folks Who Live on the Hill," a late-1930s classic by Jerome Kern and Oscar Hammerstein II that Wilson had sung in performance. But her recording was tossed out for being too "jazz-standardy." In an intriguing move, Burnett had her record Jakob Dylan's Wallflowers ballad "Closer to You" as a standard. "A singer of Cassandra's caliber should be able to sing any kind of song that touches her, and that she can touch," he told *JazzTimes*. "And then it becomes what it is she does. And I think it would loosely become 'jazz'—in the old, coarse sense of the word."

Burnett, Wilson said, had an elusive quality in the studio, raising questions in soft tones, almost under his breath, and then disappearing. "I got a sense early on that he commanded the space in a way that was indicative of a very evolved spirit," she told the *JazzTimes* columnist Nate Chinen. "Most producers like to be hands-on; they're there, they're ever-present, they're hovering and indicating and instructing.

And T Bone is just the opposite. If those qualities are there, they're very discreet."

"He makes you feel like you don't have time restraints even though you do," she told me. "We talked in the way that Southerners talk, in stories—very casually and, you know, you say a thing without saying it." (It bears pointing out that Wilson was going through a rough patch at the time. Her mother was in the early throes of Alzheimer's, and Wilson's personal life was in turmoil. Burnett's emotional support was as important as his creative support.)

The recording of *Thunderbird* was spread out over many months, during which time Burnett, his hip-hop-savvy co-producer Keefus Ciancia, and Wilson shared changes in the music via file exchanges. Working with various samples, some from outside sources, Ciancia and audio engineer Mike Piersante put the finishing touches on the album at Electromagnetic, using Burnett's vintage console. From out of town, Burnett and Wilson checked on the mixes via Internet. Welcome to the modern world of making records.

Two of the songs ended up in Wim Wenders's 2005 film *Don't Come Knocking*, starring Sam Shepard: a stormy arrangement of "Strike a Match," which as sung by Wilson in a tricky time scheme takes on dramatic new meaning, and "Lost," a shimmering duet by Wilson and Marc Ribot. But *Thunderbird* fell far short of zeitgeist penetration. The album peaked at No. 184 on the *Billboard* Top 200—forty-three places lower than her Grammy-winning *New Moon Daughter*. Wilson settled back into her usual mode for a few albums, recorded a romantic set of originals with the Italian guitarist and producer Fabrizio Sotti, and then leaped into the fray again in 2015 with a boldly conceived, darkly orchestrated Billie Holiday tribute to which Burnett contributed on guitar and Van Dyke Parks with string arrangements.

Performing songs from the album at Chicago's Thalia Hall, backed by a band with avant-garde leanings that treated the songs and arrangements to scrappy textures, Wilson further revised her Billie concept. But though the venue is known for its first-rate acoustics, I found it difficult to get past the harshness of the live sound. Was I hearing too many jagged digital lines and not enough analog curves? Or had I bought so deeply into Burnett's concept of sound that I was experiencing the music through his ears? More on that later, but first some thoughts on Burnett's next jazz experiment.

It wasn't surprising when Diana Krall, who has had her own serious flirtations with pop and happens to be married to Elvis Costello, turned to Burnett to produce an album. Unlike Wilson, Krall has spent most of her career basking in jazz tradition, adopting as models the early, easy-swinging piano trios of Nat King Cole and the joyful stride of Fats Waller. But Elvis had nudged her toward pop in co-writing songs for her 2004 album *The Girl in the Other Room*; with her husband on board as a guest contributor, she brought in Burnett to handle her 2012 effort, *Glad Rag Doll*—a throwback album of a different sort that collected favorite songs of her father's dating back to the 1920s and 1930s.

With her whispery/husky vocals, commitment to swing, and proud ties to tradition, Krall would seem to be a stronger candidate for a "real life jazz" album than would Wilson. But in some ways, *Glad Rag Doll* is even more of a stylistic outlier than is *Thunderbird*. Backed by Burnett's edgy sessioneers, Krall frequently seems like she is on a different page than the one being written for her. Her attributes as a vocalist do not include the ability to impose her will on a song: Though her ramshackle, Dave Brubeckian sound on an old Steinway upright fits the bill, her vocal is too thin for Betty James's wide-body, blues-rockabilly workout "I'm a Little Mixed Up." Once "There Ain't No Man That's Worth the Salt of My Tears," a 1920s hit for Annette Hanshaw, leaves the station, powered by Marc Ribot's space-age accents and Bellerose's rambunctious New Orleans beat, Krall can only try to keep up. And you can almost hear her sighs of relief at the conclusion of a cosmic banjo and reverb treatment of Doc Pomus's "Lonely Avenue," Ray Charles's recording of which was one of Burnett's favorites.

Glad Rag Doll does have its moments. On the title song, Krall's lilting contralto is partnered with Ribot's Spanish-style acoustic guitar to lovely effect. "Let It Rain" is a fetching pop-soul ballad swept along by Bellerose's loose, raggedy strokes. And ultimately, Burnett—who says he never thinks about a record's commercial prospects in the studio, instead concentrating only on how well things are flowing—did okay by Krall, chart-wise. *Glad Rag Doll* did not go platinum, as have most of her albums, but it rose to No. 6 on the *Billboard* chart and was certified as a gold album. It is fair to ask, though, whether Burnett did right by Krall and jazz in an artistic sense. "It was such a blast to work with [Burnett]," she told the *Seattle Times*, adding, "That album was a life-changing experience for me, in every way. I'm just feeling so comfortable with myself now." But judging by the speed with which Krall returned to the safety of the commercially slick producer David Foster for her next album, apparently comfort wasn't enough.

As a producer, Burnett has trusted bluegrass and blues and gospel to stand up on their own, but there is little sense here that he trusted jazz to do anything of the sort, pushing Krall so far out of her comfort zone that she is on alien soil. Will *Glad Rag Doll* be remembered as a Diana Krall album or a T Bone Burnett album? Where does the producer end and the artist begin? And does it matter? Burnett has never been fond of musicians taking a proprietary view of their work, as in "my solo" or "my part." He approaches art—which he aspires to make with every recording, however commercial—with a one-for-all-and-all-for-one perspective.

"All art comes out of community," he told *Drowned in Sound*, "and when communities can get together and not fight over who gets what piece, and instead can say 'this is ours—let's make it great,' it just ends up being better. As soon as someone says 'this is mine,' then it all starts fragmenting and fracturing, so to get the spirit of a piece of art right, everyone has to be generous."

Being generous also means sharing in failures. "When something is not working out," said Jay Bellerose, "T Bone always blames it on the whole, never on the guitar part or the drum part. He's gentle about tipping things in a different direction. Sometimes he'll toss out a reference to get people on track, like 'Make it more like [Miles Davis's] *Bitches Brew*.' Some great music has been created with tension, but he goes another way. He's always about keeping morale up."

Whatever position you take on album ownership, one thing is clear: if Burnett once took satisfaction in disappearing into the finished product and "not messing with the groove," he was now leaving as unmistakable a John Hancock on recordings as have Daniel Lanois and Phil Spector. The deeper he pushed into the 2000s, the more refined that bottom-rich, percussively shaded sound became, and the more common the sonic foundations for artists as different as John Mellencamp and Lisa Marie Presley. An increasing number of critics and colleagues expressed their reservations about Burnett's production style.

The straight-talking indie producer Steve Albini, whose mainstream projects include Jimmy Page and Robert Plant's *Walking into Clarksdale*, asserts that producers shouldn't shape things to their own tastes. Posting on *ProSoundWeb*, he wrote that Elvis Costello was "dramatically better with Nick Lowe's less mannered production" than Burnett's. "I want the band's record to be theirs—really, completely theirs," he wrote. In his otherwise positive review of Gregg Allman's 2011 album *Low Country Blues* (which we'll get to in the next chapter), the *Rolling Stone* writer David Fricke was critical of the "austere, consciously antique production. . . . It's as if Burnett tried a little too hard to create the illusion of empty bedrooms and roads that go on forever, when it's all in that voice." Hearing Allman with fresh ears was the last thing his hard-core followers wanted. As crazy as it seems, some sound experts, self-appointed and professional, find *Raising Sand* unlistenable.

Unexpectedly, Burnett redeemed himself as a jazz producer, and made his deepest and truest push into the music, on the Broadway veteran Betty Buckley's 2014 album *Ghostlight.* A lifelong friend of his going back to their youth in Fort Worth, Buckley is still best known for wringing every last drop of emotion from "Memory" in the original 1982 Broadway production of *Cats*. But her beautifully restrained reading of "Body and Soul" here is one of the best versions of that jazz staple in years. And her impassioned treatment of "Throw It Away" by the late jazz singer Abbey Lincoln, a neglected songwriter, helps correct that injustice.

In their notes, Burnett and Buckley say they imagined the setting of the performance as a 1940s nightclub, but it feels more like a swank, darkened theater. With the guitarist Bill Frisell, an inspired choice, heightening the dreamy atmosphere with his twinkling high-string effects—and occasional psychedelia—the sound of *Ghostlight* is so comforting in its shimmer, so alive in the dark, the songs take on an almost lullaby-like quality in seeking comfort in memories. What is this thing called jazz? The easy answer is just about anything you want it to be. But when an artist achieves a true jazz moment, as occurs here more than once, you're left knowing how futile it is to try and define that triumph in words. As Billie Holiday said, don't explain.

CHAPTER 23

Blues Man

Rock fans are used to seeing their idols come and go; only a few freakish bands have the dinosaur instincts (and cash reserves) of the Rolling Stones. But it is possible for someone who thrilled to great bluesmen in their youth to be still following them deep into their adulthood. In the case of a precious few of those fans, like Burnett, it is also possible for them to be working side by side with their heroes. He reached such a pinnacle in producing Willie Dixon, widely considered the blues' greatest songwriter, and B. B. King, the king of the blues in more than name.

Hidden Charms, Dixon's Burnett-produced 1988 album, emerged from the two sharing a song publisher, Bug Music, which had just signed a deal with Capitol Records. Dixon had founded the Blues

Heaven Foundation a few years earlier to promote the music and help blues artists recover song royalties. *Hidden Charms* was part of his campaign to reclaim his own compositions. (In 1994, two years after his death, a jury found that he had been duped into signing away a third of his song rights to his ex-manager.) Burnett, who became one of the most outspoken advocates of musicians' rights, was helping the Chess Records legend fight that good fight.

Largely consisting of lesser-known originals, Dixon's first vocal effort in many years was no masterpiece, though Burnett certainly had one in mind when he gathered together the longtime Chess pianist Lafayette Leake; the guitarist Cash McCall, a protégé of Dixon's; the harmonica player Sugar Blue of fleeting Rolling Stones fame; the jazz bassist Red Callander; and the drummer Earl Palmer. The musicians, who needed time to gel, found themselves at odds with one another in trying to decipher Dixon's cryptic directions. And Dixon came down with throat problems, sabotaging Burnett's plans to record the album live over four days with no overdubs.

On top of everything else, the noted roots music author Peter Guralnick (now best known for his two-volume Elvis Presley biography), on hand to report on the sessions for *Musician*, took after Burnett for his stressed-out manner, which he wrote "suggests a thoroughly urban insecurity grafted onto the innocent aspect of a Hans Brinker with bangs." Well, as literary allusions go, it was less predictable than was Ichabod Crane. (David Mansfield was sure to appreciate the skating reference.) And *Hidden Charms* did win a Grammy for Best Traditional Blues Album. Then, twenty years later, came B.B.

For Burnett, hearing King live and on record as a kid was life changing. He first saw the "Beale Street Blues Boy" at Dallas's Central Forest Ballroom and Green Parrot Club and never forgot the "big, dreamy, ethereal sound" of those shows. He also treasured King's blazing hits from the 1950s on Modern/Crown, which bore the inimitable stamp of the producer-arranger-mentor Maxwell Davis. "I loved those records, their size and freedom and beautiful, beautiful arrangements," Burnett told me during the recording of what turned out to be King's final album, *One Kind Favor* (2008). In producing it, he drew generously from those early memories.

In the eighty-two-year-old King, who died in 2015, Burnett had one of the most iconic figures, in the true sense of the word, in popular culture. Combining Robert Johnson's country blues (King's parents were sharecroppers), Louis Jordan's party-hearty jump and boogie, and Lonnie Johnson's single-string, jazz-inflected sound, he was an embodiment of the music in all its geographical and stylistic range. King was also known worldwide for his multitude of genre-crossing duets with Tony Bennett, Luciano Pavarotti, Willie Nelson, and U2, his Kennedy Center Honors recognition, his airline and car commercials, and the Memphis and New York supper clubs bearing his name.

Various producers over the years had attempted to "update" King, with disappointing results. Since crossing over into the commercial big time with *Completely Well*, the 1969 album featuring the string-overdubbed monster hit "The Thrill Is Gone"—the culmination of producer Bill Szymczyk's own efforts to pry King loose from formulas that weren't serving him well—the bluesman had largely been heard in compromised settings. As albums like B.B.'s self-produced *Blues on the Bayou* (1998) attest, he could deliver the goods when he wanted to, but at other times he sounded uninspired, preaching to a choir that didn't ask much of him. For all his fame and all his honors, many or even most of his followers had never been exposed to the gutty sound with which the Memphis native attained stardom in Los Angeles. Burnett wanted to uplift him by putting him in touch with his roots.

Burnett sifted through dozens of songs King discovered as a boy and performed in the 1950s. Together, they settled on well-known tunes like the Mississippi Sheiks's "Sittin' on Top of the World" and Howlin' Wolf's "How Many More Years" and lesser-known songs like T-Bone Walker's "Get These Blues Off Me" and the modern R&B artist Oscar Lollie's "Waiting for Your Call." He convinced King to step away from his usual ways of doing things and reflect on those classic Maxwell Davis arrangements, which revealed the arranger's big band background (he had played tenor saxophone for Fletcher Henderson and arranged for Louis Jordan) and played up King's love of the swing-era sounds of Benny Goodman, Duke Ellington, Count Basie, and Jimmie Lunceford. King agreed to that strategy with a wink and a nod: "I hear a lot of people saying now, 'Those things you used to do, they're something else,'" he told the *Los Angeles Times*. "But they didn't like 'em when I was doing 'em!" But, he told *Rolling Stone*, "Those old records still sound pretty good."

At Village Recorder in Los Angeles, Burnett created a double quartet for King with Dr. John on piano, Neil Larsen on organ, and Jim Keltner and Jay Bellerose on drums. The presence of Dr. John (aka Mac Rebennack), with whom King had worked previously, was key, reflecting Burnett's belief that taking an artist out of his comfort zone doesn't mean removing all comforts. The first thing that strikes you about the music, aside from its density and deep tonality, is the joyful energy that radiates from it, even—or especially—when King is lamenting the loss of a lover ("If you would only listen to me baby / We would still be together today," he declaims on Lonnie Johnson's "My Love Is Down") or contemplating mortality ("See that my grave is kept clean," he sings on a punchy reading of Blind Lemon Jefferson's song by that name—the "one kind favor" of the album title). The second thing that hits you is the bruising force of King's vocals, which, coming from a man on the far side of life, couldn't sound more alive and present.

"His voice is more powerful than it's ever been," Burnett told *Mix*. "B.B. is rightly regarded as one of the best guitarists ever, but I also believe he's a better singer than he is a guitarist, so I really wanted to focus on his singing. His voice has mellowed into this almost Billy Eckstine vibrato, which is deep and rich and powerful."

And then there are Darrell Leonard's impeccable eight-man horn arrangements. On many blues recordings, the horns have a locked-in feel. On *One Kind Favor*, they play an ever-changing and at times unpredictable role, sometimes appearing for a full chorus and sometimes for a few bars. Tucked behind King, the only soloist on all but one of the songs, the horns act like a platform for his stinging lines. In rhythm, they comp behind him like a pianist behind a soloist. In full swing, they are a moveable feast for King's vocalizing, pushing him toward jazz. The musicians sat close to one another in a circle, with Burnett positioned between King and Dr. John so he could hear both of them play in real time. He didn't bother with earphones. "I knew if I could hear Mac and if I could hear B.B.—I knew they were good, that was a take," he told *Tape Op*.

As you might expect with Dr. John at the piano, there's a strong New Orleans element to the music, particularly on the title song and "Sittin' on Top of the World," which are alive with second-line rhythms and the good Doc's strolling and strutting figures. In highlighting that part of King's style, which has long featured a distinctive mambo beat, *One Kind Favor* was in keeping with Burnett's ongoing celebration of the borderless glories of American music. Using old, crusty tube amplifiers, among other period equipment, Burnett and his longtime engineer Mike Piersante roughed up King's guitar, acting in recognition of the fact that for all the technical advances there have been in the modern era of sound, there is no improving on what was achieved at the height of the studio era. You have to think that *One Kind Favor* would have impressed Maxwell Davis. Young T Bone likely would have been as well.

So would Tom Dowd, the producer responsible for the Allman Brothers Band's memorable output at Atlantic Records. When, at the behest of his manager, Gregg Allman met with Burnett in 2009, the bluesy singer-keyboardist was still so shaken by Dowd's passing that he hadn't been in the studio as a solo act since and had no desire to end that streak. But during his talk with Burnett, an admirer of Dowd, Allman found they shared similar tastes in songs, album concepts, and recording techniques. "Damned if T Bone ain't just about like Tommy Dowd!" he concluded, as related to *LancasterOnline*.

Allman had a long history of popularizing blues classics with the Allman Brothers: Sonny Boy Williamson's "One Way Out," T-Bone Walker's "Stormy Monday," Blind Willie McTell's "Statesboro Blues," Willie Dixon's "I'm Your Hoochie Coochie Man." As with B. B. King, Burnett envisioned Allman going beyond such familiar tunes and taking on older, less well-known songs. From an external drive he had acquired containing thousands of old blues recordings—"extreme back-in-the-game stuff," as Dr. John described them to the *New York Times*—Burnett chose around two dozen and asked Allman to pick fifteen. Allman hadn't heard many of the songs, a large percentage of which were swing-mode numbers featuring horns, but after listening to them over a period of six weeks he made his selections, adding to the mix a personal favorite, Muddy Waters's "I Can't Be Satisfied."

"Basically, what I looked for was something I could do justice to vocally," wrote Allman in his memoir *My Cross to Bear*, "and also that we could light some real nasty music to."

The project hit an early snag when Burnett asked Allman to show up at the studio without his band. It was only after two weeks of mulling things over that Allman agreed. His first encounter with Jay Bellerose may well have made him wonder what he had gotten into. "Jay only used one stick; the other hand would have a tambourine or a maraca," Allman wrote in *My Cross to Bear*. "He tied these things to his leg, hollow like wax grapes, with paper clips, match heads, BBs in 'em, and they put little tiny microphones around his feet. When I first got to the studio, there were drums all over the place. It looked like a drum yard sale—not one drum matched another one. Some of them looked like they were from the Middle East or the Far East. I looked for the mounting on them—no mountings, all wood."

But his reservations disappeared when he heard Bellerose play—and when he spotted Dr. John, with whom he had been friends since the Allman Brothers opened for him in a Boston club in the 1960s. Rebennack appeared on and cowrote a song on Allman's 1977 album *Playin' Up a Storm* and had worked with him on other occasions. "T Bone knew that him being there would put a certain fire in my ass," Allman said. "It was so good seeing Dr. John, both of us being sober."

From the start, Burnett was up to a spookier kind of gospel than he was on *One Kind Favor*. The opening tune, Sleepy John Estes's "Floating Bridge," has the feeling of odd assembled parts: Dennis Crouch's super-heavy, popping bass; Dr. John's slightly distorted piano; Doyle Bramhall's ghostly, reverberating guitar; and Bellerose's scraping, scratching, cardboard-texture drums. A new arrangement of "Rolling Stone" is part tribal march and part chain gang exercise. Drumbeats don't get heavier or more convulsive than they do on the unsung Chicago blues composer Melvin London's "Little by Little." Well, actually, the drumming is even heavier on Skip James's "Devil Got My Woman," on which Colin Linden plinks out mournful notes on Dobro over what sounds like four or five bass drums.

With the Brothers, Allman's vocals, as strong and distinctive as they are, often seem to mark time between guitar exchanges. In this purposefully confined setting, heard up close, front and center, the singing is the main event. You wouldn't think a man who had been through so much and was in such bad shape physically—a chronic hepatitis C sufferer, he was coming off liver transplant surgery—would sound this good. But there is an ease and clarity in his vocals, without any loss of soulful power, that we hadn't heard before. "I'm hooked, Lord / I can't let her go," he wails in clenched desperation on the Bobby Bland tune "Blind Man," drawing sympathy from Leonard's five-piece horn section, here channeling the soulful swagger of Ray Charles's great late-1950s band. On "Just Another Rider," a mid-session addition he co-wrote with fellow Allman Brother and Gov't Mule leader Warren Haynes, he slips into southern rock mode, but anchored by bass trumpet, baritone saxophone, and two tenors. B. B. King's "Please Accept My Love" gets an unexpected rock 'n' roll treatment, with a tinge of doo-wop.

Allman was amazed at—and a little nervous about—how quickly the recording proceeded. "First takes scare me to death, they really do," he said in program notes for an appearance at the Uptown Theater in Napa, California:

> On about three or maybe four of 'em, Bone comes over to the microphone, "Alright, we got it." I say, "Well wait, hold it, hold it! What do you mean got it? We just ran it down!" "No, we got it." I went back in the control room, I said, "Man, I know I can get it better than that." He says, "What's wrong with that?" I said, "Well, nothin's wrong with it, I just think I can do it with a little more interesting feel." So we went back out there, I tried, man, I tried as hard as I could. Nope.

"We got 15 masters in 11 days," he said. "Let me tell ya, they just went Pop! Pop! Pop! Pop!"

If *One Kind Favor* and *Low Country Blues* sound like companion pieces, that is because Burnett recorded them with a nearly identical sound field: Dr. John on the left, recessed; vocals in the middle, up front, just ahead of the bass and drums; and guitars and/or horns on the right. "T Bone used these old, ancient mikes, those old square ones with the holes in them—they look like they should be in front of Groucho Marx," wrote Allman. "He would set those up all around the room; he had a different way of doing things, no doubt."

But more than the stereo alignment and choice of instrumentation, it is the spirit of these albums that links them. How often do artists as established as King and Allman have the opportunity to simultaneously reclaim their past and define their present in such timely, relevant fashion? And how often do they rediscover the wonders of the music that drew them to it in the first place? For all of Burnett's savvy studio strategizing with King and Allman, for all his conceptualizing, it is the purity of feeling that emanates from these recordings, the oneness the artists have with the blues that makes the recordings special. Allman, who said that working on *Low Country Blues* was "a true highlight of my career," didn't win a Grammy for it. Ironically, the album lost to the Tedeschi-Trucks Band's *Revelator*, featuring the longtime Allman guitarist Derek Trucks, nephew of the original Allman Brothers member Butch. But the album enjoyed the second-best debut ever for a blues album and charted higher than any of Allman's other solo records ever had.

King, who won a Grammy with *One Kind Favor* for Best Traditional Blues Album, said he was sad when the sessions were over. So was Burnett. "You know, I don't know how many more albums B.B. is going to make," he told me. "He's nearing the end of his working life. Going back to the beginning had a lot of meaning, not just for him, but for everyone involved." R.I.P B.B.

CHAPTER 24

Senior Adviser

In 2009 in Nashville, during sessions for the aborted *Raising Sand* sequel, Burnett received a call from Elton John. It is hard to imagine they had never spoken or had a personal encounter in all their years in music. At sixty-one and sixty-two, respectively, the American and the Englishman shared many experiences and had many mutual acquaintances. One of those acquaintances was Leon Russell, whom John had idolized as a young singer-pianist during his first visits to the States and Burnett had mixed with professionally during his early years in Los Angeles.

John, feeling guilty about falling out of touch with Russell, who was living in obscurity and poor health, was putting together a project to restore the Tulsan's reputation—an album on which the two of them would sing and play side by side. John had become disillusioned with the recording process; however, impressed by the sound of *Raising Sand* and the albums Burnett had done with Elvis Costello, he contacted the producer.

Make all the jokes you want about working the AARP circuit (something Bob Dylan was happy to do as cover boy of the membership organization's magazine). Burnett was at a time in his life where, having dealt with his share of starry-eyed rockers and insecure artistes, he was happy to produce veteran musicians who, while not always a leisurely walk through the park, knew what making records was about. Of all the artists he had worked with, Sir Elton was among the most significant. With his consistently high level of achievement as a singer, songwriter, and hitmaker over the decades, he embodied the dream of self-willed success Burnett once had for himself as a singer-songwriter. An Englishman who embodied the great American rock 'n' roll myth—"a kid walks out of his home with a song and nothing else, and conquers the world," as Burnett described it at USC—John had been touched by the countryfied spirit of Sun Records. "We're both cut from the same cloth," he told the *Hollywood Reporter*, referring to Burnett. "We both love the same kind of music."

The Union, the John-Russell collaboration, got underway in January 2010. If ever a project testified to Burnett's resourcefulness as a producer, and his Zen-like (and Pollock-like) openness to letting a recording unfold on its own organic terms, this was it. The sixty-eight-year-old Russell, who was in frail shape to begin with, had to have emergency surgery for a brain fluid leak shortly after the sessions began. Unavoidably, what was to have been a bilateral co-starring effort became an advanced exercise in music minus one. Backing tracks were recorded during Russell's absence for him to sing and play over when he returned. But when he did, ten days later, he was not up to speed. Most of the songs, written during the sessions, ended up being composed by John and his longtime lyricist Bernie Taupin. For those who expected a set of rollicking, gospel-charged, dueling-piano numbers, the concentration on ballads had to be disappointing, notwithstanding the deep emotions of the Civil War lament "Gone to Shiloh" (featuring Neil Young on vocals) and "When Love Is Dying" (featuring Brian Wilson).

For all that, *The Union* is a buoyant effort, especially when its roof is being raised by the drumming of Keltner and Bellerose. With its gospel swagger on tunes such as "A Dream Come True" (inspired by a Mahalia Jackson video Burnett played for the artists), the album sometimes recalls *The B-52 Band & the Fabulous Skylarks*. It's a gesture of affection and respect for Russell not only from John, but also from Burnett, who had to be gratified by the role the album played in leading to the 2015 release of Les Blank's long-lost documentary about Russell, *A Poem Is a Naked Person*.

Burnett's subsequent solo project with John, *The Diving Board*, is a very different kind of album. Recalling the thrills of John's American debut, a six-night run at the Troubadour in August 1970, Burnett convinced John to return to the stripped-down, piano-trio format with which he announced himself to the United States but had never documented on a studio recording (the trio album *17-11-70* was taken from a live radio broadcast). His instrument up front in the mix, John gets to flaunt his musicianship, something that had been buried beneath lavish production schemes in the past. His vocals, too, come through forcefully, animating with clear-eyed intensity his song cycle about an artist looking back and wanting to return home. Even when he adds an instrumental effect or two for atmosphere, Burnett keeps the focus where it belongs. John has never sounded more radiant.

The Burnett-John partnership lives on. In the summer of 2015, the artists completed work on a follow-up to *The Diving Board*. "That one was a parlor record," Burnett told *Billboard*. "This is a festival." They also worked together on *American Epic*, a documentary miniseries and recording project about the recording industry during the 1920s executive-produced by Burnett, Jack White, and Robert Redford. As part of the filming, John, Beck, Alabama Shakes, Merle Haggard, Nas, and other guests recorded on the primitive equipment producers used in the field in the early part of the twentieth century in their search for undiscovered talent. "He got my love of recording back," John told the *Hollywood Reporter*. Just imagine: making an album could be fun.

CHAPTER 25

Audio Activist

"People in Hollywood, we should go up there with pitchforks and torches to Silicon Valley," Burnett rabble-roused in October 2013 in a *Hollywood Reporter* story. This the day after that trade publication and *Billboard* honored him with the Maestro Award, given annually to "artists who have made a lasting contribution to film and television music." What had him riled was the "assault on the arts by the technology community," as he put it a few months later in an op-ed column in the *Los Angeles Times*—an attack he said has resulted in inferior sounding recordings and a systematic devaluation of music in the name of profit.

As he told the *Reporter*:

> If somebody had come down from Silicon Valley 30 years ago and said "I've got this new technology, and you're gonna be able to see all around the world, transfer your stuff all over the world, you're gonna be able to send things, you'll be able to see your friends, you'll be able to hear music—all you have to do is give up your privacy and your royalties," everybody would have said, "Get the f—— out of town! Right now! Get out of here!" Instead, these guys came down with their shtick, and everybody went "Well, how can we make money from this great new technology?" "Oh, you're not gonna make *money* from it. Everything's gonna be free. Just give us the intellectual property we can send around in our pipes, everybody will subscribe, and then we'll be rich. Not *you*, though."

Considering how content today's earbudded listeners are to sacrifice high fidelity for convenience, and how indifferent those who see free downloads as part of their birthright are to the underpayment of musicians, there may be no greater end in sight to Burnett's war on MP3s ("the worst blights ever on Earth") than there is to the "war on drugs." Do Sam Smith and Foo Fighters fans really care that MP3 was, as Burnett says, "never intended as a standard for audio sound"? Do Kendrick Lamar and Chvrches fans really care whether streaming is undermining the perception that there is "an inherent value placed on art"?

More than three decades into the digital era, most listeners equipped to make an A/B comparison would agree that CDs, which contain only 15 percent of the information contained on the original master tracks, lack the warmth, clarity, and depth of analog recordings. Most discerning listeners would also agree that MP3s don't sound as good as CDs because the compression of the music in standard formats allows even less information to come through. But for all the hope invested in rising vinyl sales, only a small percentage of music consumers (a term Burnett hates as much as his friend Elvis once hated "mature") are investing in turntables. It is tough strapping those things onto your back for the daily commute. And as politically charged as Burnett and other veteran artists including Rosanne Cash,

Neil Young, and Prince are about equitable revenue sharing, young musicians are divided on the issue. "Obviously I wish that everyone would pay for the art that they enjoy," the singer Torres told *Newsweek* in an informal 2015 poll of indie artists. "But that was never an expectation for me, and I'm not naive enough to believe that selling a few thousand copies of my record is going to be enough to sustain myself in this industry."

As a sound artist, Burnett sees himself as a descendent of Bill Putnam, founder of Chicago's vaunted Universal Recording and Hollywood's United Audio, who redefined recording with his bold innovations in studio design and engineering (he broke new ground in such areas as mastering, multitracking, reverb, separation, and isolation). Burnett didn't know Putnam well—the man credited with creating the modern recording console died in 1989. But Burnett was schooled on his methods and philosophies by Allen Sides, an acolyte of Putnam's who bought United (by then known as United Western Recorders) in 1984 and renamed it Ocean Way.

For Burnett, Putnam's analog recordings (of Frank Sinatra, Count Basie, and the Beach Boys, among others) set an imposing standard that even the best and most sophisticated modern technology is unable to approach. For a producer who you sometimes suspect hears notes and tones the way the Norse god Heimdall heard grass growing, the transfer of classic albums to CD—which Burnett compares to taking a Polaroid of a painting and throwing out the painting—was nothing less than a national disgrace. "We have better stuff in the iPhone now to make records with than when they were converting all these beautiful analog records that were made over a century," Burnett told the *Hollywood Reporter*.

Put on the mono vinyl version of *Sgt. Pepper's Lonely Hearts Club Band*, he said, and you hear the room sing. But turn up the early CD pressing of "A Day in the Life" and the distorted high notes make you leave the room. Digital sound, he told *Sound & Vision*, causes stress via its sampling technology by requiring your ears to "fill in the blanks." He claims it can actually harm you with its harsh underlying noises, which you may not be able to detect through your handheld device but can hear on home systems. The jury is out on those charges and, with all the money invested in digital music, likely will remain out until there is sufficient anecdotal evidence—or until listeners start bleeding from the ears.

For many years, recordings were held to uniform standards set by the Recording Industry Association of America and National Association of Broadcasters. But because digital music is heard on so many different devices and in so many different formats, no such standards now exist. Their absence was painfully evident when, in 2007, Burnett got back the first pressed copies of *Raising Sand* from the plant. He was dismayed to discover that the CDs sounded noticeably worse than the master tapes he had sent out. He discovered that the operators at the plant, faced with a backlog of orders, had taken it on themselves to speed up the pressings of *Raising Sand* by reducing the time of the stamping process for each disc. Instead of following the required four-second CD setting, they had switched to the two-second CD-ROM setting, which made a significant difference in the quality of the sound.

"For someone who's been doing this for 40 years and spent so much time trying to get the sound right, the way we want it, to have it then leave our hands and have maybe 10 people with no connection to the work making important decisions about how it sounds is unacceptable," Burnett told *Mix*. Using the filmmaker George Lucas's surround sound technology, THX, as a model—as evident by Metallica sounding appreciably better via video game technology than on CD, the film business holds itself to higher sound standards than does the record business—Burnett worked on a new "proprietary audio technology." He called it XOΔE, based on the Greek letters for CODE. It was unveiled in 2008 via John Mellencamp's starkly powerful album *Life, Death, Love and Freedom*, a collection of postcards from purgatory that hark back to the parched ballads of Woody Guthrie, the prison blues of Son House, and the death laments of Dock Boggs.

In a jointly signed note, Burnett and Mellencamp promised that CODE, imprinted on a standard DVD-Audio disc, gave the music "a resonance, depth, and presence that is unprecedented in the digital age." For audiophiles numbed over the years by a never-ending parade of gold CDs and Super Audio Compact Discs, "definitive" remasterings and remixings, umpteen releases of Miles Davis's *Kind of Blue*, green applicator pens that promised to make CDs sound as warm as vinyl—and let's not forget Quiex II Limited Edition Pressings of promotional copies of *Proof through the Night*—the selling of CODE smacked a bit of P. T. Barnum. And, in fact, CODE used the same basic 24-bit/96 kHz technology as the DVD-Audio and SACD releases of the late 1990s. (Bit rates are the amount of data processed each second. Sampling rates are the number of samples, or measurements, taken each second from a recording. The higher the rates, the better the sound.)

Chesky Records, the independent New York jazz and classical label, had already "astonished even the hardest-to-please audiophiles" (or so its promotions read) with its 24/96 audio DVD recordings. (The astonishment wore off: "We are still in the Stone age of audio," wrote the label co-founder David Chesky on Facebook in 2015.) And Neil Young drew on the same technology for his late-arriving, Kickstarter-funded Pono music system, which promised "a revolution in music listening" but instead delivered what the leading tech writer David Pogue characterized as an update of "The Emperor's New Clothes." (While acknowledging the pricey Pono's limitations, various recording personnel said that anything pointing in the direction of improved sound was worth supporting.)

Surprisingly, *Life, Death*—an album that might well have benefited from more of a push on its artistic merits—turned out to be the one and only Burnett production released in CODE. Though songs from Elvis Costello's *Secret, Profane & Sugarcane* were offered as demonstration models in that format when the technology was first trotted out, the full recording was issued as a conventional CD. So was Mellencamp's Burnett-produced 2010 album *No Better Than This* (recorded with a single mike on an old Ampex tape recorder in a Savannah church, a San Antonio hotel room, and Sun Studios in Memphis), and his 2014 effort *Plain Spoken*, for which Burnett ended up in the diminished role of executive producer.

The only other CODE-certified albums are also from 2009: *Moonalice*, by a retro-psychedelic California group of that name led by the venture capitalist Roger McNamee, a friend of Burnett's; and the Boston rocker Will Dailey's *Torrent, Volumes 1 & 2*, a compendium of EPs that Burnett was not involved in recording. Mike Piersante, whose collection of Grammys reflects his own importance in the industry, said that Burnett's retreat from CODE was due in part to the awareness that other people in the field with greater resources were working toward the same end. "We feel that CODE propelled the technology, and offered a higher standard," Piersante told me. "Everyone's starting to do it. It's all gonna come to fruition, better sound. It's really happening."

Ultimately, Burnett's devotion to higher recording standards is about more than sound—and an industry "bent on self-destruction." His activism speaks on a loftier level to the nature and value of art, the nobility of the artist, respect for the consumer, the ongoing enrichment of civilization. Testifying in 2006 before the National Recording Preservation Board in Los Angeles, he quoted a favorite line from the abstract expressionist Barnett Newman: "Time washes over the tip of the pyramid." As an artist, he aspires to achievements that sit near that tip, where they will survive the passage of years. When he was recording bands at Sound City, he told the NRPB, "the idea was to get it on the radio and make some money and move on. . . . Nobody thought rock and roll would last. So there was no sense of permanence. And maybe that was one of the good things about it too; there was no self-consciousness about its place in history or anything like that. But at this point, I'm . . . 58 years old. . . . You begin to realize that the things you do in your life actually have meaning and are important." ("Today's digital formats are not inherently safe harbors of preservation," concluded a study commissioned by the NRPB.)

An indication of Burnett's commitment and/or obsession with the cause was reflected in his responding to just about all of the mostly snarky remarks posted on the music industry web log *hypeblot* following his appearance at the 2010 Future of Music Policy Summit in Washington, DC. There, he told young musicians to "stay completely away from the Internet," that putting their music on the web or otherwise allowing it to be distributed in "unlistenable" MP3s degrades their efforts and music in general. "Sorry," posted Shiloh, "but that is really bad advice for artists—at least those who want their music to be heard by other people." Added Cathy, "I guess carbon paper is also going to make a comeback now. Should we stop using fire too?"

During the long flight back to Los Angeles, Burnett did his best to turn the other cheek in responding to such comments. "Would you consider the possibility that I wasn't saying something stupid?" he replied to Kevin, who was quick to call him exactly that.

> If you are a musician, I am on your side. I am fighting for a fairer, more ethical future for musicians. I have been doing this for a long time, and I have to say, in all honesty, that as larcenous as the record companies have been, the Internet makes them look like Robin Hoods. I am fully aware of the possibilities of putting together and managing a database on the Internet. The Internet is a powerful tool for sharing information—great for research. It is, however, an indisputable fact that digital technology does not capture music as fully as analog technology. . . . Digital is not the end of technology. In my view, for music, it is a detour.

"If I were just starting out today," Burnett continued, "knowing what I know now, I would have nothing to do with the Internet. (I would probably have nothing to do with selling recordings—at least in the framework we are currently laboring under.) I would not advertise myself. (The Internet, at the moment, most closely resembles an advertising platform. The goal of most Internet companies is to narrow our focus. Does that sound like an advance to you?) I would not market myself. I would spend every minute of the day I could playing and listening to music. Learning. Getting better." And, he wrote to the user EarOnDalton, "I hope the best for the future, but I do not have the kind of fervid belief in technology that causes the citizens of iTopia to behave in as close minded, threatened, and hostile a way as fundamentalists in any other religion."

"No battle that can be won is worth fighting," posted Burnett, in a classic T Bone–ism. However you choose to read that, there can be no doubt that, CODE or no CODE, he is in the fight for the long haul.

CHAPTER 26

Dylanologist

"I was well on my way to being a chronic and world class ne'er do well when Bob Neuwirth called me to come play the Other End in the Village with him," Burnett writes in his foreword to Sam Shepard's *Rolling Thunder Logbook*, recalling his years of "knocking around the high studios and low dives of Bohemian America making ketchup tomato soup and sleeping in guest rooms." When he came face-to-face, as it were, with the scuffling folkie played by Oscar Isaac in the Coen Brothers' film *Inside Llewyn Davis*, he recognized the reflection.

Like Llewyn Davis, Burnett struggled for recognition when he first hit the Village. How could he not have, lost in the shadow of Bob Dylan? Though *Inside Llewyn Davis* is set in the winter of 1961, before the arrival of Dylan (and Neuwirth) on the scene, Isaac's character is framed in the context of the Dylan legend. A good but not great artist whose major gift is for alienating those around him (sound familiar?), he, too, like young Burnett, has many limitations he must face. What better coach could Isaac have had than this advanced degree holder in Dylanology, who was not only a living witness to important chapters of the man's career and an inhaler of his songs but also knew what it was like to try to compete with him.

Oscar Isaac Hernandez, born to a Guatemalan mother and Cuban-Jewish father and raised in Miami, was trained at Juilliard and mastered the Travis fingerpicking style of Dave Van Ronk, whose real-life story informs the film. (His posthumous autobiography *The Mayor of MacDougal Street*, compiled from interviews by Elijah Wald, was a primary source for the Coens.) But he was not familiar with the music in the film or the artists the characters were based on, however loosely. Burnett had him immerse himself in Tom Waits recordings to expose him to the kind of durable, artfully forged identity the filmmakers wanted his character to project through his songs. (To these ears, the intensity and gorgeously closed-in quality of Isaac's vocals bring to mind Joe Henry's style of folk-based music.) Going beyond archetype, Burnett and the actor spent months building a backstory for Davis—who his parents were, where he grew up, where he went to school—and deciding how he should dress and wear his hair and carry his guitar case.

After it was established that Davis was from Queens (where both Woody Guthrie and Louis Armstrong lived during those years), Burnett had Isaac siphon some of the doo-wop and R&B that was popular in the borough. As with *O Brother*, all the songs were prerecorded, but only as templates for the live performances. Burnett was amazed by Isaac's ability to perform as many as thirty run-throughs of a song the same exact way, in the same exact tempo, without the help of a click track, to allow the Coens to cut between takes. Dylan fans are accustomed to hearing him perform vastly different versions of a song from one night to the next. But during the early 1960s, the songs were carefully arranged; sometimes the shape of the arrangements projected more individuality than did the singing and playing.

Burnett highlighted that aspect of the music with his clever arrangement of "The Death of Queen Jane," a transformed English ballad that Davis performs at his big Chicago audition for F. Murray

Abraham's impresario Bud Grossman (based on Dylan's manager, Albert Grossman, he utters the much-quoted line, "I don't see a lot of money here"). With its nods to Dylan's "Queen Jane Approximately" (from the 1965 album *Highway 61 Revisited*) and Lou Reed's "Sweet Jane" (from the Velvet Underground's 1970 gem *Loaded*), the arrangement speaks to the enduring legacy of the folk revival as it was absorbed by folk-rock and then underground rock.

There is no lack of gloom on the soundtrack—"The Death of Queen Jane," "Hang Me, Oh Hang Me," "Fare Thee Well." That suits Isaac's hapless character, whose musical partner (voiced by Marcus Mumford) broke up their act by jumping off the George Washington Bridge. The more you get to know Davis, the more you think it was a mistake for him to have his first solo album titled *Inside Llewyn Davis*: Who would want to go there?

For all the film's depressive airs, it was a "mini-masterpiece of ludicrousness" (*Huffington Post*) that became the popular centerpiece of the film. Written in baton-passing bursts by Burnett, the Coens, and Justin Timberlake (he plays Jim to Carey Mulligan's Jean in a strait-laced duo), "Please Mr. Kennedy . . . Don't You Shoot Me into Outer Space" was based on a chain of 1960s novelty tunes. On Larry Verne's "(Please) Mr. Custer," from 1960, a knee-knocking cavalryman begs not to be sent into battle. College attractions the Goldcoast Singers recorded the Cold War–themed "Please Mr. Kennedy" in 1962 ("I don't want to play no Russian roulette . . . I'm too young to die yet"). And on another song of the same name, released in 1961, the Motown singer Mickey Woods fervently argues that if he is sent to Vietnam, his girlfriend will run off with someone else. In one of his . . . lesser achievements, the label head Berry Gordy Jr. dashed off the lyrics to that version.

Burnett got the ball rolling by writing a dozen verses in his best Ogden Nash style ("My wife is young, with a healthy libido / And I don't want her to be a widow"), also paying homage to the political satirist of the day, Tom Lehrer. While shopping for an instrument for Timberlake in Tarzana, Burnett and the former *NSYNC idol retreated to the office of Norman's Rare Guitars, where Timberlake constructed a melody around Burnett's words and set them in a

Coasters-type groove. Burnett's "takeoff on a parody of a satire," as he put it, became another of his multiple-layered games that leaves the listener to decide what is disposable and what is worth saving. The Coens rebooted, rejiggered, and recalibrated the lyrics, and "Please Mr. Kennedy" was further dumbed up in a chaotic studio session that had the cowboy-hatted Adam Driver (of *Girls* fame) throw down strangeness with his bass vocalisms from another planet. "It was fucking crazy, what was happening," Driver told *Vulture*.

Inside Llewyn Davis may not be the Coens' most eventful film, but it is their most deeply felt in its lyrical treatment of both the failed hopes of the folk revival, and the promise embodied in the movement's messiah, Dylan. The Town Hall concert produced by Burnett featuring cast members and a slew of name artists including Gillian Welch, Conor Oberst, Colin Meloy of the Decemberists, and Jack White was even whiter than an episode of the 1960s TV series *Hootenanny*. Aside from the Carolina Chocolate Drops' Rhiannon Giddens, whom Burnett was grooming for stardom, the only featured African American performer was Keb' Mo'. That was an odd blemish considering Burnett's commentary on the film's website about how "the liberal world" had taken the folk standard "500 Miles"—which he hears as a slave song—and made it "part of the culture in a way that people could hear it, you know, and not be too guilty." Considering the lengths to which Burnett has gone to elevate great voices of all colors in our culture, it would be churlish to read too much into this imbalance, particularly considering how pervasively present the spirits of Lead Belly, Robert Johnson, Blind Boy Fuller and Blind Lemon Jefferson—to name a few of Dylan's great heroes—were in the music.

Has there ever been a time when Dylan wasn't on Burnett's mind? Oh, to have been inside his head in early 2014 when he received a box of newly discovered unfinished lyrics from the hallowed *Basement Tapes* sessions, with instructions from Dylan that he was free "to do what he pleased" with the scribblings. For Burnett, who calls Dylan the Homer of our times, this was like receiving a fresh batch of Dead Sea Scrolls in the morning post. Imagine, he would say, having the opportunity to collaborate across time with the twenty-seven-year-old Dylan as he settled into one of his most prolific periods?

When news of the recovered lyrics broke, the question on everyone's mind was, were these lyrics vintage Dylan or slush-pile rejects? The answer was, Who cared? Anything Dylan wrote, even if it was scrawled in the margins of the comics section, was treasurable. In the spirit of the original *Basement Tapes* sessions, which took place in a house (called "Big Pink") in upstate New York during the summer of 1967, when Dylan was holed up with members of his touring band—soon to be known as the Band—Burnett assembled a team of exceptional young artists and had them bring the lyrics to life over a concentrated two weeks in the studio. This all-star ad hoc band included Rhiannon Giddens, Marcus Mumford of Mumford & Sons, Jim James of My Morning Jacket, and Taylor Goldsmith of Dawes—plus the grizzled veteran Elvis Costello.

Hiding from the hordes outside of Woodstock as he recovered from a motorcycle accident, Dylan wrote songs at a faster clip than at any other time in his career. He and his cohort—Levon Helm, Robbie Robertson, Rick Danko, Garth Hudson, and Richard Manuel—recorded them demo style with no intention of releasing them. The plan was to supply Dylan's music publishing company with material for mainstream pop artists to cover—a goal realized via such recordings as Manfred Mann's "Quinn the Eskimo" and the Byrds' "You Ain't Goin' Nowhere." But of course the Woodstock recordings did see the light of day via early bootlegs; *The Basement Tapes*, a double album released by Columbia in 1975; more bootlegs; and then, in November 2014, the authorized 139-song mother lode, *The Basement Tapes Complete: The Bootleg Series Vol. 11*.

A template was in place for *Lost on the River: The New Basement Tapes*, as the Burnett project was titled. Working with previously unpublished lyrics by Woody Guthrie, the British folk-protest singer Billy Bragg and the progressive American rock group Wilco set them to music on *Mermaid Avenue*, an enthusiastically received 1998 release that spawned two more volumes. Dylan's own Columbia-distributed Egyptian label had released *The Lost Notebooks of Hank Williams* (2011), on which Dylan, Merle Haggard, Levon Helm, Jack White, Rodney Crowell, and Holly Williams (Hank's granddaughter) set to music a dozen newly discovered Williams lyrics. And Wilco leader Jeff

Tweedy's former Uncle Tupelo band partner Jay Farrar, accompanied by such artists as Jim James (going by Yim Yames), released another batch of previously unrecorded Guthrie lyrics, *New Multitudes* (2012).

What made *Lost on the River* different, aside from the fact that its benefactor was still alive and well, was its art-by-subgroup approach. Dylan's jotted-down lines, steeped in fate and fame and romance, American history and geography (Kansas City, the Florida Keys, and rivers play lead roles), were divvied up and passed around, in some cases leading to multiple adaptations of the same lyric. For the speed-writing savant Costello—who recorded *Secret, Profane & Sugarcane* with Burnett in three days—setting the lyrics to music and recording the songs, live, in two weeks, was not so daunting a challenge. But for his young bandmates, all of them multi-instrumentalists, this crash course in Dylanology got pretty intense. They had never worked together before, nor had they ever worked so quickly. In requiring them to do so, Burnett was not only making them reach inside themselves to discover untapped abilities, he was also introducing them to the way great artists once worked when they were turning out an album or two every year rather than one every three or four or five.

Recorded at Capitol's state-of-the-art facility, *Lost in the River* had little chance at—and little interest in—capturing the scruffy vitality of the music Dylan and the Band captured in their musty cellar. Featuring a generous number of outside musicians (was that really Johnny Depp on guitar?) and backup singers (including the Haim and Levell Sisters—and S. I. Istwa, the pseudonym of Simone Burnett), this was a highly polished production. No matter how much the musicians say they were able to channel the loose, off-the-cuff vibe of the Big Pink sessions, it is clear from the Showtime documentary *Lost Songs: The Basement Tapes Continue*, that they had to overcome fits of self-consciousness. (Though that was not always such a daunting task: Goldsmith, who professed believing he was the contributor from whom the least was expected, makes good on his determination to prove himself worthy of inclusion. His impeccable melodic touch is responsible for a pair of grabbers: "Card Shark," which boasts the strongest melody on the album, and "Liberty Street," which boasts a surging gospel chorus. And the frettingly out-of-her-element Giddens, who had no experience in this kind of setting, brings depths of mystery and womanly resolve to the folk tune "Spanish Mary" and a soaring, heel-kicking energy to "Hidee Hidee Ho.")

The 107-minute Showtime film, of which Burnett was one of the producers, squanders a golden opportunity to convey to viewers exactly what this studio superstar does, on a project in which he has a personal as well as business investment. We can see that he delegates a lot of responsibility to the artists—James is seen doing much heavy lifting as an arranger and psychedelic sound strategist. And Mike Piersante, Jay Bellerose told me, did heroic work in overcoming sudden technical snafus that might have proven too much for another engineer. But Burnett's screen time is largely limited to smiling comings and goings and asking artists if they want to record another take. Even taking into account the possibility that his subject was too busy with other projects to be fully engaged in this one, the director Sam Jones (known for the Wilco documentary *I Am Trying to Break Your Heart*) had an obligation to get him to weigh in on the making of this unexpected "sequel"—and his relationship with Dylan.

In the end, *The New Basement Tapes* is a more interesting tribute album than most, with some smartly crafted songs and a deep, reverberant sound. But for all the hype it got, it is an overly polite footnote to Dylan's *Tapes* (which did *Lost in the River* no favors by appearing in its mega format the week before the Burnett album came out, leading some consumers to think they were one and the same). One was left wondering how much livelier *The New Basement Tapes*—and the New Basement Tapes, the awkward name given the band for its late-night talk show appearances—would have been had Burnett himself stepped into the breach.

That would have been a bold move to be sure, especially for an artist still torn between the desire to perform and the need to work on the sidelines. But Burnett had proven himself an excellent interpreter of Dylan's songs. He had in his kill squad a tight-knit unit with Band-like range and flexibility. And the audience that Burnett had developed for himself as a "legendary producer" might well have paid to hear him ripping into those never-before-heard Dylan lyrics that so transported him: "I see by the papers that / He came from the old religion but possessed no magic skill / Descending from machinery he left nothing from his will." Burnett might have found one of his most rewarding new beginnings.

But like most great artists, Burnett is too committed to his own vision to step more than momentarily into someone else's. In his guise as king of Americana, he draws greater personal rewards from elevating gifted young artists and seeding the future with singers and songwriters who will carry our great music tradition forward than he does from massaging his own reputation. And for an artist who moves from job to job as freely and mysteriously as he does, even hanging for a prolonged stretch with the seriously talented members of the *New Basement Tapes* band would tax his patience. Just how uncomfortable he is being boxed in was made clear when network television tested his staying power.

CHAPTER 27

Televisionary

In October 1999, Burnett carved a little piece of TV immortality for himself by appearing on the ABC sitcom *Dharma & Greg* as a sideman of Bob Dylan. In the closing scene of "Play Lady Play," a rather cheery Dylan auditions the drummer Dharma (Jenna Elfman), who thinks she has found her calling after subbing in her teenage neighbor's garage band. Seated in a chair, sporting his familiar dark shades and black suit, the poker-faced Burnett plays lead guitar on a polka-style tune and a lively little blues instrumental. A year later, it was announced that Burnett and Elvis Costello had created an hour-long comedy-drama series for the WB network about "four models turned rock stars." If ever a release had prank written all over it, this one did. But what if? *Charlie's Angels* meets *Josie and the Pussycats*? The

Runaways on the runway? Nothing came of that project. But the signs were there that a guy who hadn't seemed to have a future in TV was eyeing the medium as another way to diversify.

In late 2009, he became an executive producer and executive music producer of *Tough Trade*, a Nashville-based series about a country music dynasty "with a penchant for drink, debauchery and divorce." The series, to star Sam Shepard as a singing legend and the real-life country star Trace Adkins as one of his brood, was green-lighted by the fledgling cable network Epix as its first original scripted series. But the show got axed after its pilot was shot and four other episodes were written. Two years later, Burnett picked up where he was let off when he joined the screenwriter Callie Khouri, whom he had married in 2006, as one of the creative forces behind the ABC series *Nashville*.

Not counting a nonstarting pilot she had created several years earlier with the producer Steven Bochco (of *Hill Street Blues* and *NYPD Blue* fame), *Nashville* was the first TV venture for Khouri, a native of San Antonio who was raised in Paducah, Kentucky, halfway between Nashville and St. Louis. Burnett saw in the show the potential for depicting Nashville artists and their creative process in a more realistic way than had been done before, and for giving a national platform to young musicians who were badly in need of one at a time when it was almost as difficult to get on the radio as on *American Idol*. He and Khouri worked closely in choosing songs for their cast, which largely consisted of actual musicians, and developing their characters' backstories.

Things got off to a great start. Burnett spoke of happily deferring to Khouri's vision while he and co-producer Buddy Miller, a stalwart singer, songwriter, and guitarist, undertook the recording of dozens of songs, many of them new and most of them performed live—an unheard-of approach for a TV series. Envisioning themselves as producers at a hit factory like Stax or Motown, Burnett and Miller turned out a succession of collections from the show.

Burnett cast his net wide for songwriters, old and new, established and rising. Among the seasoned pros he and his staff enlisted were David Poe, Vince Gill, Elvis Costello, Patty Griffin, Steve Earle, and the great Ray Price. The smart, emerging talent he called on from the

Nashville community included Kacey Musgraves, the Pistol Annies member Ashley Monroe, the Civil Wars' Joy Williams, Hillary Lindsey, and Cary Barlowe, whose "Telescope" was a rough and ready, finger-popping high point for Hayden Panettiere's character, Juliette. (In a rare prime-time victory for the blues, Burnett also snuck in Blind Lemon Jefferson's "Matchbox Blues" as a feature for Chip Esten's character, Deacon, an ace sideman with dreams of stardom and drinking problems, who may have been partly inspired, like Bad Blake, by Stephen Bruton.)

Burnett's vocal coaching notwithstanding, Connie Britton's character, Rayna Jaymes, wasn't convincing as a Shania Twain–type star. But the pop-influenced music—which he pointedly said was not country—was a cut above the TV norm, and the show's glimpses into the songwriting process were reasonably convincing. His hopes that *Nashville* would "strike a blow for the importance of music in our country," as he told *Rolling Stone*, were lifted by the show's popularity.

From the start, though, there were behind-the-scenes power struggles between the production company in Nashville and the studio back in Los Angeles, and tensions between the cast and the producers. Chances of maintaining any kind of high standard faded. Four episodes in, the showrunner was replaced. After the strong early ratings slipped, things got a whole lot soapier: Characters got shot, crashed their cars, and overdosed. Couples uncoupled and recoupled. Clare Bowen's poor, mother-abused character, Scarlet, melted down onstage. And the true identity of Rayna's older daughter's father was revealed, leading to fisticuffs and worse between Deacon and Eric Close's character, Teddy. After his own run-ins with producers not named Callie, whom he derided for not treating her with respect, Burnett announced that the first season would be his last and that Buddy Miller would take over as primary music producer.

Dodging questions from the media about trouble on the set, Burnett initially said his exit was planned from the start, that he had only signed on to do thirteen episodes. Eventually, however, he opened up. "It was a knockdown, bloody, drag-out fight, every episode," he told the *Hollywood Reporter*. He criticized the show's sketchy approach to the music, calling for more complete performances of the songs and a fuller integration of them into the story: "It's no good in a show like this to do what everybody already knows."

"Network television really is about selling advertising," he said. "I don't hold that against them, it's just the reality. So everything is driven by what's gonna sell more advertising. Now, that's a game I'm happy for them to play. But if that gets in the way of telling the truth, then I'm sorry, I've got to go with telling the truth. In the old days in the movie business when I was coming up, all the movie executives used to talk about the actors as if they were petulant babies. And these days, I'm seeing more and more it's the executives who are the petulant babies."

Despite its frustrations, *Nashville* proved rewarding for Burnett, who got a chance to develop potential stars in the Australia native Bowen (though her Burnett-produced debut, slated for 2015, didn't appear by year's end) and the British import Sam Palladio. And as someone who now divides his time between Nashville and Los Angeles, he developed an appreciation for the city as "the Alamo for the music business," he told the *Hollywood Reporter*. "All of the young writers, young musicians are all going there. I just signed [LA-based] Mini Mansions, and I'm talking to them about moving to Nashville. They're a pop rock & roll band, but they can work out of there like crazy. It's not country anymore. I mean, Jack White's there, the Kings of Leon are there." In the fall of 2014, Burnett parted with his longtime LA-based agent, Larry Jenkins, and signed with the Brooklyn-born, Nashville-based heavy Ken Levitan, founder of Vector Management.

The visibility Burnett gained from working on *Nashville* lifted his celebrity status another notch. And with his next, drastically different venture into television, *True Detective*, he made a slew of new fans. Along with the mesmerizing performance by the film star Matthew McConaughey, who rode a hot streak into the HBO series, Burnett's eerie electronic score and ridiculously far-ranging soundtrack helped make the show the cable channel's biggest hit in more than three years.

The series creator and writer Nic Pizzolatto's plot recycled some familiar serial killer elements, including the bizarre ritualistic murder of a young woman. And women had other reasons to dislike the show. "While the male detectives of *True Detective* are avenging women and children and bro-bonding over 'crazy pussy,'" wrote the *New Yorker* critic Emily Nussbaum, "every live woman they meet is paper-thin." But viewers had never been exposed to a character quite like McConaughey's enigmatic Rust Cohle, a onetime Texas narcotics detective now serving up cosmic thoughts as a Louisiana state cop, or a soundtrack quite like Burnett's, which in providing undercoating for the themes of sin and redemption shoehorns in everyone from the bluesman John Lee Hooker to Georgia's spiritually charged McIntosh County Shouters to the psychedelic 13th Floor Elevators.

The songs, heard in barrooms and cars and out of thin air, frequently for no more than a few seconds, had the series' more compulsive viewers mapping every title. If they weren't familiar with artists like 1960s British folk singer Vashti Bunyan or the Canadian alt-country group Cuff the Duke before watching *True Detective*, rest assured they were afterward. Though the first season of *True Detective* was set and shot in Louisiana, Pizzolatto banned the use of Cajun music and swampy bayou sounds. Unlike HBO's music-centric, New Orleans–set *Treme*, which was all about regional flavor, this series was after an other-regional reality. Beginning with Burnett's inspired, out-of-left-field selection of the Handsome Family's brooding "Far from Any Road" as the show's theme song, the only place the musical elements point to is T Bone World.

"It's all about the character," Burnett told *Mother Jones*. "The depth of character is the breadth of music you get to use. So all I have to do is imagine what they're listening to, and imagine the stories rattling around in their heads. How do you strengthen that? How do you make that resonate? It's about having the songs become part of the storytelling."

"He's alone in a room, and he's looking at photographs of dead women," Burnett said, discussing a scene with Cohle. "What kind of music is he listening to? Well, he's not going to be listening to music about his truck, or music about how tight his jeans are, or music about how much beer he's had to drink before he gets in the truck! He's gonna be listening to some Captain Beefheart."

Or not. As with the Dude, Burnett's assignation of the cult artist Beefheart to Cohle—"Clear Spot" in this case—has more to do with Burnett's own strong identification with the artist's blues sensibility, outsider status, and painterly visions ("The sun big brown / Mosquitos 'n moccasins steppin' all around") than the musical tastes of the character. But who knows what kind of far-out stuff is floating around in Cohle's thoughts?

The Handsome Family—the Albuquerque-based husband-wife duo of Brett and Rennie Sparks—were on tour in New Zealand when they got an e-mail from HBO informing them that the cable network was thinking of using their 2003 song for a series. "We considered it for two seconds and laughed for about 15 minutes," Brett told the *Washington Post.* Only after the song became a minor sensation did they contemplate why it worked so well. "It's really about things taking place in the middle of nowhere," said Rennie. "It's about tricks and death and something sinister, and I think they—the song and the show—live in the same emotional landscape."

True Detective is hardly the first TV series in which soundtrack choices play an important role. In setting a dark but inviting tone, "Far from Any Road" had nothing on Gangstagrass's "Long Hard Times to Come," the theme of *Justified*, and Jace Everett's "Bad Things," the opening theme of *True Blood.* And shows ranging from *The Sopranos* (which spawned both a single and double CD of its songs) to *Mad Men* to *The Americans* have drawn emotional weight from keenly chosen end-credit tunes. But few TV themes have had the immediate impact of "Far from Any Road." Said Rennie, "A few days after the first show aired, we got an e-mail from a guy from Tehran, Iran, about how he just put our song as his ringtone and we get e-mails from places like Kyrgyzstan and we're actually charting in Ukraine right now, which is totally insane."

True Detective went a step further with Burnett's haunting score, which with its array of sci-fi tones (tinnitus sufferers beware) imbues the scenes with surreal meaning. He said he approached the show not as eight hour-long episodes but as one eight-hour movie. To devise a coherent score, he wrote what he called "a big-time epic movie melody" for the final episode and worked backward from there. "I wrote a set of intervals that could be broken down into many different configurations, so the DNA of the melody is in all of the music," he told *Mix*. "Parts of it will appear in a scene, and another one comes over here, but in the end, the whole thing is revealed."

Though Burnett had fooled around with electronic music in his teens, he had never taken it any further. To prepare himself for *True Detective*, he studied the works of Bartok, Stravinsky, and Debussy, among other modern classical composers. "People compose in tone now," he told the *Daily Beast*. "There was a sense in classical music in the 1930s that everything had been done. Then Stockhausen and these composers started going off in different directions. John Cage started composing not in melody and pitch anymore, really, but in tone. So you started getting all those beautiful tone compositions."

"I think melody exists in speech," he said. "Melody exists in life. There's a drone that's going on around us all the time, and we're all speaking and blending with it. But I think the reason that melody doesn't get old is that tone is the essential reality of melody. Pitch is a way to refer to a melody, but the tone is what really forms the note. In their tones, people have hundreds of different pitches at all times."

Burnett also studied Walter Schumann's score for *The Night of the Hunter*, which made the creepiest noir of all time even creepier; Maurice Jarre's music for *Dr. Zhivago*, which in integrating "Lara's Theme" into the story was for him the apotheosis of film scoring; and Danny Elfman's music for Tim Burton's films, including *Batman*, *Edward Scissorhands*, and *Big Fish*. Collaborating on the score for *The Hunger Games* with Elfman and the Arcade Fire's Win Butler and Régine Chassagne, Burnett got to study movie composing on the job, but those lessons ended when Elfman was fired from the 2012 film.

"We had written several beautiful pieces," Burnett told *MTV News*, "but the director [Gary Ross] for some reason wanted to take over the music. We were doing this kind of broken future that would have made a lot of sense, but the director couldn't handle it." (Though Burnett did not compose the film's score, he did oversee the official companion album, *The Hunger Games: Songs from District 12 and Beyond*, which yielded the hit "Safe & Sound" by Taylor Swift and the Civil Wars, debuted in the top spot of the *Billboard* 200 and ranks among the most popular of franchise movie soundtracks.)

Burnett recorded the score for *True Detective* at his home studio with a cast of regulars including Patrick Warren on Mellotron and the Moog-like Swarmatron; Darrell Leonard on bass trumpet, didgeridoo (a long wind instrument of Australian origin), synthesizer, and conch shell; and the weird sound specialist Keefus Ciancia on keyboards. The recordings got passed around from musician to musician, additions were made, and, working with the engineer Jason Wormer, Burnett put his final stamp on the music.

For the disappointing second season of *True Detective*, set in a corrupt industrial city outside of Los Angeles, Burnett replaced "Far from Any Road" with Leonard Cohen's brooding and unsparing "Nevermind"—a typically inspired choice by the producer, even if it made many Handsome Family fans unhappy. Burnett's stealthy use of different lyrics from "Nevermind" (taken from Cohen's 2014 album *Popular Problems*) for different episodes of the show matched up brilliantly with the obscured truths in Pizzolatto's script. As Cohen sings, "The story's told with facts and lies."

Season 2 featured songs Burnett wrote with Rosanne Cash and the sultry folk-country singer Lera Lynn, whose recurring, ghost-like onscreen role boosted the young artist's career. Cash provided a glimpse into their collaboration via e-mail:

> The writing process with T Bone has been very natural and easy. He has given me themes, and I've sent the lyrics to him, and he's written the music. He gave me the first theme (a woman's lover turns into a bird) and I wrote the lyrics and he put it to a very dark, beautiful melody. He asked me if I wanted to write another, and I said sure—he gave me the theme, I wrote the lyrics, he put music to them.
>
> Last week he casually asked if I wanted to write something on reunion and separation and I said I'd love to. Then I went on the road and as I landed at JFK today, I turned on my phone and had an e-mail from him saying "Are they finished? We're recording tonight." (!!) I had a verse, so I started working on it, finished it today and sent it to him. So I imagine it's being recorded even as we speak.

For the sixth episode, "Church in Ruins," Burnett told *Entertainment Weekly*, he had the noir writers John Fante and James M. Cain in mind: "I had the line 'You were a loner, you were alive among the walking dead. He was a liar who would not atone, still he went to your head.' I had that melody and verse and Lera finished it off from there."

The second season soundtrack was less crowded than the first in terms of incidental tunes. But featured numbers like Bobby "Blue" Bland's "I Pity the Fool," heard in the tense moments leading up to the shotgunning of Colin Farrell's disheveled cop character, Ray, packed a mighty wallop. Floating across the transom of heaven and hell, time and space, black and white, Bland's gospel shouts dramatized the stubborn quest for glory in the face of abject failure, investing the scene with a rough-hewn grace that left it lingering in memory.

CHAPTER 28

Back to the Futurist

No less a roots authority than Hank Williams Jr. said the only artists anyone ever needed were his old man, Elvis Presley, and Frank Sinatra. So it shouldn't have been a surprise when Burnett interrupted his 2014 session at Nashville's House of Blues Studio with Striking Matches to play the young duo some Ol' Blue Eyes—or actually some Young Blues Eyes, namely, "In the Wee Small Hours of the Morning." Sarah Zimmermann wasn't giving him what he wanted vocally on "When the Right One Comes Along," an aching ballad she wrote with her fellow singer-guitarist Justin Davis. "Do that!" he said to her, referring to the 1955 recording. "Pretend you're Frank!"

In pulling Striking Matches into the timeless orbit of Sinatra and his arranger, Nelson Riddle, Burnett succeeded in putting them in the right emotional frame of mind. "Wee Small Hours" is a masterpiece in tone and articulation, a disarming performance without a single overstated note. Letting their guard down, the duo nailed "When the Right One Comes Along" in one take (thinking they were rehearsing—a classic Burnett tactic). But in playing them what they called the "Frank track," Burnett also fired a shot in his campaign to widen, and deepen, the context in which music's future hears its past.

Striking Matches, who got on Burnett's radar by writing "When the Right One Comes Along" and "Hanging on a Lie" for Sam Palladio and Clare Bowen's *Nashville* characters, describe their music as "an amalgamation of everything that has influenced us over the course of our lives, which comes from rock and roll, country and blues." In other words, like so many other artists in Nashville, Austin, New Orleans, and other hotbeds of American music, they are products of the Americana movement—a label that has vaulted past alt-country and roots music as the preferred catchall term.

There are plenty of reasons to disdain "Americana." Like "world music," which essentially umbrellas anything and everything that originates outside of the United States or the English-speaking world, it presumes to commodify artists and recordings of dramatically different stripes. What exactly is "the authentic voice of American roots music" that the Americana Music Association, a Nashville-based trade organization founded in 1999, claims to advocate for in its mission statement? It is not Frank Sinatra, as uber-American as his music is (though his protégé Tony Bennett might be able to cash in his duets with Willie Nelson, the Dixie Chicks, and Sheryl Crow, not to mention the big hit he had in 1951 with Hank Williams's "Cold Cold Heart," for a spot at the Ryman). It is not jazz (even if Cassandra Wilson did sneak in a performance at the AMA's annual awards show in 2014). And because classical music is thought to exist in a separate galaxy, it is not the heartland music of Aaron Copland and Samuel Barber, as quintessentially American as those composers are.

Those exclusions don't sit well with Burnett, who has dedicated himself over a span of decades to opening this culture's eyes to the essential oneness of American musical styles and the continuum on which they rest. But there is no denying the higher profile many blues, country, and folk artists have attained thanks to the Americana movement—and not just the younger set. Greats like Merle Haggard and Willie Nelson have gotten a second or third wind from the renewed attention the Americana crowd has given them.

Not so long ago, the newly minted country icon Sturgill Simpson, the blue-eyed soul band St. Paul and the Broken Bones, and the folk duo the Milk Carton Kids never would have crossed paths, let alone shared the same stage—as they did at the 2014 AMA event. And Burnett, who in the midst of *O Brother* madness accepted a lifetime AMA award for "executive achievement," was excited to see such national treasures as the late Levon Helm, Mavis Staples, Rosanne Cash, Emmylou Harris, and Rodney Crowell honored by the Grammys, thanks to the Americana category established in 2009 (never mind that they were feted out of the full glare of the awards, as pre-broadcast side items).

The question is, how do you maximize whatever expanded awareness and appreciation there is for Americana-branded artists at a time when few record companies are willing to spend any money on them and few noncollegiate radio stations play them? Though Burnett said this has not been a conscious decision, he has refocused his attention on emerging talent as a producer. In 2013, he struck a deal with Capitol Music Group to take on his newly established label, Electromagnetic Recordings, which he told *Variety* would be "a base for which I can invest in some very good young artists" as well as Gregg Allman and other established favorites. According to the official announcement, he would also "serve as a producer and A&R resource for the CMG labels, and as a liaison for the company to the music, film and television communities." In early 2015, he entered into an exclusive publishing arrangement with Spirit Music Group for his song catalog in North America, and a joint venture under which Burnett will sign and develop songwriters for the New York–based company.

As we saw with DMZ, ambitious plans have a way of getting run over by economic reality. But in 2015, four albums by emerging artists bore his imprimatur as producer: Striking Matches' *Nothing but the Silence*, released on IRS Nashville, Capitol Music Group's Nashville imprint; the New Wavey LA pop-rock band Mini Mansions' *The Great*

Pretenders, issued on Electromagnetic; and, most importantly, Rhiannon Giddens's *Tomorrow Is My Turn* and the Punch Brothers' *The Phosphorescent Blues*, both released on Nonesuch.

Of these releases, Giddens's has created the most excitement. As we have seen, Burnett has done some of his best work with female vocalists. Among the ones I haven't mentioned are Brandi Carlile, whose career-making 2007 album *The Story* benefited from his surprise move to have her band record its road-tested songs with vintage instruments; the Canadian-born Australian Wendy Matthews, whose 1992 album *Lily* went double-platinum Down Under; Natalie Merchant, whose 2001 album *Motherland* is one of the best of her post–10,000 Maniacs efforts; and the sleekly harmonizing neo-traditional country duo the Secret Sisters, who got to complete a Dylan demo, "Dirty Lies," on their 2014 effort *Put Your Needle Down*. One of the reasons the women fare so well with him is that in an era in which so many female pop singers imitate the vocal acrobatics of Mariah Carey, he won't tolerate those who "attract attention to the fact that they're singing," as he told *Performing Songwriter*. "I just want them to say the word. That word has its own meaning; you don't have to give it meaning, so just say it."

In Giddens, he found someone who "just says it" and then some. The North Carolina native, who emerged with the Carolina Chocolate Drops (their 2009 debut, *Genuine Negro Jig*, was produced by Joe Henry), has a powerful, opera-trained voice but practices the kind of winning, unmannered folk diplomacy that made Harry Belafonte so popular in the late 1950s and early 1960s, via his Carnegie Hall recordings. On *Tomorrow Is My Turn*, she reaches across a broad spectrum of styles and eras as an entertainer first and a teacher of traditions second. The beauty of the album is how she transcends history even as she avails herself of it.

In a departure from his usual approach, Burnett had Giddens draw up her own list of songs, asking her to come up with tunes she would put on her "dream album." She chose music by strong-willed female artists that had been going through her head—a wide selection ranging from the 1930s blues singer Geeshie Wiley to the 1960s jazz sorceress Nina Simone. *Tomorrow* boasts smart string and horn arrangements by the Punch Brother Gabe Witcher, but this is, decisively, a vocal album. Planting her feet firmly and projecting—really projecting, something too few singers do anymore—Giddens brings spellbinding power to songs such as Sister Rosetta Tharpe's rocking "Up above My Head" and the hard-bitten Patsy Cline vehicle "She's Got You," which has never sounded more convincing.

Giddens's first gig with Burnett was as a contributor to *The Hunger Games: Songs from District 12 and Beyond.* "He wanted 'Appalachian music from 300 years in the future,'" Giddens told the *New York Times.* She delivered it by turning Hazel Dickens's stark bluegrass reverie "Pretty Bird" into a jig-like ballad, "Daughter's Lament." Burnett then enlisted her for the *Another Day, Another Time* concert at Town Hall, held in September 2013 to promote the Coen Brothers' *Inside Llewyn Davis*, where she had the crowd whooping with the Odetta staple "Water Boy." And then came the trial by fire of *Lost on the River*, an experience she documented in the original song "Angel City," with which she concludes *Tomorrow Is My Turn.* Some producers, in the interest of preserving the cover version concept of *Tomorrow*, might have gotten Giddens to save that tune for another album. Burnett included it to extend the album's chronology into the present—and announce that, in fact, today is Giddens's turn.

Like many listeners, Burnett was drawn to the Punch Brothers by their scary brilliance as musicians—by the ingenuity with which they floated above bluegrass and classical music and jazz—and the star potential of their mandolinist Chris Thile (who in the summer of 2015 was named the new host of the long-running NPR favorite *A Prairie Home Companion*). Burnett signed the band up for the all-star Speaking Clock Revue, which visited New York and Boston in 2010 and recorded an album, performed with them as guest guitarist at the Hardly Strictly Bluegrass Festival in San Francisco, and featured them on the soundtracks of *The Hunger Games* and *Inside Llewyn Davis.* The Punch Brothers also were the house band for the *Another Day, Another Time* concert.

Even knowing Burnett as well as they did, Thile, Witcher, and their Punch siblings didn't know what to expect when they went into Ocean Way during the summer of 2014 for what proved to be a month's worth of recording. Though the producer introduced drums to their airy sound, overdubbed some strings, and played some guitar to sharpen the musical texture on *The Phosphorescent Blues*, their fourth full-length album, he mostly left them to their own freewheeling devices. With its sudden episodic shifts and tricky time signatures, the ten-minute opener "Familiarity" is the album's grabber, creating excitement by being more than the sum of its interludes. With its plea for human connection in the age of text messaging, the song is the heart of the album. "Singing while T Bone was in the control room," Thile wrote on the band's website, "I felt what it was like for an actor to work with a great director. He would find ways to get me into my own lyrics."

The Punch Brothers may not be the Hot Five of their era—and considering how many side projects the individual members are involved in, they may well not last any longer as a group than did Louis Armstrong's famous band. But in the end, you can forgive Burnett for suggesting, and maybe even believing, that they're on the same level. The Punch generation sorely *needs* to have a Hot Five—and a Ray Charles and a Bing Crosby and an Ella Fitzgerald—to set the bar high. We are told that kids these days place little value in the future; they don't even take one for granted. Through their involvement in American tradition and their up-to-the-moment ingenuity in creating meaningful ripples in it, young artists like Giddens and Thile awaken us to the timelessness of possibility.

Music that isn't reinvented remains stuck in place. Reinventing—reharmonizing, restructuring, reshaping, recontextualizing—doesn't mean going where no artist has gone before. In the best cases, it means finding new and personal modes of expression by building on and expanding available models. Punk music didn't come out of a vacuum, but rather reprocessed and readrenalized elemental rock. As radical as rap and hip-hop first seemed, they had James Brown and Gil Scott-Heron, P-Funk and Chic, whispering in their ears. The freest of free jazz artists are shaped by the blues-based breakthroughs of Charlie Parker and those musicians who influenced him.

As a producer prized for his authentic touch in treating roots-based styles, Burnett might not seem like this kind of trailblazer. But in freeing up traditional sounds in such a way that they can speak to the future, and the future can knowingly speak back to them, he belongs in the company of artists who have pushed the music forward. "To remember is incredibly important. But I think one has to be selective in what he remembers at the same time. I've never wanted to be an anachronism. What I want to remember from the past is the wit of people like James Thurber and S. J. Perelman," he told the *Los Angeles Times*, "and the heart and soul of people like Hank Williams and Muddy Waters. But I don't think it's nearly as important to keep the style and surface of what all that was alive."

Burnett has no monopoly on pursuit. It is in the Declaration of Independence. But after all these years of being surrounded by satisfied individuals who define themselves by what they have achieved, and how much money they have made, he continues to define himself by what he aspires to for the culture: new ways of making music and framing sound, of applying and integrating art, of inciting and provoking change—of daring ourselves to be better and, of course, to sound better.

Once he attaches himself to a young artist with the right stuff, he is likely to stay attached. When the gospel-folk band Ollabelle was left in the lurch following the demise of his DMZ label, for which he produced their self-titled 2004 album, he used his influence to get them on Alison Krauss's Great High Mountain Tour and secure them a gig as harmony vocalists on *Across the Universe* (2006), the film director Julie Taymor's darkly fanciful Beatles musical, of which he was music producer. Unhappy with the mix on Ollabelle's second album, *Riverside Battle Songs* (on Verve Forecast), produced by Larry Campbell in close association with him at his home studio (Mike Piersante did the engineering), he remixed it gratis.

"His old friends and new friends are never on vacation in his mind," Sam Phillips said to me. The same can be said of old songs and new songs—including the ones that haven't yet been written. After a long hiatus, Burnett was composing songs again. In late 2015, it was announced he was writing the music and lyrics for *Happy Trails*, a Broadway musical about Roy Rogers and Dale Evans—replacing, ironically, the Disney composer Alan Menken (known for *The Little*

Mermaid and *Aladdin*) and his partner, Glenn Slater. On the weather map of possibilities—or, okay, fervent wishes—a new T Bone Burnett album was blowing in from the West, somewhere in the wide open spaces between Electromagnetic City and the Athens of the South. As long as his hopes and dreams stay in motion, you have to figure, the man is reasonably satisfied.

THE KILL SQUAD: A SHORT LIST OF LONGTIME MUSICAL ASSOCIATES

CARLA AZAR, DRUMS

Azar was tipped off to Burnett in 2001 by Joe Henry. Burnett didn't need any convincing after seeing her play with her experimental LA trio Autolux, which became the first band he signed to DMZ, the short-lived label he formed with the Coen Brothers. Though record label changes and a horrendous injury to Azar's elbow slowed the band's momentum after its impressive 2004 Burnett-produced debut *Future Perfect*, they have remained in the game, and Azar has become a star. Among her recent credits were playing with Jack White and appearing as a drummer in the Michael Fassbender film *Frank*.

Schooled on classic rock, Azar is a ferocious drummer in the manner of her idol Keith Moon and has embraced synthetic drums, programming, and "sick beats." "She never plays anything straight," Burnett told *Modern Drummer*. "She's always doing something beyond. And she can play more quietly than anybody else I know and still groove." That Jim Keltner, one of the most individual-minded drummers, became enamored of playing in a two-drum setting with her speaks volumes about her abilities.

JAY BELLEROSE, DRUMS

No single musician has been more important in the development of Burnett's mature deep-end sound than Bellerose, an extravagantly inventive and intuitive drummer with the ability to change the aural atmosphere in the studio. Many or most drummers establish their comfort zone and stay there. Bellerose sets things up differently for each song, customizing sounds and textures to the needs of the song, and is happy to keep trying new things to achieve the desired effect.

A native of Maine, Bellerose started out playing jazz, idolizing Gene Krupa. He attended Boston's prestigious Berklee College of Music for one year before an instructor, recognizing his uniqueness—and basic unteachability—told him to take off. Bellerose followed a girlfriend to California in the late 1980s and, after a difficult period during which no one in Los Angeles cottoned to his idiosyncratic approach, found a foothold.

His first significant gig was in 2000 with Joe Henry, who hired him for a tour, sight unseen, based on the recommendation of the bassist Jennifer Condos (now Bellerose's life partner of twenty years). She had been blown away seeing him play cardboard boxes at a party. Bellerose had actually agreed to join the band backing former Talking Heads front man David Byrne, but chose to play with Henry because he liked his music and, he told me, "I didn't see myself playing with Byrne." (Ironically, Henry was Byrne's opening act.)

"Jay is like a painter," Henry told me. "He's completely and unfailingly song-oriented. He has a genius for keeping the pulse going, with some subliminal kind of tone. It's tricky for a drummer to be present with a singer, to give the singer a foil and some ballast. He serves the singer by pushing against them with his phrasing, something you feel more than hear."

KEEFUS CIANCIA, KEYBOARDS

Ciancia first worked with Burnett on the soundtrack for *Divine Secrets of the Ya-Ya Sisterhood.* The film featured "Drug State," an exotic groove piece with a melody borrowing from "My Funny Valentine" created by Burnett and Vincent & Mr. Green—Ciancia's goth-style duo with the singer Jade Vincent. With his hip-hop seasoning, Ciancia has a talent for subtly underwriting the beats into other styles. He is also an acknowledged master of weird effects.

"I honestly don't know what some of the sounds are," Burnett told *Mix*. "I'll e-mail him and say, 'What the hell is a harp-piano?' and he'll write back, 'Yes!'" "I call him the 'texturizer,'" said Cassandra Wilson, whose album *Thunderbird* he co-produced. "I've never seen anyone do such intensive work on a sound, an idea, a thought, an impression, or a feeling."

JIM KELTNER, DRUMS

An Oklahoma native, Keltner first hooked up with Burnett in the late 1960s, when he was a member of the Fare, a Texas band young Burnett was producing. He made a name for himself in Los Angeles playing with the likes of Gábor Szabó, one of the leading jazz guitarists of the day. He soon entered the ranks of the Wrecking Crew, as the city's fabled collection of super-prolific but virtually anonymous studio aces would be known. Among his first records was the Gary Lewis and the Playboys track "She's Just My Style," a big hit for the comedian Jerry Lewis's son produced by fellow Tulsan Leon Russell.

In the fall of 1968, after subbing for Delaney & Bonnie's drummer, Keltner began playing with that husband-and-wife band regularly and appeared on their 1969 album *Accept No Substitute*. He made a splash with Joe Cocker's Leon Russell–directed Mad Dogs and Englishmen band. As a drummer who could adapt to anyone's style without compromising his personal approach, he built up a remarkable résumé boasting recordings and live dates with John Lennon, George Harrison, and Ringo Starr as well as Bob Dylan, Jimmy Webb, Ry Cooder, Steely Dan, and Barbra Streisand.

Though he is one of rock's finest groove-oriented drummers, his playing has a coolly understated, seemingly effortless quality. As different as he is from Charlie Watts, the Stones' Zeusian rock of time, they share a centered, poised quality that reflects their shared background in jazz. "Keltner broke the mold of what drummers were supposed to do," said Jay Bellerose, who has played in a dual drum format with Keltner on various Burnett recordings. "He keeps a different kind of time; his concept is more elastic and forgiving. He floats and breathes and makes you dance. He has always been a song and lyric guy, and very performance-oriented."

DARRELL LEONARD, HORNS, ARRANGEMENTS

Even though he has been one of Burnett's most valuable weapons in the studio since the days of Sound City, Leonard remains one of his best-kept secrets. An Iowa native schooled in the high-powered music program at North Texas State (now called the University of North Texas), he met Burnett in the late 1960s when the Third Avenue Blues Band, of which he was a member, recorded at the Fort Worth studio. (The touring group's drummer, Bill Maxwell, has played and done arrangements for Burnett over the years as well.) Leonard has played on and/or contributed charts to dozens of Burnett albums.

"T Bone sends me stuff and asks whether we should put horns on it," he told me. "I see whether we can make it work. People often call and say, 'Can you give us some Memphis Horns, that kind of sound?' We try to paint outside the box, using different combinations of horns, including French horn. We try to make the horns part of the rhythm section, not the kind of arrangements where it's 'Here come the horns!'"

MIKE PIERSANTE, ENGINEER

Piersante may not play with the kill squad unit, but he deserves recognition as a full-fledged member for all he has done to enhance their sound. Burnett met him while producing the Wallflowers at Sunset Sound, where "Mikey" was a second engineer. It proved to be a memorable first encounter. "In that era, the second engineer was a whipping boy for clients of that ilk," Piersante told me. "But T Bone found a way to treat me as part of the party, if not an equal. At one point, he went around the room asking people what they thought about something. He looked at me and asked me what I thought—the first time a producer had done that. I knew right then that this guy was different."

Before making Piersante his regular right-hand man in the studio, Burnett had used different engineers for different recordings, depending on what they would bring to a particular project. Having him on permanent call as engineer and mixer brought a consistency to the recordings that enabled Burnett to develop the complex sound for which he is known. Piersante, who has won numerous Grammys for his work with Burnett, said he learned from the legendary Texas producer many of the techniques and methods he practices, crucial concepts in control and separation among them.

"I'm the captain of his vision," Piersante told me. "I know what he wants to hear. To a large extent, that has freed him from having to worry about the sound." And when he does worry? "T Bone is like Clint Eastwood in *Unforgiven*," Piersante said. "He goes into this slow-motion mode, the calm in the storm. Even in a hail of gunfire, he never panics."

MARC RIBOT, GUITAR

Since emerging from New York's experimental scene in the mid-1980s, Ribot has left his idiosyncratic imprint on virtually every form of music. Best known by rock fans for his boldly inventive work with Tom Waits, who calls him "the Lon Chaney of the guitar," he can at any moment reflect the influence of Duane Eddy or Thelonious Monk, Charley Patton or Charlie Christian, Andres Segovia or Lou Reed. He is lionized in jazz for his remarkable solo improvisations, his interpretations of the free jazz giant Albert Ayler's works, and his Cuban crossover efforts with his band Los Cubanos Postizos.

Ribot, who first worked with Burnett on Elvis Costello's *Spike*, is all over Burnett's discography. He has made crucial contributions to such Burnett albums as *The Criminal under My Own Hat* and *The True False Identity*, as well as a long list of Burnett productions ranging from Sam Phillips's *Cruel Intentions* and *David Poe* to Robert Plant and Alison Krauss's *Raising Sand* and Diana Krall's *Glad Rag Doll*.

During his long association with Burnett, Ribot has influenced his colleague's guitar playing with his skewed approach. But he is never looking to stand out. "I don't want to impose some agenda on a song," Ribot said in a *Downbeat* interview. "I respect the ability to read the song, to figure out the song's intentions."

ACKNOWLEDGMENTS

First and foremost, thanks to T Bone Burnett, whose remaining on the sideline, as disappointing as it was, in no way diminished the quality of his company these many months. I can't imagine spending time with a more fascinating subject, or one who is more inspiring in his refusal to settle for less. (That includes helping me to obtain better photos for this book.)

Neither did Burnett's nonparticipation preempt his generosity in allowing me to reach out (as they say these days) to those close to him. Sam Phillips removed a weight from my shoulders with her early blessing of the book (the McCarthy salad was really good, too) and made herself available for all follow-up queries. I am also indebted to the impressive and well-spoken Simone Burnett for sharing her thoughts so openly.

Joe Henry, a prince of insight and instant articulation, was steady with his support, friendship, and enthusiasm. I can honestly say that all the people in Burnett's circle with whom I talked were exceptionally friendly and helpful. Special thanks go to David Mansfield, Rosanne Cash, Bob Neuwirth, Jay Bellerose, Darrell Leonard, and David Graves.

Though I didn't know it at the time, *A Life in Pursuit* began as a cover profile I wrote for *No Depression.* While putting that piece together, I spent a fair amount of time cussing and moaning about the ridiculous deadline and nonexistent budget, both of which ruled out any chance of me talking with my subject in person. But those feelings were overcome by my gratitude to the magazine and its editors,

Peter Blackstock and Grant Alden, for the opportunity to look into the phenomenon that was and remains Joseph Henry Burnett.

I am also beholden to David Menconi, editor of the University of Texas Press American Music Series, for helping make it possible for me to return to the Burnettian landscape to conduct a wider and deeper investigation, and to my UTP editor, Casey Kittrell, for all his support. To manuscript reviewer Dan Durchholz, thanks for saving me from citing *Friday Night Fever*, among other fluffs.

A heartfelt *grazie* to my spiritual advisers for the project, Ann Chaney and Chris Stacey; my Steppenwolf friends Martha Lavey and Terry Kinney; my gracious studio connection Juanita Copeland; my pressed-into-service archivist Bill Cochran, who did some serious digging through old cassettes (whatever they are); and the Country Music Hall of Fame's Becky Miley, who helped me explore their archive.

Paul Natkin, a Windy City institution, was his usual giving self in providing photos he took of Burnett. Jean Sievers came through in the clutch in helping me to score a great shot taken by her client Jeff Bridges. And I am not sure what I would have done in terms of acquiring images without the generosity of Don Duca, Sherry Rayn Barnett, Frank Ockenfels, Joseph Guay, Nancy Lamb, Rick Benedict, Tate Wittenberg, Randall Michelson, Mark Nobles, Bob Shaw and Tom Cording.

Next to last, but in no way next to least, a round of appreciation for my agent, Lynn Johnston, and for the dear friends, noted authors all, who lifted this project through their readings of the manuscript and/or the inspiration they have provided. I bow to my cornerman par excellence, Don McLeese, who never loses faith; Mike Lenehan, the best writer-editor I know; John Milward, who set an early standard in Chicago for rock criticism; and my former WNUR "Lightning Round" partners, the jazz eminences Kevin Whitehead and John Corbett.

Finally, where would I be without my soul and my heart's inspiration—Marianne, Willa, and Genevieve.

SELECTED DISCOGRAPHY

PRIME T BONE

The Alpha Band, *The Arista Albums*
(Arista, 2005)

A collection of the three albums recorded in the late 1970s by the collective trio, in all their eccentric, prophesizing glory. The most easily dismissed of them, *The Statue Makers of Hollywood*, is one of Burnett's real ear-openers.

Truth Decay
(Takoma, 1980)

Widely regarded as Burnett's solo debut, this album of garage-style rockabilly and spiritual expression established him as a songwriter who mattered. One time through "Driving Wheel," "Boomerang," and "Shake Yourself Loose" and you are hooked.

T Bone Burnett
(Dot, 1986)

A favorite among many fans, this career outlier is a beautiful, heartfelt exercise in spiritual self-reflection, lifted by its exquisite acoustic playing. "River of Love" started here.

The Criminal under My Own Hat
(Columbia, 1992)

Half acoustic, half electric, half angry, half hopeful, the album has the immediacy of automatic writing and atmospheric touches that provide comfort even as they unsettle.

The True False Identity
(Columbia, 2006)

Burnett's first album in fourteen years, his boldest ever, tells you where he has been with its tribal rhythms, thick swamp sound, and lancing lyrics.

Twenty Twenty: The Definitive T Bone Burnett
(Columbia/DMZ/Legacy, 2006)

Not your ordinary overview, this two-disc collection includes all manner of remixed and redone songs—seven from his 1983 Warner album *Proof through the Night*. It is worth having all the alternate versions.

PRIME PRODUCTIONS

Los Lobos, *How Will the Wolf Survive?*
(Slash/Warner Bros., 1984)

The great East LA band's 1987 follow-up, *By the Light of the Moon*, also produced by Burnett (with Steve Berlin), may be deeper and more cohesive. But this was the baby that launched Los Lobos, and it has lost little of its rhythmic bite or anthemic power.

The Costello Show, *King of America*
(Columbia, 1986)

Elvis in the land of plenty (aka Los Angeles), where he hit it off so well with the American stalwarts with whom Burnett teamed him that his own band, the Attractions, barely made it onto the record. An acoustic high-water mark in 1980s rock.

Sam Phillips, *Martinis and Bikinis* (Virgin, 1994) and
Fan Dance (Nonesuch, 2001)

The first album is the culmination of the immaculate popcraft practiced by Burnett and his former wife. *Fan Dance* is a work of minimalist magic, streaked with lyrical shadows and lifted by acute poetic insight.

Robert Plant and Alison Krauss, *Raising Sand*
(Rounder, 2007)

Who would ever have guessed that the Led Zeppelin wailer and the bluegrass thrush (as *Variety* liked to call female singers) had the makings of a great duo? Burnett, of course, but it took his genius in the studio to achieve such transcendence.

John Mellencamp, *Life, Death, Love and Freedom*
(Hear Music, 2008)

Stark meditations on mortality, treated to the earthiest, most doom-tuned sound Burnett has come up with as producer. "If I Die Sudden," one of the highlights, trips toward infinity with some Burnett's most freakishly resonating guitar playing.

Elton John, *The Diving Board*
(Capitol, 2013)

A throwback album in the best sense, this beautifully framed masterpiece captures John in the classic piano man mode with which he first thrilled the masses. He has never sung or played more deeply or more affectingly.

SCREEN GEMS

The Big Lebowski: Original Motion Picture Soundtrack (Mercury, 1998)

Burnett's first soundtrack for the Coen Brothers uses the Dude's trippy visions as an excuse to program artists as oddly far-ranging as the legendary street musician Moondog, the Hollywood composer Henry Mancini, and the sultry folk-jazz singer Nina Simone.

O Brother, Where Art Thou? Music from the Motion Picture (Lost Highway/Mercury, 2000; deluxe edition, 2011)

Americana starts here—at least it does if that is what you want to call the music of Ralph Stanley, Dan Tyminski, Alison Krauss, Gillian Welch, the Fairfield Four, and the many other artists introduced to millions of listeners by this endlessly enriching soundtrack. To never hear Stanley's "O Death" is not to live.

Cold Mountain: Music from the Miramax Motion Picture (Sony, 2003)

The mega-budgeted film was a commercial disappointment, and the soundtrack did not get nearly the attention of *O Brother*'s. But with its mix of deep tradition and pop professionalism (Burnett and Costello wrote "The Scarlet Tide" in the ballroom of the Hotel Bel-Air in Los Angeles—"an ideal place to write a lament about the American Civil War," writes Costello in his memoir), this album offers its own unique lesson in musicology.

Crazy Heart: Original Motion Picture Soundtrack (New West, 2010; deluxe edition, 2013)

Ryan Bingham's "The Weary Kind" got much of the attention, and an Oscar. But the story of faded country star Bad Blake (played by Jeff Bridges, who does his own singing) draws deeper meaning from the parcel of songs Burnett co-wrote with his lifelong friend Stephen Bruton. The soundtrack led to *Jeff Bridges*, a Burnett production released in 2011 on the storied Blue Note label.

True Detective: Music from the HBO Series
(Harvest, 2015)

This collection of vocal performances, most of them recorded for the hit crime series, doesn't represent Burnett's superb archival work or his eerie electronic score. But listening to the album assures that you will return to the show to appreciate the full scope of his achievement.

SELECTED BIBLIOGRAPHY

Albini, Steve. Posts on *ProSoundWeb*, January 2–3, 2005. http://repforums.prosoundweb.com/index.php?topic=4925.75.

Allman, Gregg. *My Cross to Bear*. New York: William Morrow, 2012.

Altman, Billy. "A Music Maker Happy to Be Just a Conduit." *New York Times*, February 24, 2002.

Appleford, Steve. "Exile's Return: T Bone Burnett's Feverish Mixed Emotions Permeate a New Album Tinged with Idealism and Outrage." *Los Angeles Times*, October 18, 1992.

Baccigaluppi, John. "Gillian Welch and David Rawlings: Producing Themselves." *Tape Op*, September–October 2011.

Belcher, David. Review of Elvis Costello and T Bone Burnett, The Playhouse, Edinburgh. *Glasgow Herald*, November 12, 1984.

Belth, Alex. *The Dudes Abide: The Coen Brothers and the Making of* The Big *Lebowski*. "Kindle Single," Amazon Digital Services, 2014.

Berkery, Patrick. "T Bone Burnett: A Producer with Teeth." *Modern Drummer*, October 2008.

Bonner, Michael. "An Interview with T Bone Burnett: This Music Is the Music That Grew Up Out of the Ground . . ." *Uncut*, January 17, 2004.

Brogan, David. Review of *The Talking Animals*. *Chicago Tribune*, February 19, 1988.

Bruton, Stephen. Interview in *Tone Quest Report*, November 2002.

Burnett, T Bone. "Burning Love." *Musician*, December 1985.

———. Commencement speech, USC Annenberg School of Communications, Los Angeles, May 16, 2014. https://www.youtube.com/watch?v=quNnZKLVWoA.

———. Dedication to Sam Shepard, *Tooth of Crime*. Nonesuch, 2008.

———. In conversation with Greg Kot, Future of Music Coalition Policy Summit, Georgetown University, Washington, D.C., October 4, 2010. https://www.youtube.com/watch?v=1s8zpB3ABh4.

———. Interview with Bob Boilen. *All Songs Considered.* National Public Radio, May 15, 2008. http://www.npr.org/sections/allsongs/2008/05/15/90471395/guest-dj-t-bone-burnett.

———. Interview with Bob Boilen. *All Songs Considered.* National Public Radio, August 23, 2011. http://www.npr.org/2011/08/23/139880668/t-bone-burnett-on-10-years-of-o-brother-where-art-thou.

———. Interview with David Dye. *World Cafe*. National Public Radio, October 31, 2011. http://www.npr.org/2012/05/21/141863684/t-bone-burnett-on-world-cafe.

———. Interview with Terry Gross. *Fresh Air*. National Public Radio, December 12, 2012. http://www.npr.org/templates/story/story.php?storyId=122526723.

———. Liner notes, *Proof Through the Night and The Complete Trap Door.* Rhino/Warner, 2007.

———. Liner notes, *Twenty Twenty: The Essential T Bone Burnett.* Columbia/DMZ/Legacy, 2006.

———. Posts on *hypebot*, October 2010. http://www.hypebot.com/hypebot/2010/10/t-bone-burnett-new-artists-should-stay-completely-away-from-the-internet-.html.

———. Posts on *Steve Hoffman Music Forums*, 2000. http://forums.stevehoffman.tv/.

———. "T Bone Burnett's Plea: The Piper Must Be Paid." *Los Angeles Times*, June 4, 2014.

———. "25 Things to Remember about George Bush When You Go to the Polls." *Spin*, November 1992.

Canby, Vincent. Review of *The Tooth of Crime: Second Dance. New York Times*, January 12, 1997.

Chinen, Nate. "Cassandra Wilson: Golden Age." *JazzTimes*, May 2006.

Christgau, Robert. Review of *Omnipop. Robert Christgau, Dean of American Rock Critics*, n.d. http://www.robertchristgau.com/get_artist.php?name=Sam+Phillips.

———. Review of *Truth Decay. Robert Christgau, Dean of American Rock Critics*, n.d. http://www.robertchristgau.com/get_artist.php?name=T-Bone+Burnett.

Chusid, Irwin. *Songs in the Key of Z: The Curious World of Outsider Music.* Chicago: Chicago Review Press, 2001.

Cockburn, Bruce. Comments from "Nothing but a Burning Light, the Radio Special CD." *The Cockburn Project* blog, 1991. http://cockburnproject.net/songs&music/iw.html.

———. *Rumours of Glory*. New York: HarperOne, 2014.

"A Conversation with T Bone Burnett." *Inside Llewyn Davis* website, n.d. http://www.insidellewyndavis.com/about/a-conversation-with-t-bone-burnett.

Costello, Elvis. Liner notes to *King of America*. Rykodisc, 2005.

———. Liner notes to *Spike*. Rykodisc, 2001.

———. Review of *The Talking Animals*. *Musician*, March 1988.

———. *Unfaithful Music and Disappearing Ink*. New York: Blue Rider Press, 2015.

Crane, Larry. "T Bone Burnett: Recording and Love." *Tape Op*, September–October 2008.

Cromelin, Richard. "After Fourteen Years Away, He's a Changed Man." *Los Angeles Times*, May 30, 2006.

Davis, Clive. *The Soundtrack of My Life*. New York: Simon & Schuster, 2013.

De Barros, Paul. "Jazz Singer, Pianist Diana Krall Fulfills Decades-Old Prophecy." *Seattle Times*, April 11, 2014.

Dylan, Bob. *Chronicles, Volume One*. New York: Simon and Schuster, 2004.

Ebert, Roger. Review of *Divine Secrets of the Ya-Ya Sisterhood*. *Chicago Sun-Times*, June 7, 2002.

———. Review of *Walk the Line*. *Chicago Sun-Times*, November 17, 2005.

Farah, Joseph. "I'm Not Stupid Enough to Want to Be Famous." *Today's Christian Music*, Fall 1982.

Ferguson, Jon. "A Rejuvenated Gregg Allman Working on Tour, Movie and a New Album." *LancasterOnline*, October 24, 2013. http://lancasteronline.com/features/entertainment/a-rejuvenated-gregg-allman-working-on-tour-movie-and-a/article_634b5196-b2db-53b2-ba7d-aad1136e4eff.html.

Ferman, Dave. Review of T Bone Burnett at Caravan of Dreams, Fort Worth. *Dallas Morning News*, December 6, 1986.

Flanagan, Bill. "Counting Crows Learn to Fly." *Musician*, May 1994.

———. "First Let's Kill All the Drummers." *Musician*, September 1987.

———. *U2: At the End of the World*. New York: Delacorte Press, 1995.

Fricke, David. Review of *Low Country Blues*. *Rolling Stone*, January 18, 2011.

Friskics-Warren, Bill. "Orphan Girl of the Hollywood Hills Finds a High Lonesome Musical Home in the Heart of the Appalachians." *No Depression*, July 1996.

Gallo, Phil. "Inside Move: T Bone Burnett Returns." *Variety*, July 28, 2002.

Gleiberman, Owen. Review of *Cold Mountain. Entertainment Weekly*, December 22, 2003.

Gold, Adam. "T Bone Burnett on 'Nashville,' Elton John's Comeback and Retiring as a Producer." *Rolling Stone*, December 18, 2012.

Goodman, Frank. "A Conversation with Daniel Tashian." *Puremusic*, December 2007.

Granger, Thom, ed. *The 100 Greatest Albums in Christian Music*. Eugene, OR: Harvard House, 2001.

Greene, Andy. "Robert Plant Says Gritty New LP Will 'Sound Right at a Jamaican Party.'" *Rolling Stone*, May 12, 2014.

Griffin, Sid. *Shelter from the Storm: Bob Dylan's Rolling Thunder Years*. London: Jawbone Press, 2010.

Gritten, David. "T Bone Burnett Interview: I Work with the Coen Brothers Any Chance I Get." *The Telegraph*, December 14, 2013.

Guarino, Mark. "Famed Producer T Bone Burnett Reclaims His Songwriting Roots." *Chicago Daily Herald*, May 19, 2006.

Guinn, Jeff. Review of T Bone Burnett at Caravan of Dreams, Fort Worth. *Fort Worth Star-Telegram*, December 6, 1986.

Guralnick, Peter. "Willie Dixon." *Musician*, September 1988.

Gutch, Frank. "Lost in Space: The Epic Saga of Fort Worth's Space Opera." *Rock and Reprise*, 2008.

Hall, Michael. "The Greatest Producer You've Never Heard of Is . . ." *Texas Monthly*, January 6, 2014.

Hampton, Howard. "The Edge of the Country." *Village Voice*, December 16, 1986.

Harrington, Richard. "A Producer's Record Crop: T Bone Burnett Has Mined a Mountain of Roots Music." *Washington Post*, April 25, 2004.

Hart, Brother Patrick, ed. *The Literary Essays of Thomas Merton*. New York: New Directions, 1985.

Harvey, Dennis. Review of *The Late Henry Moss. Variety*, November 19, 2000.

Hausknecht, Gina. "T Bone Burnett Biography." *Musician Guide*, n.d.

Hendrickson, Matt. "T Bone Talks." *Smoke Music Archive*, 2009. http://www.smokemusic.tv/content/t-bone-talks?page=0%2C0.

Hilburn, Robert, and Chris Willman. "Rock of Ages: There's a New Spirituality in Pop Music." *Los Angeles Times*, June 7, 1987.

Hill, Michael. "Punch Brothers." Feature on *The Phosphorescent Blues* for the band's website, 2015. http://www.punchbrothers.com/about/.

Hiltbrand, David. Review of *The Talking Animals. People*, March 28, 1988.

Himes, Geoffrey. "The BoDeans' Heartland Rock." *Washington Post*, June 6, 1986.

———. "A New Wave of Musicians Updates That Old-Time Sound." *New York Times*, November 5, 2006.

———. "T Bone Burnett and the Skyliner Sound." *Texas Music*, July 1, 2008.

Hochman, Steve. "Burnett Hopes Radio Will Accept His Gospel." *Los Angeles Times*, February 22, 2004.

Hoekstra, Dave. "Burnett's 'Identity' Found in the Woods." *Chicago Sun-Times*, May 21, 2006.

Holden, Stephen. "Sounds around Town." *New York Times*, February 19, 1988.

"Inventory: Twenty-Six Songs That Are Just as Good as Short Stories." *AV Club*, May 26, 2007.

Irving, Jim, ed. *The Mojo Collection: The Ultimate Music Companion*, 4th ed. Edinburgh: Canongate Books, 2007.

Jackson, Blair. "T Bone Burnett: Looking Back, Looking Forward." *Mix*, July 1, 2006.

———. "*Mix* Interview with Producer Artist T Bone Burnett about Recent Work with B. B. King, John Mellencamp, Elvis Costello and more." *Mix*, October 1, 2008.

———. "Music for 'True Detective': T Bone Burnett Digs Deep for Eerie HBO Drama." *Mix*, April 1, 2014.

Jason. Review of *The Unwritten Works of Geoffrey, Etc. Rising Storm*, April 26, 2007. http://therisingstorm.net/whistler-chaucer-detroit-and-greenhill-the-unwritten-works-of-geoffrey-etc/.

Kasten, Roy. "O Brother! Producer and Guitarist T Bone Burnett Joins Robert Plant and Alison Krauss at the Duo's Fabulous Fox Performance." *Riverfront Times*, September 17, 2008.

Kim, Wook. Review of *Omnipop. Entertainment Weekly*, August 23, 1996.

Kot, Greg. "An Act of Hope: T Bone Burnett Tries It Once More, with Feeling." *Chicago Tribune*, November 8, 1992.

———. "This is Not a Love Song: Sam Phillips' Latest Album Infused with Pain after Her Breakup from T Bone Burnett." *Chicago Tribune*, June 11, 2004.

Krauss, Alison. Interview with Liane Hansen. *Weekend Edition Sunday*. National Public Radio, October 28, 2007. http://www.npr.org/templates/story/story.php?storyId=15675741.

LA Weekly staff. "The Definitive Guide to the Music of *The Big Lebowski*." *LA Weekly*, March 7, 2013.

Lanois, Daniel. *Soul Mining: A Musical Life*. London: Faber & Faber, 2010.

Light, Alan. "A New Start and a Gumbo of Old Sounds." *New York Times*, January 14, 2011.

Lubitz, Rachel. "A Conversation with the Handsome Family, the Band behind the 'True Detective' Theme Song, 'Far from Any Road.'" *Washington Post*, March 5, 2014.

Macnie, Jim. "Marc Ribot and Nels Cline: Gargantuan Impact." *DownBeat*, July 2011.

Massey, Howard. "Talking with T Bone Burnett Is Like Entering an Alternate Universe of Free-Flowing Creativity." *Performing Songwriter*, June 2008.

———. "T Bone Burnett: A New Dimension in Sound." In *Behind the Glass: Top Record Producers Tell How They Craft the Hits, Vol. 2*. San Francisco: Backbeat Books, 2009.

Maymudes, Victor, and Jacob Maymudes. *Another Side of Bob Dylan: A Personal History on the Road and off the Tracks*. New York: St. Martin's Press, 2014.

McDonnell, Thomas P., ed. *A Thomas Merton Reader*. New York: Image Books, 1974.

McLean, Duncan. Review of Elvis Costello and T Bone Burnett, The Playhouse, Edinburgh. *Edinburgh University Student*, November 15, 1984.

McLeese, Don. Liner notes to Jimmie Dale Gilmore's *Braver Newer World*. Elektra, 1996.

———."They Cried Wolf about Los Lobos: Album Squashes Rumor." *Chicago Sun-Times*, January 18, 1987.

———. "Top Pop Albums." *Chicago Sun-Times*, December 30, 1990.

Merton, Thomas. *The Waters of Siloe*. Boston: Houghton Mifflin Harcourt, 1979.

Mettler, Mike. "30 Minutes with T Bone Burnett." *Sound & Vision*, June 1, 2006.

Milward, John. "From T Bone Burnett, Music with Character." *Philadelphia Inquirer*, May 19, 1988.

Morris, Chris. *Los Lobos: Dream in Blue*. Austin: University of Texas Press, 2015.

Morthland, John. Review of *Braver Newer World*. *Texas Monthly*, July 1996.

———. Review of *Fort Worth Teen Scene! Vols. 1–3*. *Austin Chronicle*, August 6, 2004.

Murray, Noel. "Steve Berlin of Los Lobos on REM and Sharing the Planet with Paul Westerberg." *AV Club*, September 14, 2012.

Nellis, Krystina. "Inside Llewyn Davis: DiS Meets T Bone Burnett." *Drowned in Sound*, January 22, 2014. http://drownedinsound.com/in_depth/4147342-inside-llewyn-davis—dis-meets-t-bone-burnett.

Newcomb, Brian Q. "T Bone Burnett Stakes Out New Ground on 'Criminal.'" *Billboard*, August 15, 1992.

Nobles, Mark A. *Fort Worth's Rock and Roll Roots*. Charleston, SC: Arcadia Publishing, 2011.

Nussbaum, Emily. "Cool Story, Bro: The Shallow Deep Talk of 'True Detective.'" *New Yorker*, March 3, 2014.

O'Donnell, Kevin. "T Bone Burnett Spills More Secrets of *True Detective* Season Two." *Entertainment Weekly*, July 18, 2015.

Ostler, Scott. "T Bone Burnett Quietly Makes Beautiful Music." *San Francisco Chronicle*, February 8, 2014.

Overstreet, Jeffrey. "Sam Phillips: The Looking Closer Interview." *Patheos*, September 24, 2004. http://www.patheos.com/blogs/lookingcloser/2004/09/sam-phillips-the-looking-closer-interview/.

Pareles, Jon. "Great Career Just 'Came Along.'" *New York Times*, May 16, 2006.

———. "A Solo Spotlight for a Powerful Voice." *New York Times*, January 23, 2015.

———. "When It Takes Three People to Make a Duet." *New York Times*, October 21, 2007.

Patoski, Joe Nick, and Bill Crawford. "The Long, Strange Trip of Ed Bass." *Texas Monthly*, June 1989.

Paumgarten, Nick. "Brilliant Mistakes: Elvis Costello's Boundless Career." *New Yorker*, November 8, 2010.

Pilato, Bruce. "T Bone Burnett Feasts on Chewy Label Deal." *Variety*, January 7, 2014.

Pond, Steve. "T Bone Burnett: Surviving the Wild Side." *Rolling Stone*, November 24, 1983.

"Producer of the Year." *TCU Magazine*, Summer 2002.

Ragogna, Mike. "A Conversation with T Bone Burnett." *Huffington Post*, September 29, 2010. http://www.huffingtonpost.com/mike-ragogna/emhuffpost-exclusiveem-el_b_742868.html.

———. "Hymns, Harrows, Harvests and More: Chatting with John Hiatt, Gillian Welch and Umphrey's McGee's Joel Cummins." *Huffington Post*, August 3, 2011. http://www.huffingtonpost.com/mike-ragogna/hymns-harrows-harvests-mo_b_916771.html.

———. "*Women and Country*: A Conversation with Jakob Dylan and More." *Huffington Post*, May 25, 2011. http://www.huffingtonpost.com/mike-ragogna/emwomen-and-countryem-a-c_b_516582.html.

Ray, Michael. "T Bone Burnett: American Producer and Musician." *Encyclopedia Britannica*, September 26, 2014. http://www.britannica.com/biography/T-Bone-Burnett.

Rhodes, Joe. "T Bone Burnett: The Insider Comes Out to Play." *Los Angeles Magazine*, July 2006.

Righi, Len. "On the Trail of Los Lobos with Saxman Steve Berlin." *Morning Call*, March 21, 1987. http://articles.mcall.com/1987-03-21/entertainment/2558793_1_saxophonist-steve-berlin-los-lobos-mexican-folk-music.

Riley, Tim. *Hard Rain: A Dylan Commentary*. New York: Vintage Books, 1993.

Robbins, Ira, and Regina Joskow, ed. *The New Trouser Press Record Guide*. Rev. ed. New York: Collier Books, 1989.

Romano, Andrew. "Interview: T Bone Burnett, the Coen Brothers' Musical Guru." *Daily Beast*, December 13, 2013. http://www.thedailybeast.com/articles/2013/12/13/t-bone-burnett-the-coen-brothers-music-guru.html.

Ryan, Mike. "'Please Mr. Kennedy': How an Intentionally Bad Song Turned Out So Great." *Huffington Post*, December 2, 2013. http://www.huffingtonpost.com/2013/12/01/please-my-kennedy-inside-llewyn-davis_n_4344365.html.

Sachs, Lloyd. "Cassandra Wilson: Beyond the Blues." *No Depression*, May–June 2006.

———. "The Invisible Man." *No Depression*, January–February 2004.

———. "Musical Couple in Traffic Jam." *Chicago Sun-Times*, October 10, 1999.

———. "Peter Case: A Guitar Makes a Band." *No Depression*, September–October 2007.

———. "Rock Solid Rebel: Texas Original Jimmie Dale Gilmore Shatters Stereotypes with an Unpredictable Approach to His Music." *Chicago Sun-Times*, February 27, 2000.

———. "Sam Phillips Refuels with 'Dance,' TV Gig." *Chicago Sun-Times*, November 14, 2001.

Sasfy, Joseph. "Tuning Up for the 80s." *Washington Post*, October 21, 1982.

Schonfeld, Zach. "What Do Indie Musicians Really Think about Music Streaming?" *Newsweek*, July 23, 2015.

Scott, A. O. Review of *O Brother, Where Art Thou? New York Times*, December 22, 2000.

Selvin, Joel. "Anatomy of a Hit: Luck, Timing and Talent." *San Francisco Chronicle*, May 6, 1994.

Shepard, Sam. *The Rolling Thunder Logbook*. New York: Da Capo Press, 2004.

———. *The Tooth of Crime: Second Dance*. Reprint ed. New York: Vintage Books, 2006.

Shewey, Don. "Sam Shepard's Identity Dance." *American Theater*, July–August 1997.

Simmons, Sylvie. *I'm Your Man: The Life of Leonard Cohen.* New York: Ecco, 2012.

Sloman, Larry "Ratso." *On the Road with Bob Dylan.* Rev. ed. New York: Three Rivers Press, 2002.

Soeder, John. "Robert Plant and Alison Krauss Find Common Ground in Rootsy American Music." *Cleveland Plain Dealer*, July 12, 2008.

Stanley, Ralph. *Man of Constant Sorrow: My Life and Times.* New York: Gotham, 2009.

Suebsaeng, Asawin. "T Bone Burnett on How He Chooses Music for 'True Detective.'" *Mother Jones*, January 24, 2014.

Sullivan, Kevin P. "'Hunger Games' Soundtrack Producer Reveals Truth about the Music You Never Heard." *MTV News*, November 18, 2013. http://www.mtv.com/news/1717665/hunger-games-soundtrack-t-bone-burnett-danny-elfman/.

"T Bone Burnett: Proust Questionnaire," *Vanity Fair*, December 31, 2013.

Thomson, Graeme. *Complicated Shadows: The Life and Music of Elvis Costello.* Edinburgh: Canongate, 2005.

Tianen, Dave. "Rocky Start with Burnett Almost Derailed BoDeans' First Album." *Milwaukee Journal Sentinel*, March 5, 2009.

"Tommy Keene: Pop's Forgotten Genius." *Rockerzine*, March 19, 2012. http://www.rockerzine.com/2012/03/tommy-keene-pops-forgotten-genius/.

Troyer, Chris. "Wed., 20 October 1982: Seattle, WA, Kingdome." *The Who Concert Guide*, November 11, 2007. http://www.thewholive.net/concert/index.php?id=486&GroupID=1.

Tucker, Ken. Review of *Truth Decay*. *Rolling Stone*, October 2, 1980.

Turner, Steve. "Bob Dylan Finds God: A Classic Article from the Vaults." *The Guardian*, September 11, 2012.

Vadion, Diane. "Scoring a Hit: The Year's Most Iconoclastic Soundtrack Proves What's Wrong with Most." *Spin*, January 2001.

Verlinde, Jason. "An Interview with Stephen Bruton." *Fretboard Journal*, Winter 2008.

Vine, Katy. "T Bone, Well Done." *Texas Monthly*, March 2001.

Vineyard, Jennifer. "T Bone Burnett Explains His Musical Influences." *Vulture*, March 3, 2013. http://www.vulture.com/2013/03/t-bone-burnett-explains-his-musical-influences.html.

Wexler, Jerry. *Rhythm and the Blues: A Life in American Music.* New York: Knopf, 1993.

Willman, Chris. "Capitol Records' VP of A&R T Bone Burnett on Elton John's 'Beautiful' New Record, Taylor Swift vs. Apple and Making Music for 'True Detective.'" *Billboard*, August 14, 2015.

———. "Elton John on T Bone Burnett: 'He Got My Love of Recording Back; I Thought I'd Lost That.'" *Hollywood Reporter*, October 30, 2013.

———. "The Music behind 'The Big Lebowski.'" *Entertainment Weekly*, April 3, 1998.

———. "'Nashville': It Was a Drag-Out Fight." *Hollywood Reporter*, October 30, 2013.

———. "T Bone Burnett Comes Down to Earth in LP." *Los Angeles Times*, April 23, 1988.

———. "T Bone Burnett vs. Silicon Valley: 'We Should Go Up There with Pitchforks and Torches.'" *Hollywood Reporter*, October 31, 2013.

Wilonsky, Robert. "Born Again." *Dallas Observer*, September 5, 1996.

Winn, Steven. "Memorable Moss: Sam Shepard's Family Drama Comes to a Remarkable Climax after an Uneven Start." *San Francisco Chronicle*, November 16, 2000.

Yonkee, David. "As the Crows Fly: Counting Crows Celebrate What It Calls Its Best Record Yet." *Vancouver Province*, June 15, 2000.

"Your Interview with T Bone Burnett." *No Depression*, October 6, 2011.

Zollo, Paul. *Songwriters on Songwriting*. 2nd ed. Boston: Da Capo, 2003.

INDEX

Note: the photo section follows page 110.